Deleuze and Memorial Culture

To Michael Zaretsky

Deleuze and Memorial Culture

Desire, Singular Memory and the Politics of Trauma

Adrian Parr

EDINBURGH UNIVERSITY PRESS

Transferred to digital print 2013

Edinburgh University Press Ltd
22 George Square, Edinburgh

Typeset in 11/13pt Adobe Sabon
by Servis Filmsetting Ltd, Manchester, and
Printed and bound by CPI Group (UK) Ltd, Croydon, CR0 4YY

A CIP record for this book is available from the British Library

ISBN 978 0 7486 2754 7 (hardback)

Contents

Acknowledgements

The research and writing of this book received assistance from many people in different ways. I would especially like to thank Ronald Bogue, Ian Buchanan, Claire Colebrook, Felicity Colman, Tom Conley, Verena Conley and Carol MacDonald for their support. Eli Zaretsky provided me with academic advice for references in the area of psychoanalysis that I am most grateful for. An earlier version of Chapter 7 appeared in the journal *Angelaki*, Volume 2 (2006) http://www.informaworld.com, while a shorter version of Chapter 8 was published as part of the Association of Collegiate Schools of Architecture 2007 conference proceedings. I would like to thank both the journal editors and the ACSA committee for their permission to reprint this material. Lastly, a Presidential Fellowship from the Savannah College of Art and Design provided me with financial assistance to conduct research in preparation for the writing of this book and I would especially like to thank President Paula Wallace for her support.

I would also like to thank my son Lucien, daughter Shoshana and Margaret Sabolik for their patience during my long periods of absence. My Hungarian grandmother, Rosa, and her experiences during World War Two and the memories of her mother provided me with inspiration to write on traumatic memory and public remembrance. Finally, my husband Michael Zaretsky has not only given over his time to proofread, comment and discuss every last corner and detail of this project, but he has continually provided me with critical suggestions for improvement, unconditional encouragement and unwavering confidence without which I can honestly say this book would never have come to fruition.

Introduction

How we remember also affirms how we live our lives today and tomorrow: defensively or joyfully. Memory is dynamic and its movement is largely ungraspable. It can open new linguistic, economic, historical, and energetic combinations that either normalize or reinvent how the social field organizes itself. Yet the movement of memory cannot be clearly situated within space and time. Memory, unlike remembrance itself, is not *in* space and time, although it can be said to produce space-times. Memory does not happen to a body, it subsists throughout it. A body doesn't remember a defined slice of time, for memory is in excess of the chronological compartmentalizing of discrete temporal units. So, where do we start when we begin to think about memorial culture? How do we collectively grapple with trauma as it gnaws its way through the social field? Perhaps with a mixture of aggression, tears, outrage, overwhelming sorrow, and silence. How does culture answer to the memories that linger on in the wake of a trauma collectively experienced and the feeling that a community has been pushed to what seems like the end of the world? Questions such as these underpin a now commonly quoted statement Theodor W. Adorno made in 1949 that after the holocaust to write poetry is simply barbaric. This challenge has been met by the blossoming industry of memorialization – holocaust museums and memorials, holocaust remembrance day and so on. Actually, the building of memorials has become an entirely independent genre in contemporary art and architecture. So, what might Adorno think of this? Perhaps we need to respond to him through an exercise of our imagination by considering the quality and affect of the time through which he spoke.

The essence of history framed by a teleological principle of progress that Karl Marx predicted would culminate in the end of History once the class society was overthrown was quickly suspended post World War Two. For if history has a goal or meaning then it can also be measured in terms of consequences, yet the consequence of the holocaust was that millions were murdered. What could involuntary death on such a large scale as this possibly prove? To even consider that genocide has a truth-value, or that the objective of genocide can be justified by historical progress, or to attempt to calculate the deaths of men, women, children, and the elderly in terms of historical costs and benefits seems crude at best. The reality was that standing alone with its back to the wall humanity really confronted head on the difference between existence and essence. What seeped to the surface was the brutal fact that existence is without essence. Many people were forced into the realization that all we do is simply live; sometimes directions emerge through the motions of life but no single direction ever fully commands the unpredictable and unfathomable movement that life can take at any given moment.[1] Towards the loneliness of life and the continual changes it invokes humanity turned away from the certainties and comforts of historical progress. The time Adorno spoke from has long since buried all but one historical truth – the truth that the present always has the potential to gut the past anew while lowering its shield in the face of the future.

Adorno spoke at a time when humanity had been forced to its knees, and left kneeling there it discovered it no longer believed in itself. Yet, it was humanity that had forsaken itself, not life that had abandoned humanity. Life does not close its eyes, life does not look away; life wildly endures without guarantees. Indeed, are there any truths that history can teach us in light of this? John Lukacs proposes 'the truths of history, the real meanings, are to be discovered in what history can teach us about the framework of the Logos, if you will: about the significance of human existence: about the splendor and the misery of our condition.'[2] Yes, history may teach us something about reason but perhaps not in the way that Lukacs intends. Hannah Arendt is fully aware of the limitations of this kind of humanism when she points out that the whole idea of humanity creating itself – an idea common to Leftist humanism – is contrary to the 'factuality of the human condition.'[3] She vehemently pronounces: 'nothing is more obvious than that man, whether as member of the species or as an individual, does *not* owe his existence to himself.'[4] History, if it teaches us anything, can only in effect describe to us the limits and, dare we admit it, the insignificance of human existence.

Rather than assuming the past can be contained and resurface unscathed in the context of the present, memorial culture, much like Adorno, can remind us that attempting to recapture and extract the meaning behind the stench and smoke of the holocaust is an inherently futile exercise. This is not only because the very essence of the past can never be fully represented but also because the movement of memory poses a very real problem to do with essences per se. Adorno's denouncement of writing poetry after the holocaust brings to our attention the ethical problem memorial culture poses and it is one that is split in two directions: towards the practical and ontological. Further, he clearly situates the ontological categories – to be or not to be barbaric – within the ethical question of how to respond to barbarism and the sociopolitical realities this invokes. Maybe then, memorial culture is utopian memory thinking: one where culture inhabits the disruptive dimension of traumatic memories, which also entails a little bit of forgetting, while simultaneously bringing forth a sense of agency. The utopian dimension of memorial culture simultaneously presents the movement of collective agency and the materiality of concrete life. Hence at its most successful, it avoids monumentalizing the past, choosing instead to tension the past with the present, while joyfully looking to the future. And, to borrow from Fredric Jameson, it compels us to think the break utopia announces, rather than providing us with a conventional picture of what life would be like after the break.[5]

In the pages that follow we will explore how culture at times organizes and at other times experiments with the disruptive social life of trauma. It is this combination of cultural production and collective traumatic memory that can help us peel back the skin and tissue of repression so as to uncover the utopian demand that memory stirs forth. In this respect, memorial culture may be considered a corporeal movement of memory thinking. This mode of thinking is both idealistic and realistic not because it represents the essence of trauma in its entirety, or the causes and effects of singular events; rather, utopian memory thinking is ultimately about how the social field conceptually, imaginatively, and materially grasps and labors over the sociopolitical contradictions collective trauma exposes. Therefore, as cultural production (memorial culture), it is a social activity that organizes the energies, affects, and forces of memory. The mistake to avoid, if we follow the philosophical advice of Henri Bergson and Gilles Deleuze on this point, is thinking about the present as the effect of the past. In fact, in order to affirm the movement of memory as a past that coexists in the present we need to try to move beyond realism and idealism all together.

How we understand collective trauma and the methodology we use to consider memorial culture is pivotal here. In particular, it is not so much the solutions to trauma that memorial culture provides that this book is concerned with, rather how memorial culture establishes historical problems by experimenting with the social and political realities of collective remembrance. According to Deleuze there is a methodological difference between true and false problems and the methodology for arriving at true problems is intuitive. Agreeing with Bergson, Deleuze explains that intuition 'is not a simple pleasure, nor a presentiment, nor simply an affective process.'[6] Clarifying, he explains the four prevailing characteristics of Bergsonian intuition. The first is that intuition does not infer; it presents life from the interiority of life itself. The implication of this is that we begin to look to the problems dictating the edges and insides of memorial culture, the way in which a methodology of intuition establishes *an other* memory; such cultural practices seek to reinstate the singularity of trauma by restoring different connections to memory. The second characteristic is that intuition rediscovers. In other words, instead of inventing memory we 'rediscover the immediate because we must return to find it.'[7] In this sense, we begin to understand memorial culture not simply as the re-creation of the past but the restoration of memory thinking, understood to be a utopian demand that arises out of what Jameson describes as a narrative opposition. In terms of subjectivity he explains this 'involves a distinction between consciousness – as in an impersonal presence to the world which is always with us as long as we exist – and the self, which is so often an object of consciousness, but also of biography, and its stories, of fantasy and trauma, of "personal" ambitions and private life, in short, of narrative as such.'[8]

The third characteristic of Bergsonian intuition is that the intuitive method respects the supple differences defining 'being' by seeking out the difference in things, not trying to simply resolve the conflict trauma invokes. In the context of our discussion here this would mean not assuming memorial culture consists of finding and collating the 'facts' of the past into a systematic epistemology or representation, and as Jameson advises it is a matter of inventing new versions of the disruptive aspect of such antagonisms. For this reason, this book will follow lines of differentiation, how collective remembrance produces variation. Put differently, how the movement of time does or doesn't actualize or give rise to difference.

It is into the wilderness that traumatic memory takes us. The journey may be confounding, not because it demands we refrain from responding, as many have simplistically interpreted Adorno,[9] rather because the epic quality of trauma forces culture to stutter and historical consciousness to stumble and it is here where memory tumbles around mixing up the specificity of the present with the complexity of the past. In effect traumatic memory can make cultural production stagger, reducing society to tears. Ultimately, in all their force these tears are beyond representation. This book will explore the affective movement of memory as it skirts fixed organization, describing it through the use of Deleuze and Félix Guattari's concept of desire and, more specifically, the three syntheses of desire – connective, disjunctive, and conjunctive. The connective synthesis is the productive dimension of libidinal energies, affects, and forces; the disjunctive synthesis refers to breaks occurring in the flow of these energies and their subsequent recording; and finally the conjunctive synthesis of consumption produces a subject or subjectivity.

Collective trauma pushes and prods the social field to the point where the disordered flows of intensity and affect emerge as the raw material of memory labor. It is for this reason that the conceptual framework of desire as social may bring us closer to what Adorno meant when he decried that after the holocaust to write poetry is barbaric. In regard to memorial culture, the legitimate form of the synthesis of desire would be a cultural practice that does not symbolically negate or represent the libidinal force, energy, and affects of collective trauma; instead the libidinal charge of trauma is deployed to reorganize and even disrupt the social imaginary in an effort to produce change. That is, the legitimate synthesis of utopian memory thinking occupies the libidinal charge traumatic memory produces so as to put these energies and affects to work in an effort to overcome habit and the limitations of our present circumstances: a practical experiment with the empirical material of memory and the real conditions of history.

Posing the question of how culture articulates and harnesses different libidinal energies and, at times, contradictory investments of desire, the central thesis of this book is that memorial culture registers both paranoid (fascistic) and open (schizoid) investments of desire. As the social field remembers, grieves, mourns, weeps over, and shares a sense of collective trauma, a political community emerges. At times the social force of collective trauma and turbulent political realities merge and other times they collide. In either event their combination is never entirely rational or logical. In what follows, we will pursue the ways in which cultural production taps into the rage, pain, and ardor characteristic of trauma with our overriding premise being: memorial culture cannot be sustained without the will of the public to remember and the desire to continue remembering.[10]

In the absence of social investment memorial culture would quite simply collapse and, it is to this connection between desire and sociality that the opening chapter intends to turn. It will be argued that as a form of social organization, trauma is not just managed and created through the process of social remembrance it also organizes a social habitat. That is, the fundamental issue is not what makes trauma a signifying event or experience but 'what causes it to move, to flow, and to explode'?[11] The answer Deleuze and Guattari give to this problem is 'desire.' The fascistic investment of desiring-production integrates trauma, turning it into a secure signifier into which all the messiness of trauma is rendered manageable. This prompts the following questions: how does the public subordinate itself to the labor of memory? Further, is this subordination symptomatic of a failure to repeat the past in a future-oriented way? Sketching out the theoretical framework that will be used to pursue such questions, Chapter 1 explores the sociality of collective remembrance and mourning, looking to the libidinal energies traumatic memory activates. We ask whether the revolutionary force of these energies are incarcerated and neutralized by the figure of Oedipus, as Sigmund Freud was to posit, or if indeed, the sociality of memorialization may in fact constitute a mode of social production and political potency. Using Deleuze and Guattari for guidance we will amend Freud's concept of desire and his use of an original site of trauma to bring into focus the socially productive force of traumatic memory in the context of cultural production. Outlining the first synthesis of desire – production and connection – and using Wilhelm Reich's thesis on the sociality of desire, this chapter will demonstrate the importance of looking to social oppression over and above that of individual repression (as Freud does) in our discussion of memorial culture.

If the essence of trauma is beyond representation interestingly the unrepresentability of trauma is also what makes it the prime subject of authoritarian power: as will be discussed in the context of Mark Rothko's color field pictures. That is, as a blank slate trauma is completely open to fascistic investment, one where all the messiness of trauma is resolved through a sublime identification (the reactive exercise of wish-fulfillment) with an ideal pictorial space. Authoritarian investments of desire (illegitimate syntheses of desire) include the excluded unrepresentable trauma and the sociality that comes from sharing trauma, by actually including it as a source of redemption. As Chapter 2 argues, this is why the sublime vision Rothko presents during the 1940s to the mid-1960s verges on the fascistic, because the life of trauma (in all its unmanageability) is turned into a limit-figure, a point of identification that functions like the law of the Father (as Freud was to advance) in which, as Jameson suggests, 'the structure of the Utopian wish-fulfillment' is 'itself slowly swung about into its object,' whereby form becomes content 'transforming the Utopian wish into a wish to wish.'[12]

Turning to Deleuze and Guattari for guidance we will examine how the experience of trauma is given transcendent meaning, arguing this produces a despotic connective synthesis to be made. For instance, while the abstract visual language of an abstract color field picture may articulate the problem of representation that Adorno raises in response to the holocaust, it can also mobilize the libidinal energies motivating trauma and fear within an Oedipal triangle – understood here as one that produces an alienated individual who finds investment in part objects, whereby the picture becomes the part object. If abstraction not only represents the silence that trauma invokes, but a more authoritarian identification with emptiness and the beauty of an ideal space constituted through the softened edges of Rothko's luminous floating rectangles, we need to urgently revise the way in which we put Adorno's challenge to de-aestheticize to work. In order to begin this journey we look to the concept of utopia as advanced by Jameson and Deleuze, proposing that perhaps it is not so much the content of memorial culture – understood as a transcendent space – but rather the affective force of memory to produce a utopian demand where Adorno's call to de-aestheticize is revived. Using Jameson, and in particular Ian Buchanan's response to Jameson's assertion that utopia is a dialectical practice that functions much like a promise-machine, we propose that it is only once memory is put to work as a utopian demand that memorial culture is pushed toward a newfound hope in the unforeseeable possibilities the future poses.

In Chapter 3 we look at how trauma can produce a legitimate connective synthesis. To do this, we address Maya Lin's Vietnam Veterans Memorial and in particular how it confronts the untimely dimension of trauma and the enormity of over 58,000 American lives lost by invoking a crack of unfamiliarity. That is, in Chapter 3 we examine how this memorial conserves blocks of sensation, using Deleuze and Guattari's assertion that all art is the being of sensation, a being that consists of the threefold connection between percept (pre-personal forces), affect (transformation), and house (a structure that mediates forces). In it we argue that prior to Lin's memorial there was a tendency towards a more monumental typology in memorial design. Monumentalizing the past immobilizes the social vitality of memory, defining and demarcating a limit-interpretation to it. We ask: what if the past was not immobilized, rather it unabashedly unleashed the provocative, violent, and despairing tendencies of the social field? How might this take cultural form? Pursuing these questions in the context of Lin's design we note the plane of composition she creates in her use of form, material, site placement, and organization, along with the conceptual development of a wall-becoming-window. Together these elements compose a compound of sensation that conserves the shockwaves the Vietnam veteran experience sent throughout American society, politics, and culture.

Quoting Walter Benjamin, Jameson observes that genuine memory determines 'whether the individual can have a picture of himself, whether he can master his own experience.'[13] To add to Jameson on this point, genuine memory also demands a little bit of forgetting in order to dialectically engage history and master experience and this is the fundamental point of Chapter 4: either we cannot represent the inchoate movement of traumatic memory (abstraction) or the concrete reality of trauma is suspended entirely (irony and pastiche). In the case of the former, as was argued in Chapter 2, this misplaced emphasis can produce an illegitimate connective synthesis of desire. Meanwhile, as is proposed in Chapter 4, the latter situation exemplifies an illegitimate emphasis at the level of the disjunctive synthesis; for when memorial culture is limited to connecting dependent terms memory fails to condition or affect the milieu in which it is itself concretely effected, hence the utopian break Jameson speaks of never takes place. Using statistics compiled by the Pew Research Center for the People and the Press on public viewing trends of news coverage for 9/11, it is suggested that media coverage of traumatic events may in effect fuel too much remembrance. It is argued that the visual power of collective trauma comes from its affective capacity and this is sometimes appropriated as a vehicle of repression.

If ever there was a danger in too much social remembrance then the public consumption of the documentation of US military abuses of Iraqi detainees at Abu Ghraib magnifies how this can occur when collective trauma is turned into a memory football – kicking one kind of uncomfortable memory to the other side of the field as a prelude to activating a sense of national strength, and as a way to counter the unsavory memories of 9/11. Chapter 5 proposes the images of 9/11 were stifled once the equally powerful albeit ethically compromising array of images detailing the torture of Iraqis entered the American social field. Looking to the affective dimension of visual culture we argue that documentation does not simply record an event it affects the investment of the libidinal charge and energies collective trauma brings into play. Using Foucault and the argument that power is dissociated from the body so as to paradoxically increase its power while also reversing the revolutionary energies that this may bring into effect, we propose that the power of the Abu Ghraib images lies in the way they supplanted the visual memory of 9/11 images with a new image of US strength and might.

Keeping in mind that 'desiring-machines work only when they break down, and by continually breaking down' the question our analysis of trauma produces is continued in Chapter 6 where we ask: how can trauma skirt the despotism of Oedipalization?[14] Here the Amish response to the slaughter of half of their schoolgirl population in Lancaster, Pennsylvania provides us with an interesting point of departure. The Amish did not advocate amnesia but a leaner more disciplined mode of public remembrance and as such trauma gave rise to what Deleuze has described as an orgiastic, not an organic representation. The concept of an orgiastic representation embraces the utopian demand of traumatic representation, whereby memorial culture discovers its own limitations in respect to organizing the unmanageable movement of traumatic effects and energies. When trauma is no longer the dominant point of reference around which memorial culture organizes itself (organic representation), representation begins to rediscover the monstrosity of trauma within itself. Put simply, it starts to operate unconventionally.

In Chapters 7 and 8 we turn to the relationship between traumatic memory and the built environment looking to the connection between public remembrance and the design and development of sites where traumatic events once took place. For example, in what way was the ground zero site in New York City defined by the libidinal charge 9/11 left behind? Governor Pataki's description of the Freedom Tower scheduled to replace the now fallen Twin Towers in New York assumes not only that safety and security can be built and set in concrete and glass, but also that safety and security define the architecture and urban space of ground zero in the wake of 9/11. He announced:

> Together we faced the challenge of redesigning the Freedom Tower and today we see the result is a better, safer, and prouder symbol of freedom for our skyline. This new design reflects a soaring tribute to freedom and a bedrock commitment to safety and security. The Freedom Tower will not only be a tremendous icon, it will also be an economic engine generating thousands of jobs for New Yorkers.[15]

This statement is entirely committed to the idea that the relevance of memory in the context of contemporary cultural production is purely symbolic: a dual symbol of democratic freedom and economic liberalism. While his position presupposes that the future form and function of the Freedom Tower will somehow be causally determined by the events of 9/11, he also seems blind to the fact that the full force of what happened on that day was the result of an indeterminate variable being inserted into the symbolic objects of capitalism and western democracy.

Baudrillard notes that terrorism 'is the act that reduces an irreducible singularity to the heart of a system of generalized exchange.'[16] What we end up with is a change in the rules so to speak, or more pertinently a complete suspension of them. Pataki denies the fact that the movement of memory doesn't just define, it also changes built space; it disrupts its organization as much as it reinvents it. Consequently, the commitment to safety and security that he focuses the public's attention on seems irresponsible and naive at best. There is neither absolute safety, nor security if one wants to talk about the vitality and validity of freedom in the same breath. Sadly though, the eagerness to live on and survive the terrorist attacks, symbolized here by the Freedom Tower, only reinforces the power and effectiveness of the suicide bomber who is 'as eager to die as the Americans are to live!'[17] In respect to the Manhattan ground zero site where the World Trade Center Towers crumbled on 9/11, it will be argued that trauma functions like a *logos* working to organize space around a newfound emphasis on tightened security controls, producing robust buildings and a design principle of risk reduction. Yet the real risk arises when civic life becomes arbitrary, because then life is reduced to a mere formality.

The manner in which the problem of traumatic memory is articulated in urban design is therefore clearly part of the problem of how design practice and theory explicitly organize urban life around a passive/active dichotomy. Here we go on to critically engage the in-depth and detailed study of terrorism in the context of urban design put forward by urban theorist Jon Coafee. He suggests that the territorial metaphors of 'wild' and 'safe' areas be used to separate threatening spaces from secure ones, not only implying that distance creates protection but that urban space is a passive container that can be secured through state planning and design initiatives.[18] Coafee's wild spaces of the city may be likened to the forces of terrorism that threaten to unravel the economic, social and political relations defining a city. However, he seems to articulate 'risk' in negative terms, and in so doing he reinforces the scaffolding of normative urban space defined against security and predictability, instead of problematizing and critiquing it. It is proposed that urban life is untidy and chaotic; however, when traumatic memory is put in the service of spatial striation – a space we occupy by measuring, counting, and organizing hierarchically – urban life turns into a formal problem of security enhancement and risk management. In effect, the focus on striating space stifles the vitality of the urban environment. At what point does an urban environment stop working as one? In short, the answer to this question is: when the cacophony of civic life stalls. This proposition invites us to look to another, less reactive example in Chapter 8. Studying architect Daniel Libeskind's Jewish Museum and Peter Eisenman's Memorial to the Murdered Jews of Europe in the city of Berlin, along with the traces left behind from the fall of the Berlin Wall in 1989, it is argued that the topography of contemporary Berlin could best be described as intensive, whereby the vitality of memory topographically differentiates memory from itself, producing a future-oriented urban environment.

Chapter 9 puts to work the final synthesis of desire: the conjunctive synthesis. In it we follow popular viewing trends of disaster coverage in America, noting the high rate of consumption for such events as compared to other politically significant events and popular entertainment shows. What the findings of the Pew Research Center suggest is that memorial culture is big business. Given the widespread reification of trauma in the media, through Hollywood, and the rising tourist industry to sites of holocaust destruction, we ask where the revolutionary force of memorial culture might lie? How can memorial culture interrupt the process of reification by putting the productive power of trauma – its social energies and affects – to work differently? If remembering traumatic events is another form of consumption then it seems that memorial culture is also another mode of economic production. What Deleuze and Guattari tell us is that economics is not just monetary, it also constitutes creative energies, these being the creative economics of social forces to reorganize the social capital of public remembrance so that collective memory struggles against being seamlessly integrated into the capitalist system.

This book does not profess to comprehensively survey the art of memorials. Instead, it presents a series of case studies concentrating on certain contemporary traumatic events and the cultural activity of memorialization, in order to exercise Deleuze and Guattari's concept of desire within the social framework of public remembrance. As such, the chapters are structured around the legitimate and illegitimate form of the three syntheses of desire: connective, disjunctive, and conjunctive. Overall, the paradigm of memorial culture being offered here is one where memory either affirms, legitimates, and advances a paranoid (fascistic) investment of social desire, or it stirs forth an open polyvocal (schizoid) one. The latter is a critical and joyful movement; the former immunizes us against the past while rendering the future mute. This is what Baudrillard warns us against when he says you 'weep over your own misfortune, and at the same time you are the best. And what gives us the right to be the best is that from now on, we are victims.'[19] Society need not pit death against life in an endless sense of suffering, injustice, and victimization; it can joyfully embrace the hardships and injuries of the past by choosing not to suffer in the face of it. This can only happen though once the *jouissance* of memorial culture is freed from the debilitating mechanism of a traumatic memory that condemns public remembrance to a melancholic look to the past without any glimmer of hope for what the future may hold.

Although memorial culture may not heal the wounds of collective trauma, the vitality of collective acts of remembrance, such as the forgiveness the Lancaster Amish community initiated in response to the killing of half their schoolgirl population, ultimately has nothing to do with curing or controlling social grief and everything to do with reclaiming a sense of joy and inventively engaging the energies, affects and forces grief stirs forth. The concept of 'memorial culture' originates at this crossroad starting with Deleuze and Guattari's definition of desire as social and ending with an idiosyncratic use of their concept of 'singularity' to revise their somewhat scathing assessment of memory in favor of a more positive praxis of memory thinking that taps into what we will call 'singular memory.' The proposition is that desire drives memory labor and singular memory ferociously instantiates a mode of remembrance always in excess of itself. The concept of singular memory implies a qualitative metastable memory, the content of which defies definition, measurement, and coherent representation. This is a slippery memory that is always more than its own internal organization. Singular memory is affective in so far as it is a memory *with* the world, not a single memory *in* the world, and for this reason it constitutes an ethical force, one that has the power to energize and activate the sociality of memory.

Notes

1. The realization that life merely exists and that existence does not necessarily have any meaning could also be described as an existential philosophical shift in focus. The groundwork for existential thought may have begun prior to World War Two with Søren Kierkegaard and Friedrich Nietzsche but the key figures commonly associated with existentialism include post World War Two philosophers like Jean-Paul Sartre, Simone de Beauvoir and Albert Camus; in theatre the playwright Samuel Beckett; and in the fine arts, the American Abstract Expressionist Jackson Pollock. For a solid and thorough introduction to existentialism see Cooper, David. *Existentialism: A Reconstruction* (Oxford: Blackwell, 1999) and MacDonald, Paul (ed.). *The Existentialist Reader* (Edinburgh: Edinburgh University Press, 2000).
2. Lukacs, John. *Historical Consciousness: The Remembered Past* (New Brunswick, NJ: Transaction Publishers, 2004), xii.
3. Arendt, Hannah. *On Violence* (San Diego, CA: Harcourt, Brace & Co., 1970), 13.
4. Ibid.
5. Ibid., 211–33.
6. Deleuze, Gilles. *Desert Islands and Other Texts: 1953–1974* (New York: Semiotext[e], 2004), 22–3.
7. Ibid., 24.
8. Jameson, Fredric. *Archaeologies of the Future: The Desire Called Utopia and Other Science Fictions* (London: Verso, 2005), 213.
9. Lang, Berel. *Writing and the Holocaust* (New York: Holmes & Meier, 1988), 179.
10. To borrow from Deleuze and Guattari: 'Desire is an exile, desire is a desert that traverses the body without organs and makes us pass from one of its faces to the other. Never an individual exile, never a personal desert, but a collective exile and a collective desert.' See Deleuze, Gilles and Félix Guattari. *Anti-Oedipus: Capitalism and Schizophrenia*, trans. R. Hurley, M. Seem, and H. R. Lane (Minneapolis, MN: University of Minnesota Press, 1977), 377.
11. Ibid., 133.
12. Jameson, *Archaeologies of the Future*, 213.
13. Jameson, Fredric. *Marxism and Form: Twentieth-Century Dialectical Theories of Literature* (Princeton, NJ: Princeton University Press, 1971), 62.
14. Deleuze and Guattari, *Anti-Oedipus*, 8.
15. Pataki, Governor. 'Design Plan for Freedom Tower: Introduction,' *Lower Manhattan Development Corporation: Remember, Rebuild, Renew*, 30 June 2005. See: http://www.renewnyc.com/plan_des_dev/

wtc_site/new_design_plans/Freedom_Tower/freedom_tower_intro.asp. Accessed on 10 May 2006.

16. Baudrillard, Jean. *The Spirit of Terrorism*, trans. Chris Turner (London: Verso, 2002), 9.
17. Ibid., 16. In a similar fashion, but writing during the Cold War, Arendt outlined that 'power cannot be measured in terms of wealth, that an abundance of wealth may erode power, that riches are particularly dangerous to the power and well-being of republics – an insight that does not lose in validity because it has been forgotten, especially at a time when its truth has acquired a new dimension of validity by becoming applicable to the arsenal of violence as well.' See Arendt, *On Violence*, 10–11.
18. Coafee, Jon. *Terrorism, Risk and the City: The Making of the Contemporary Urban Landscape* (London: Ashgate, 2003), 217.
19. Ibid., 61.

CHAPTER 1

Desire is Social

> . . . oedipalization is one of the most important factors in the reduction of literature to an object of consumption conforming to the established order, and incapable of causing anyone harm. (Deleuze and Guattari)[1]

Memorial culture appears in many different forms. There is the institutionalized setting of public commemoration, such as the celebratory activities of Memorial Day, or the countless memorials and monuments erected in public places. In addition, there is the whole industry of memorialization, such as memorial exhibitions and museums, as well as Hollywood's rendition of real-life collective traumas in film, not to forget the blossoming industry of memorial tourism to former concentration camp sites like Auschwitz and Birkenau. Further, there are the spontaneous memorials – teddy bears, flowers, wreaths, and letters – such as those flooding the gates of Buckingham Palace in London upon the death of Princess Diana (31 August 1997), or surrounding the perimeter of ground zero in Manhattan after 9/11.[2] More recently, a new phenomenon of cyber memorialization has appeared giving people the opportunity to produce spontaneous memorials online and these commonly take the form of letters and poems.[3] Needless to say, these are all examples of how culture is involved with shaping, organizing, and situating collective memory in space and time. Yet, how the movement of traumatic memory qualitatively changes the social field is not so easily located within the neat parameters of the public memorial or monument. This is because as renowned memorial scholar James E. Young notes, 'memorials by themselves remain inert and amnesiac, dependent on visitors for whatever memory they finally produce.'[4]

Young describes, evaluates, and critically analyzes a broad array of holocaust memorials and in particular he astutely notes the ideological implications of many memorial images and spaces. He insists a memorial is not neutral, going on to explain that depending on 'where and by whom these memorials are constructed, these sites remember the past according to a variety of national myths, ideals and political needs.'[5] As Young points out, memorials generally recall tragedy and offer members of the public a place to mourn, and an avenue through which to ritualize public remembrance. Monuments, as a subset of memorials, refer to the materials used to memorialize an event or person; these tend to be celebratory and triumphal. The limitations of monumentalizing the past are many, and one of the more illusory aspects of the monument that Young identifies is that, 'rather than embodying memory, the monument displaces it altogether, supplanting a community's memory-work with its own material form.'[6]

No matter how we define the similarities and differences between memorials and monuments though, the role of both is public remembrance. Accordingly, it is important we not only consider the meaning of any given memorial, as Young's study so thoroughly attends to, but also the deeper problem of how memory affects and energies are put to work by the public. Generally, the more acute the trauma, the more libidinal charge the work of public remembrance carries. Hence, rather than attend to the meaning of collective trauma and public remembrance, our focus here will be to consider how the social field puts trauma to work as a system of socialization, the outcome of which is memorial culture. In the context of our discussion of collective trauma, it will be proposed that it is not so much the subject who initiates the system of memory socialization and the distortions it produces, rather the subject is the effect of it. In addition, when we use the concept of desire Deleuze and Guattari advance, it becomes possible to identify two very different investments this system of socialization takes in the context of memorial culture: one is schizoid (open), the other fascistic (paranoid).

Undoubtedly, once we begin to identify memorial culture as animated by fascistic investments of social energies and affects, our analytic focus begins to widen the semiotic lens provided by Young to include libidinal semiotics. The former approach looks to the genre of memorials and monuments as texts, arguing that these constitute a language in general, and after examining individual examples what Young does is demonstrate how these produce meaning. Instead of arguing the memorial or monument is the effect of a system of signification, libidinal semiotics proposes memorial culture is the effect of an investment of libidinal energies and affects. Following Deleuze and Guattari's lead here desire is taken to be social. Briefly put, to speak of a schizoid investment of desire in the context of memorial culture is to extract the polyvocal movement of social energies and affects at play in the process of public remembrance. A schizoid investment of desire occurs when memorial culture registers the social force of collective trauma, yet this registration operates as an index to prompt the affective dimension of memory to generate future-orientated connections. A fascistic investment of memorial culture, on the other hand, is when the energies and affects the labor of memory produces are coded and given a fixed use. That is, as trauma registers throughout the social field it functions as a determinate entity. This chapter intends to begin the discussion of memorial culture from the vantage point of libidinal energy so as to outline these two very different investments of social remembrance (schizoid and fascistic) that underpin subsequent discussions throughout the course of this book.

The connection between desire, trauma, and memory was first put to work in the psychoanalytic theories of Sigmund Freud. As early as his lecture on 'The Origin and Development of Psychoanalysis' (1909) Freud presents the argument that '*hysterical patients suffer from reminiscences*', in so far as 'symptoms are residues and mnemonic symbols of particular (traumatic) experiences.'[7] He begins his historical survey of the development of the psychoanalytic method, as both research and praxis, with the story of a twenty-one-year-old patient whom the Viennese physician Dr Joseph Breuer treated. Regardless of being physically healthy, the patient suffered from severe emotional disturbances. She had been ill for two years, during which time her illness had developed a series of physical and psychic symptoms: paralysis, eye disturbances, impaired vision, nausea, and an inability to drink, regardless of how thirsty she became. Freud tells his audience how her 'powers of speech were reduced' to the point where she couldn't 'speak or understand her native tongue.'[8] Finally, she was subjected to what he described as 'conditions of "absence," ' characterized by confusion and delirium to the point where her entire personality changed.[9] Freud notes that the symptoms began while the young woman cared for her ill father, who later died. Breuer discovered: 'It was actually possible to bring about the disappearance of the painful symptoms of her illness, if she could be brought to remember under hypnosis, with an accompanying expression of affect, on what occasion and in what connection the symptoms had first appeared.'[10]

Prior to Breuer's use of hypnosis no one had successfully cured hysteria in this way. Indeed, the great discovery of Breuer, in Freud's opinion, was that psychic trauma, or affective experiences, cause hysterical symptoms. The character such symptoms take are determined by the lived experiences whose memory traces they embody. For this reason, Freud, like Breuer, concluded symptoms are not an arbitrary or mysterious function of neurosis. In order to cure the patient, the analyst sets out to erase the psychic cause of the illness by repeating memories in chronological sequence. Tracing back in time analysis starts with the last or most recent memory and ends with the original traumatic memory. This process of recalling forgotten memories by bringing them to consciousness removes the symptoms.

The task of Freud is to clarify the character and cause of symptoms or what he also calls mnemic symbols. A mnemic symbol is a symptom of a traumatic experience. He explains that walking through the city we encounter monuments that preserve the memory of a sad or terrible historical happening. Monuments are mnemic symbols just like other psychic symptoms, but whereas we tend to go about our everyday lives amid such monuments in the city, hysterics and neurotics fixate on the painful experience because they continue to be strongly affected by it. Indeed, they are unable to free themselves from the past and as such for them the reality of the past is reinforced at the expense of the present. Freud concedes that although we may be able to argue that Breuer's patient was in mourning for the death of her father and her fixation of feeling on the trauma is nothing abnormal, he clarifies that the longer the fixation the more abnormal it becomes. There is a point at which any fixation of psychic life on a traumatic experience in the past moves from normal mourning to an abnormal symptom of hysteria, or neurosis, and that would have to be when the symptom, or mnemic symbols, become more debilitating.

The intensity of emotions that a trauma produces has to find a means of escape, otherwise these begin to mutate and a symptom manifests itself. Symptoms are therefore the physical result of intensive emotional disturbances that have found no means of release. Elsewhere he describes this deferred effect as *Nachträglichkeit*: the original emotions and affects of the traumatic experience are not discharged and as they are deferred emotionally colored psychic energy becomes increasingly more exaggerated and eventually symptoms appear (what is also known as 'displacement'). This is why psychoanalysis, in its theory of hysteria, assigns importance to affective processes (which in Freud's later work came to be characterized as the unconscious). These processes are both internal to the self and yet outside of consciousness. What is especially interesting is that Freud does not suggest that repeating a memory always results in cure because repeating the past in analysis may not be sufficiently cathartic in and of itself. He admits that simply reproducing the traumatic scene to the physician does not necessarily result in a cure if 'the recollection took place without any generation of affect.'[11] The point here is that the intensity of memory recall is imperative in the context of therapy. Repetition of the past therefore implies a principle of futurity.

Evidently for Freud, we not only return to the repressed past, but we return in order to produce the present and future differently. As Deleuze and Guattari acknowledge:

> Freud noted from the beginning that in order to stop repeating it was not enough to remember in the abstract (without affect), nor to form a concept in general, nor even to represent the repressed event in all its particularity: it was necessary to seek out the memory there where it was, to install oneself directly in the past in order to accomplish a living connection between the knowledge and the resistance, the representation and the blockage.[12]

Cure comes when we identify that a demonic power is at work within the self but this identification process is outside the realm of reason and judgement. In fact, as an irrational and affective process of intensive energy it is completely beyond logic and absolutely resistant to objective measurement. The critical lesson of Freud now begins to emerge: subjectivity is the result of unconscious psychic forces, not human reason and consciousness. As noted, for Freud, this means we only ever get a glimpse of ourselves if we examine the effects of trauma. But we might retort: not everyone is suffering from abnormal or debilitating symptoms of neurosis and hysteria. This is true; nonetheless Freud's theory retains its significance.

In his lecture 'Resistance and Repression' Freud describes the case of a woman who falls ill not because of a traumatic event but out of frustration. The frustration this woman experiences as a result of her husband's impotence gives rise to symptoms of obsession. Although she has no intimate relations with her husband she continues to be faithful to him on account of her intense love for him. What she ends up doing is setting her 'husband on a pedestal' and in this way she both denies and corrects his impotence. In this case, Freud explains that her symptom is 'fundamentally a wish-fulfilment, just like a dream – and moreover, what is not always true of a dream, an *erotic* wish-fulfilment.'[13] Here the symptom acts as a substitute for sexual satisfaction. Interestingly, the symptoms are the result of a compromise struck between a positive substitute for sexual satisfaction and a negative strategy that fends off or stops sexual satisfaction.

Summarizing, Freud says this situation represents 'not only the repressed but also the repressing force.'[14]

With the structure of repression, Freud was able to argue that a traumatic memory and the affect of this trauma are pushed out of consciousness. Once unconscious, trauma simmers away. When this repressed and now magnified affect returns, it does so as a symptom. As noted, symptoms are cured by making their cause conscious, implying the cure lies in being able to represent trauma. The cure of representation relies upon the premise that what is represented is somehow immune to repression. This raises the question of how to bridge the gap between repression and representation, especially if the forces of repression are so strong that what is remembered is really only what the patient 'wishes' to remember. As a subset of repression, Freud later calls the opposition encountered during psychoanalytic treatment – resistance. All analysis, he says, struggles against defense mechanisms that resist the analyst's 'effort to transform what is unconscious into what is conscious.'[15] At this point, Freud is able to understand an important contextual relationship between the move out of unconscious life and into consciousness. He notes, 'an individual process belongs . . . to the system of the unconscious' and once resistances have been broken down they can in certain circumstances 'pass over into the system of consciousness.'[16]

Yet it is not just on the analyst's couch that resistance is encountered. As a psychic phenomenon, resistance also makes an appearance in the form of shame and guilt. Freud's studies on sexual perversion invoke the concept of resistance to help explain how sexual instincts struggle against mental forces whose aim is to keep perversion at bay and support normal sexuality. Here the social inscription of the instincts reappears. In his 'Three Essays on the Theory of Sexuality' Freud outlines the relationship between perversion and pathological symptoms, explaining that in the majority of cases the 'pathological character of a perversion is found to lie not in the *content* of the new sexual aim but in its relation to the normal.'[17] So when does a perversion become a pathological symptom? Freud provides the following explanation:

> If a perversion, instead of appearing merely *alongside* the normal sexual aim and object, and only when circumstances are unfavourable to *them* and favourable to *it* – if, instead of this, it ousts them completely and takes their place in *all* circumstances – if, in short, a perversion has the characteristics of exclusiveness and fixation – then we shall usually be justified in regarding it as a pathological symptom.[18]

The list Freud provides of perverse sexual activities is long and includes: homosexuality, bisexuality, deviant sexual aims such as a fetish or the sexual use of the anus, as well as sadistic and masochistic activities.

In his studies on the sexual life of human beings Freud concludes that the 'memories and associations arising during the analysis of symptoms [in adults] regularly led back to the early years of childhood.'[19] Further, a child is filled with libidinal energies. 'Libido' is the name he gives to 'the force (in this case that of the sexual instinct) by which the instinct manifests itself.'[20] Whereas the Hungarian physician Dr Lindner had previously pointed to the sexual nature of an infant suckling at the mother's breast, Freud took this observation and turned it into an entire theory of childhood libido.[21] Children are commonly understood to be asexual beings, propounding the myth that they are also pure and innocent. The period where the sexual life of the child is most obvious occurs up to the age of five or six at which point it begins to be covered by the 'veil of amnesia' and as Freud has already noted, once these psychic energies are repressed they fester and later reappear as symptoms.[22] What psychoanalysis tries to do is lift the veil of amnesia.

Completely dependent upon others for its survival the child forms a deep attachment toward those who nurture and meet its immediate needs. Interestingly, the logic of Freud's position here is that we are, as Elizabeth Grosz puts it, 'biologically social, social out of biological necessity.'[23] Suckling at the mother's breast the first infantile sexual impulses appear.[24] Sometimes though the child wishes to continue suckling regardless of being full. Sensual sucking creates erotogenic zones in those parts of the body, such as the mouth and lips where a sexual pleasure is derived from sucking. The child then discovers that it can receive the same pleasure from its erotogenic zones independent of the mother's breast, for instance simply by sucking its thumb. The oral instinct turns auto-erotic when the child gives up on the outside object and the sexual aim 'finds its object in the infant's own body.'[25] Later Melanie Klein added to this, arguing that infants start out with a focus on part objects, such as the breast (source of nourishment and security) but this comes at the expense of the whole object. At around three to four months the infant starts to form a whole object – in the figure of the mother – unifying what were once parts of the whole.

Meanwhile, for Freud sexual life, or libidinal function, continues developing when the child then abandons its own body and takes up an outside object once more. This time it is not the mother's breast but the mother herself who becomes the love object, replacing the physical demand for pleasure with a mental attachment to the mother. What now needs to be mastered is this perverse sexual attraction for his mother and this is the heart and soul of psychoanalysis. Freud declares: 'Every new arrival on this planet is faced by the task of mastering the Oedipus complex; anyone who fails to do so falls a victim to neurosis.'[26] To summarize, Freud uses the Greek legend of King Oedipus to explain the psychic process of a child taking his mother as his love-object. Briefly, Sophocles in his tragedy tells the story of Oedipus who by decree of the Athenian oracle was doomed to kill his father and marry his mother, Jocasta. Trying to escape this terrible destiny he 'did everything possible to escape the oracle's decree and punished himself by blinding' and yet he still unwittingly committed both crimes.[27]

The Oedipus complex begins when the affections a little boy feels for his mother develop into feelings of animosity toward the other parent who is perceived as threatening. So, how does the young boy give up on his erotic feelings for his mother? During this stage the boy has also discovered he can satisfy his own sexual interests by masturbating and at around this time he also notices his mother does not have a penis. He becomes anxious not to lose his organ of satisfaction believing at some point a woman must have been castrated as punishment for doing something wrong. He connects this traumatic realization of the castrated mother to the parental threat of castration should he continue masturbating. Briefly put, fearing castration the boy succumbs to the law of the father and gives up on his mother as his primary love object. Meanwhile, the affections a little girl feels for her mother shifts onto her father, once she also realizes she lacks a penis. Becoming jealous – penis envy – girls abandon their feelings for their mother and begin to desire their fathers.[28] While her father cannot give her a penis he can provide her with a baby: a penis substitute. This is not the place to enter into a deeper discussion of the problems Freud's explanation of female sexuality raises, although it is worth noting that many commentators involved in feminist theory have cogently challenged the model of female sexuality defined in terms of lack.[29] What is interesting for our purposes here is that in his use of the Oedipus complex Freud figures the libido within a model of 'lack.' Furthermore, he binds desire to the law of signification.

In order to become a member of a social community the boy has to detach his libidinal interests away from his mother and redirect these toward another outside love-object. Part of this process entails the boy creating a newfound relationship with his father. The hostility previously felt toward his father is reconciled once he submits to the authority of the father. The 'normal sexual life of the adult' appears once the 'pursuit of pleasure comes under the sway of the reproductive function and in which the component instincts, under the primacy of a single erotegenic zone, form a firm organization directed towards a sexual aim attached to some extraneous sexual object.'[30] In response, the criticism Deleuze and Guattari advance against Freud is that the Oedipus complex completely destroys the productive potential of desire strangulating all libidinal energy within a repressing representation entailing the triangle of mummy, daddy, and me. As Eugene Holland explains 'the ruse of the law prohibiting incest (and perhaps of law in general)' is that 'it presents desire with a falsified image of what desire "wants" in the very act of prohibiting it . . . docile subjects supposedly discover what they desire at the same time that they discover they cannot have it.'[31] Deleuze and Guattari write:

> Freud made the most profound discovery of the abstract subjective essence of desire – Libido. But since he realienated this essence, reinvesting it in a subjective system of representation of the ego, and since he recoded this essence on the residual territoriality of Oedipus and under the despotic signifier of castration, he could no longer conceive the essence of life except in a form turned back against itself, in the form of death itself.[32]

That is, the cure consists of a twofold movement: repetition and reproduction, and the effect such a focus has for cultural analysis is paralyzing, as best evidenced by Freud's discussion of the artist Leonardo da Vinci.

In the essay 'Leonardo da Vinci and a Memory of His Childhood' Freud draws a connection between creative energy and the sexual instincts, the reason being that the

> sexual instinct is particularly well fitted to make a contribution of this kind since it is endowed with a capacity for sublimation: that is, it has the power to replace its immediate aim by other aims which may be valued more highly and which are not sexual.[33]

In order to justify these observations he butchers a memory from Leonardo's early years, interpreting it as evidence in support of repressed erotic feelings for his mother. Apart from the fact that the key symbol of interpretation was a mistranslation from the Italian,

Freud bastardizes the memory when he inserts it into a clear system of signification: 'the existence of a causal connection between Leonardo's relation with his mother in childhood and his later manifest, if ideal [sublimated], homosexuality.'[34] Leonardo's creative production, as I have discussed elsewhere, is reduced to mere biography; creativity is Oedipalized and worse still it 'constitutes a successful psychoanalysis, a sublime "transference."'[35] The mistake of Freud, as Deleuze conceives it, comes from how the past defines the present and future.[36]

Taking up the Stoic thesis that all signs (as signs of the present) consist of a connection between the past and future as these coexist as dimensions of the present, Deleuze announces: 'A scar is the sign not of a past wound but of "the present fact of having been wounded": we can say that it is the contemplation of the wound, that it contracts all the instants which separate us from it into a living present.'[37] Needless to say, the present has a history, but it only partially owns that history because as we contemplate the past we only partially signify it. The present can never fully articulate the entirety of the past, nor the coincidence of the past and present within the present. The contemplation of the present is a signifier for the signified contemplation of the past and future dimensions of the present; the difference between them is ontological. Although a sign may refer to the past and future it also belongs to the present as a relation between the two. In this respect, the sign is neither more of the present than it is of the past. To clarify Deleuze employs the Stoic distinction between a natural and artificial sign, the former is the dimension of the past and future in the present, the latter is the self-representational gesture that extends the present into the past and future. Indeed, in Chapter 2 of *Difference and Repetition* Deleuze insists that as a dimension of the present and the future, the past is not a separate moment in time. That is, it contracts in the present before thinking and remembrance take place in the mind and in this regard it can be said to be the 'passive synthesis' of habitual memory. In addition, in *Anti-Oedipus* he and Guattari explain that the productive nature of the unconscious consists in the 'passive synthesis itself insofar as it ensures the relative coexistence and displacement' of its two different functions – to create connections after breaking the flow of habit.[38]

The question is how can desires that belie the signifying authority of Oedipus and paternal law be produced? In the context of our future discussion of memorial culture it is critical we ask this for it is useless to argue memorialization is how the public overcomes a collective trauma or, as Young advances, memorial culture participates in the system of signification neatly representing past traumas, because both positions alienate the productive nature of remembrance from the authority of trauma leaving the whole question of desire unaddressed. The best way to understand the sociality of desiring production is to amend the Freudian conception of libido structured around an original wound that took place in the past, this being a position that quite simply incarcerates desire within a familial triangle and parental images. Deleuze and Guattari initiate their revision of Freudian desire by looking to Wilhelm Reich for guidance and in particular his idea of the sociality of desire.

Using the work of Reich, Deleuze and Guattari ask what happens if the process of socialization does not civilize the individual, but rather the individual is conceived of as the effect of distortions arising out of the system of socialization itself. Reich, for instance, provides a compelling analysis of fascism, arguing that it is not ideology that produces the masses but the other way around. He proposes the human character develops along three trajectories. The first, the surface layer of the personality, is epitomized by tolerance and self-control, working hard to curb and manage sadistic impulses by enforcing ethical norms that in turn produce socially cooperative individuals.[39] The second intermediate layer is characterized by natural impulses and is ultimately where repressed drives exist. Or, in the terminology used by Freud, this is where unconscious activity takes place. Ideology is produced here at level two of the character structure. Regulating the economy of individual sexual energies, the world of secondary drives reproduces the civilities of the cultivated layer as a distortion and here we have the first hint of Reich's thesis on the fascistic tendencies of the masses.

Thus far there is nothing new about these claims; however, what Reich adds to the mix is a biologic core. This third layer is a priori to the formation of character and is described by him as 'essentially honest, industrious, cooperative, loving.'[40] As the biologic core of natural human sociality, and unlike the second layer, the third deepest and most revolutionary layer of the human structure is not socially represented. This is because the distortions natural impulses undergo as they pass through into the second layer pervert the drives. For Reich the expression of humanity's naturally cooperative sociality has so far only happened in cultural activities such as art and music although he does conclude that to date these have not carried much influence when it comes to shaping human communities. The revolutionary spirit of the biologic core strives for truth so as to bring about social improvement. Fascism combines the rebellious feelings of the third layer with the reactionary social ideals of the first. Reich writes that '[f]ascist rebelliousness always accrues where a revolutionary emotion, out of fear of the truth, is distorted into illusion.'[41] The repression of the biologic core starts early in life as the authoritarian structures of the patriarchal family not only work to repress female independence and sexuality but also produce in children a subservient attitude to authority (father figure). 'The tie to the mother,' writes Reich, 'is the basis of all family ties. In their *subservient emotional core* the notions of *homeland and nation are notions of mother and family*.'[42] It is significant to note that Reich is not simply making a biological connection here. The tie he speaks of is a social product and this is because it creates a familial and nationalistic connection. The manner in which an authoritarian social system turns into nationalistic feeling is through sexual repression. Once natural sexual relations are externalized they also become a reactionary social force.

The idea that sexuality is a social force is not exactly new, it is also at the heart of the Freudian notion of the Oedipus complex. Neither is the sociological interpretation of the family entirely groundbreaking, for it can also be found in Marxist theory. What is interesting though is that Reich tells us that political and libidinal economies coincide. In so doing, he proposes that the gratification fascism incites is the effect of psychic conflicts between instinct and morality, a conflict that takes the form of reactionary politics and social life. For this reason 'all forms of fascistic, imperialistic, and dictatorial mysticism can be traced back to the mystical distortion of the vegetative sensations of life, a distortion that results from a patriarchal and authoritarian organization of the family and state.'[43] Žižek shares a similar view of ideology when he states:

> Ideological hegemony is thus not the case of some particular content directly filling in the void of the empty Universal; rather, the very form of ideological universality bears witness to the struggle between (at least) two particular contents: the 'popular' content expressing the secret longings of the dominated majority, and the specific content expressing the interests of the forces of domination.[44]

Fascism for Žižek is a formal principle that distorts pre-existing social hostilities. For Reich fascism also constitutes a distortion of pre-existing social organizations, although at the core of Reich's social organization there also exists a freedom-fearing authoritarian structure. Reich uses this idea to stage a heavy indictment against

Marxism.[45] The critique he levels here is primarily against the socio-economic focus of Marxism, whereby he goes onto explain this gives no consideration to the subjective elements of history. The irony here is that in being unable to put its own methodology of dialectical materialism to work the revolutionary Left of pre-World War Two Germany failed because it could not historically comprehend new social situations. What distinguished, for example, the German National Socialists from the shared political discourse of material needs and hunger at the time was the metaphysical focus of National Socialism.

If the majority is suffering on an economic level what is it about this situation that does not coincide with the psychic structure? The whole Marxist concept of class-consciousness is premised upon economic structures – class – that determines the superstructure – consciousness and ideology. However, one needs to be brutally aware of the fact that one is living in a wretched situation before change occurs.[46] Putting a real dent in the theory of raising class-consciousness, Reich points out that sometimes economics and ideology do not coincide. It is not just a matter of individuals being disenfranchised by their economic conditions, for on another level economics are also material conditions and processes embedded in the psychic structures of individuals and society. What Reich introduces into the Marxist thesis is the possibility that it is not just economics that determines ideology but ideology can also determine economic existence, in so far as psychic factors not just economics also constitute a historical force. This idea gives us a first real glimpse at the connection between desire, memory, and social organization. He says the 'ideology of every social formation has the function not only of reflecting the economic process of this society, but also and more significantly of embedding this economic process in the *psychic structures of the people who make up society*.'[47] That is, we are subject to both social ideology and our material circumstances and yet in our activities we also reproduce the selfsame ideology out of which psychic and social conditions derive. In this regard, ideology is conceived of as a material force. For instance, moral control and abstinence come into direct conflict with material joy, noting everything is 'to be recommended which hardens the body and eases the fight against immorality, such as *gymnastics, sports, swimming*, hikes and getting up *as soon as* one wakes up. *Moderation* in the consumption of food and above all of beverages. *Alcohol is to be avoided*.'[48] The fundamental limitation of the Marxist notion of raising proletariat consciousness comes from the emphasis placed on economic interests because sexual conflicts and the authoritarian nature of private life are completely ignored.

The implication of Reich's account of the mass psychology of fascism is that the individual is not unique and distinct from others; neither does an individual have a fixed and knowable nature that can be used to justify social life and order. Once we turn our back on these principles, which it should be noted are the key tenets of individualism and liberalism, the premise of an autonomous individual is held to ransom. Accordingly, the universal notion of rights, or the interests of a given social class, or even a determinate past trauma that can be objectively represented, is also invalidated. If an individual does not always consciously make a choice then the self-willed individual sustaining the concept of the 'autonomous individual' is surrendered. For Reich both subjectivity and fascism are the effect of particular investments of desire. In addition, the individual does not always act in accordance with the use of reason. Here we are reminded of the limitations of liberal theory as it gives enormous weight to 'individual will' for the production of society and as a source of social change.

Significantly, Reich argues fascism is the effect of authority structures that spring from the family. Herein consists the key lesson of Reich: it is the repressed feelings and suppressed position of a body that produce fascistic orientations. Understood in this way fascism is, as Reich outlines, the 'organized political expression of the structure of the average man's character.'[49] Just as much as a political system or ideology can organize or channel desires in a particular direction, Reich's point is that investments of desire can also nuance the social field. Likewise, Deleuze and Guattari posit and it is worth quoting them at length here:

> It is not a question of ideology. There is an unconscious libidinal investment of the social field that coexists, but does not necessarily coincide, with the preconscious investments, or with what the preconscious investments 'ought to be.' That is why, when subjects, individuals, or groups act manifestly counter to their class interests – when they rally to the interests and ideals of a class that their own objective situation should lead them to combat – it is not enough to say: they were fooled, the masses have been fooled. It is not an ideological problem, a problem of failing to recognize, or of being subject to, an illusion. It is a problem of desire, *and desire is part of the infrastructure*.[50]

For Deleuze and Guattari that infrastructure is first constituted from the synthesis of connection, meaning the productive force of the 'actions and passions' to freely produce connections and where there is no distinction between 'producing and its product.'[51]

Desiring-production resists the rules of representation and the law of signification because it articulates the real. Yet, it needs to be noted that this articulation in its combination of duration and matter can never be fully grasped through the logic of representation. In fact Deleuze and Guattari argue that Freud's tripartite formula of mummy, daddy, and me is ultimately neurotic:

> The fact is, from the moment that we are placed within the framework of Oedipus – the cards are stacked against us, and the only real relationship, that of production, has been done away with. The great discovery of psychoanalysis was that of the production of desire, of the productions of the unconscious. But once Oedipus entered the picture, this discovery was soon buried beneath a new brand of idealism: a classical theater was substituted for the units of production of the unconscious; and an unconscious that was capable of nothing but expressing itself – in myth, tragedy, dreams – was substituted for the productive unconscious.[52]

If desire does not lack anything and what it produces is real rather than fantasies or imaginary objects, what kind of 'real' does desire produce? The first order of desire is productive and when we reduce it to representation in the way that Freud does we basically strip it of its productive function. Borrowing from Reich, the formulation Deleuze and Guattari provide is that desiring-production is social production, in so far as a social field is the historical outcome of the particular investments desire takes and these can be either schizoid or fascistic.

It is not that fascistic or schizoid desiring investments are polar opposites; indeed they are implied within each other because sociality can be likened to a Whole containing both schizoid and fascistic forces virtually within itself. The role of the instincts here is to organize these investments. The fascistic or paranoid investment 'subordinates desiring-production to the formation of sovereignty and to the gregarious aggregate that results from it.'[53] On the other end of the spectrum entirely, a schizoid investment they write 'brings about the inverse subordination, overthrows the established power, and subjects the gregarious aggregate to the molecular multiplicities of the productions of desire.'[54] *Schize* refers to the rupturing process, the effect of which is a *schism* and in this way to speak of schizoid investments of desire they mean a dynamic connection that is implicitly disjunctive in its movement. Succinctly put, schizoid desiring-investments are revolutionary, open, polyvocal, liberating, and productive and can be characterized as a zigzag or rhythm. Fascist, or paranoid, investments of desire are organized around a despotic signifier; they are univocal, expressive, and can be characterized by a line or form. So how does desire actualize if it does not follow the structure of signfication? The actualized investment, as either schizoid or fascistic, moves out of virtually constituted relations and here emerges the productive nature of desire. No one actual investment of desire fully represents the possible investments of desire that desiring-production virtually constitutes. Fascistic or schizoid unconscious libidinal investments emerge empirically as the outside contracts and folds over onto the inside. In this light, is trauma necessarily negative? Or, to phrase the same question slightly differently: how can trauma be positive? Perhaps if we follow Deleuze and Guattari, this would be when the connection between trauma and remembrance subverts order and the fixity of meaning, taking on what they might call a schizoid dimension.

Keeping in mind that desire for Deleuze and Guattari is not psychological, it is social, the point in all this is that the character memorial culture takes depends on how desires are invested throughout the social field and this book is concerned with looking at instances when the culture of social remembrance becomes either schizoid or fascistic. In the pages that follow we will extract the schizoid and fascistic dimension of memorial culture by exploring examples of their investment through the connections society makes between collective trauma and the culture of public remembrance. While it would be impossible to provide a comprehensive overview of all instances of memorial culture we will limit our analysis to some of the most recent incidents such as the American reaction to the Vietnam War, Germany's response to the holocaust, remembering 9/11, the widespread dissemination of images of US military abusing Iraqi detainees at the Abu Ghraib prison, the My Lai massacre during the Vietnam War, and the American Lancaster County Amish shootings.

Notes

1. Deleuze, Gilles and Félix Guattari. *Anti-Oedipus: Capitalism and Schizophrenia*, trans. Robert Hurley, Mark Seem, and Helen R. Lane (Minneapolis, MN: University of Minnesota Press, 1983), 133.
2. It seems odd to note that there was a three-mile-long procession of mourners the *day before* Diana's funeral all the way across the globe in San Francisco. It began from the Castro District and moved to the British Consulate, lead by a truck filled with flowers and an enlarged photo of the princess.

3. The Royal Family has established a Princess Diana memorial site online: http://www.royal.gov.uk/OutPut/Page151.asp. Accessed 14 November 2006. There is another public site established by an individual – that speaks out against drunk driving and urges visitors to boycott tabloids that support paparazzi. Cargaro, Carolyn. *In Memory of Diana, Princess of Wales*, http://www.gargaro.com/diana.html. Accessed 14 November 2006.
4. Young, James E. *The Texture of Memory: Holocaust Memorials and Meaning* (New Haven, CT: Yale University Press, 1993), xiii.
5. Ibid., 1.
6. Ibid., 5.
7. Freud, Sigmund. 'First Lecture,' *The Standard Edition of the Complete Psychological Works of Sigmund Freud*, Vol. XI, trans. James Strachey (London: Vintage, 2001), 16. The First Lecture was delivered on Monday, 6 September 1909 at Clark University, Massachusetts.
8. Ibid., 10.
9. Ibid.
10. Ibid., 13.
11. Ibid., 18.
12. Deleuze, Gilles. *Difference and Repetition*, trans. Paul Patton (New York: Columbia University Press, 1994), 18–19.
13. Freud, Sigmund. 'Resistance and Repression,' *Introductory Lectures on Psychoanalysis*, trans. James Strachey (London: Penguin, 1991), 340.
14. Ibid., 342.
15. Ibid., 335.
16. Ibid., 336.
17. Freud, Sigmund. 'Three Essays on the Theory of Sexuality,' *The Freud Reader*, ed. Peter Gray (London: Vintage, 1995), 253.
18. Ibid., 253.
19. Freud, Sigmund. 'The Sexual Life of Human Beings,' *Introductory Lectures on Psychoanalysis*, trans. James Strachey (London: Penguin, 1991), 352.
20. Ibid., 355.
21. Freud mentions Lindner's discovery in 1879. Ibid.
22. It should be noted that elsewhere he says this period of infantile amnesia continues up until six to eight years. See Freud, Sigmund. 'Three Essays on the Theory of Sexuality,' 259; and Freud, 'The Sexual Life of Human Beings,' 354.
23. Grosz, Elizabeth. *Volatile Bodies: Toward a Corporeal Feminism* (Sydney: Allen & Unwin, 1994), 55.
24. In fact Freud goes so far as to assert: 'Sucking at the mother's breast is the starting-point of the whole of sexual life, the unmatched prototype of every later sexual satisfaction, to which phantasy often enough recurs in times of need.' See, Freud, 'The Sexual Life of Human Beings,' 356.

25. Freud, 'Three Essays on the Theory of Sexuality,' 272.
26. Ibid., f.9, 290.
27. Freud, Sigmund. 'The Development of the Libido,' *Introductory Lectures on Psychoanalysis*, trans. James Strachey (London: Penguin, 1991), 373.
28. Freud writes: 'Overcome by envy for the penis – an envy culminating in the wish, which is so important in its consequences to be boys themselves.' See Freud, 'Three Essays on the Theory of Sexuality,' 271.
29. For important feminist interruptions and challenges to the Freudian explanation of female sexuality see Gallup, Jane. *Feminism and Psychoanalysis: The Daughter's Seduction* (London: Macmillan, 1982); Grosz, *Volatile Bodies*; Irigaray, Luce. *Speculum of the Other Woman*, trans. Gillian Gill (Ithaca, NY: Cornell University Press, 1985); and Irigaray, Luce. *The Sex Which Is Not One*, trans. Catherine Porter with Carolyn Burke (Ithaca, NY: Cornell University Press, 1985).
30. Freud, 'Three Essays on the Theory of Sexuality,' 272.
31. Holland, Eugene W. *Deleuze and Guattari's Anti-Oedipus: An Introduction to Schizoanalysis* (London: Routledge, 1999), 37.
32. Deleuze and Guattari, *Anti-Oedipus*, 333.
33. Freud, Sigmund. 'Leonardo da Vinci and a Memory of His Childhood,' *The Freud Reader*, ed. Peter Gray (London: Vintage, 1995), 452.
34. Freud also goes on to provide a strikingly reductive analysis of homosexual activity writing the 'boy represses his love for his mother: he puts himself in her place, identifies himself with her, and takes his own person as a model in whose likeness he chooses the new objects of his love. In this way he has become a homosexual.' See Freud, Sigmund. 'Leonardo da Vinci and a Memory of His Childhood,' 461–3. What Leonardo wrote in his manuscript was the following:

    > Questo scriuersi distintamete del nibbio par che sia mio destino, perchè nella prima ricordatione della mia infantia e mi pare ache, essendo io in culla, che vn nibbio venisse a me e mi aprisse la bocca colla sua coda, e molte volte mi percuotesse co tal coda dentro alle labra.

    Translated into English this is:

    > This writing distinctly about the kite seems to be my destiny, because among the first recollections of my infancy, it seemed to me that, as I was in my cradle, a kite came to me and opened my mouth with its tail, and struck me several times with its tail inside my lips.

    Freud mistranslated the Italian for 'kite' to mean 'vulture.' The original Italian along with the translation of the Codex A, 65b; 199b appear in Richter, Jean Paul. *The Notebooks of Leonardo Da Vinci: Volume 2* (New York: Dover Publication, 1970), 414.

35. See Parr, Adrian. *Exploring Leonardo da Vinci in the Context of Contemporary Art and Culture* (New York: Edwin Mellen Press, 2003); Deleuze and Guattari, *Anti-Oedipus*, 134.
36. Deleuze discusses the importance of how we pose the problem of this connection between the drives and symptoms with Guattari. See Deleuze and Guattari, *Anti-Oedipus*, 23–5.
37. Deleuze, *Difference and Repetition*, 77.
38. Deleuze and Guattari, *Anti-Oedipus*, 325.
39. It is for this reason that Reich later compares the surface layer of the cultivated human being to liberalism.
40. Reich, Wilhelm. *The Mass Psychology of Fascism* (New York: Farrar, Strauss & Giroux, 1970), xi.
41. Ibid., xiv.
42. Ibid., 56–7.
43. Ibid., 136.
44. Žižek, Slavoj. *The Ticklish Subject: The Absent Centre of Political Ontology* (London and New York: Verso, 1999), 185.
45. More specifically he is speaking of the failure of German Marxism between the years 1917 and 1933.
46. Žižek has an interesting take on this. Following Laclau he writes: 'Leftists usually bemoan the fact that the line of division in the class struggle is as a rule blurred, displaced, falsified – most blatantly in the case of rightist populism, which presents itself as speaking on behalf of the people, while in fact advocating the interests of those who rule. However, this constant displacement and "falsification" of the line of (class) division *is* the "class struggle": a class society in which the ideological perception of the class division was pure and direct would be a harmonious structure with no struggle . . .'. Žižek, *The Ticklish Subject*, 187.
47. Reich, *The Mass Psychology of Fascism*, 18.
48. Ibid., 161.
49. Ibid., xii.
50. Deleuze and Guattari, *Anti-Oedipus*, 104.
51. Ibid., 4 and 7.
52. Ibid., 24.
53. Ibid., 376.
54. Ibid.

CHAPTER 2

Utopian Memory

There seems to be a fundamental difference between public apathy toward past communal trauma and being morbidly obsessed with such events. Anyone attempting to come to terms with the incommensurability of representation with regard to trauma has inevitably to address this difference. Ultimately, apathy towards the past provides the motivation for the self-indulgent question of 'Why bother caring?' to be posed, while critical distance encourages us to ask 'What does it really matter?' The latter is a question Theodor W. Adorno discusses in *Negative Dialectics*, but contrary to the belief that questions posed in this way are a sign of bourgeois indifference, he points out that this type of question turns one into a spectator and as such it effectively brings to our attention the inhuman aspect of human existence.[1] In what seemingly appears to be a paradoxical proposition, Adorno announces that the inhuman inheres in the human and it is here where negative dialectics begins. That is, he does not just advance the importance of being a spectator for critical self-reflection; rather the point he makes is that the authenticity of thinking comes from thinking against itself.

When Adorno puts forward in his essay 'Cultural Criticism and Society' his now well-cited dictum that to 'write poetry after Auschwitz is barbaric' he is not suggesting we give up on culture altogether (although he is certainly suspicious of political art); instead he brings to our attention the problem of re-presenting the wound of traumatic events and the difficulty any concept of the 'inhuman' poses for humanism per se.[2] Largely, this is a cultural problem of how to avoid displacing the affective power of trauma in a playful gesture of banality or resolving its unmanageable dimension via an appeal to the historical guarantees humanism provides us with. For Adorno, the concentration camp environment of Auschwitz sent the sociality of culture into crisis and for this reason it 'demonstrated irrefutably that culture has failed.'[3] This is not to suggest that he believes culture is poorly equipped to respond to the traumas of history; rather, he teaches us the important contribution culture can make in confronting the full force of trauma without undermining its singularity. As Adorno sees it, culture has both a positive and negative aspect. It is positive in so far as it promotes freedom; negative once it obstructs freedom, which is largely, in his estimation, when culture is in consonance with instrumental reason. The negative and violent character of reason comes from its complicity with forces of domination.

In the *Dialectic of Enlightenment*, writing with his fellow exile Max Horkheimer from Califorinia between 1941 and 1944, Adorno says the focus of the enlightenment project was primarily to emancipate humanity from its subordination to nature.[4] However, he insists what instrumental reason has in effect done is create a system of social rationalization, as expressed throughout the various social, political, and cultural institutions of the enlightenment project, all of which work to dominate the very freedoms they were meant to instigate in the first instance. As he sees it, what is inhuman is the rational process of reasoning that prevents us from living a fully human life. Adorno insists the attempted extinction of humanity that took place during the holocaust is also responsible for extinguishing the utopian dimension of culture. He writes:

> When the German fascists defamed the world and replaced it with the inane notion of 'art appreciation,' they were led to do so only by the rugged interests of the authoritarian state, which still feared the passion of a Marquis Posa in the impertinence of the journalist. But the self-satisfied cultural barbarism that clamored for the abolition of criticism, the incursion of the wild horde into the preserve of the mind, unawares repaid kind in kind. The bestial fury of the Brownshirt against 'carping critics' arises not merely from his envy of a culture that excludes him and against which he blindly rebels, nor is it merely his resentment of the person who can speak out the negative moment that he himself must repress. Decisive is that the critic's sovereign gesture suggests to his readers an autonomy he does not have, and arrogates for itself a position of leadership that is incompatible with his own principle of intellectual freedom.[5]

What he draws attention to here is an alienated cultural mode that has increasingly come under the sway of the hegemonic workings of reason. In this regard, it is uncompromisingly violent. The challenge is to produce an implicitly utopian culture, one that articulates itself without recourse to 'communication': an art form that is both independent and social. In retaliation against alienated culture he advances a method of de-aestheticization, or as Shoshana Felman explains, he demands art justify its own existence, meaning the utopian dimension of culture comes from the way in which it writes against itself in an act of critical self-referentiality.

How can the closed-circuit of self-referentiality ever aspire to being critical? From an empirical standpoint this seems at best idealistic and at worst, simply glib.[6] One possibility is with what Davis terms 'deracination.' He proposes that traumatic experience renders the Kantian epistemological undertaking, whereby our conceptual framework is applied to the data of our experiences, to be inadequate. This is because trauma clouds the object of inquiry so that knowledge is thrown into crisis. Referring to the discipline of history, he says this happens when 'the very nature of knowledge – of what it is we want to know and why – is at issue.'[7] He adds, 'crisis in any discipline is valuable because it renews our contact with something else that Heidegger formulates . . . when he defines a "metaphysical" question as one that "puts the very being of the questioner into question." '[8] Avoiding what he sees as the pitfalls of postmodern irony and historical play, along with the essentialism at the heart of humanist history Davis turns our attentions to a dialectic of affect, announcing that the method historians use would benefit from art forms that take traumatic impact as their first and last historical fact. All in all, identifying a disciplinary limit, he advocates a process of detached reasoning that combines both an objective and subjective stance towards objects of knowledge. According to him, the explanatory power indicative of objectivity may be reassuring. Nevertheless, it continues to strip the crisis out of trauma. Similarly, it is in the crisis that trauma invokes where Adorno identifies the utopian power of culture and for this reason he writes that by making culture the object, the critic objectifies culture, turning it into a commodity; on the other hand authentic culture suspends objectification.

As Davis sees it, the problem with objectivity is twofold. First, the subject limits the terms and conditions that engage history. Second, and as a consequence, this produces a limit on what can be known which is ultimately an authoritarian impulse and one that Adorno also alerts us to when he says that if 'thought is not measured by the extremity that eludes the concept, it is from the outset in the nature of the musical accompaniment with which the SS liked to drown out the screams of its victims.'[9] Subjectivity, Davis says, has a dialectical potential because it is a process involving self-mediation and affective transformation. What happens though if we actually put deracination to work in the context of cultural production? If subjective affect becomes the basis for how we articulate and confront the unknowable and unrepresentable experience of trauma, what might this actually entail?

The traumatic impact Davis speaks of is what led New York School painter Mark Rothko to reject academic painting and the human figure entirely.[10] Although the abstract language of Rothko's color field paintings could be discussed in purely formal terms – line, color, scale, shape, and depth – his work belies rational and objective calculation. Using thin layers of color that bleed over and into one another, the sense of a determinate boundary is infected by shifts in hue and tone. Rothko vertically composes floating rectangular forms concomitantly producing an image that makes reference to both portraiture (vertical) and landscape painting (horizontal). Over time Rothko would reduce the number of rectangles in a picture choosing to work increasingly on larger canvases so that the separation between art object and viewer was reduced to the point where the viewer would feel like they were within the picture from the moment they encountered it. In a letter addressed to Katharine Kuh on 25 September 1954, Rothko explains the largest pictures 'must be first encountered at close quarters, so that the first experience is to be within the picture. This may well give the key to the observer of the ideal relationship between himself and the rest of the picture.'[11] His earlier and later works were medium in scale, for example the social realist *Subway Scene* (1938) measures 89×120 cm, and his surrealist *Hierarchical Birds* (1944) is 100.5×80.5 cm, as compared to his color field works during the early 1960s which exploded in size becoming as large as 236.2×203.2 cm as in *Orange, Red and Red*, or *Dark Gray Tone on Maroon* that measures 340.5×188 cm. Hence, in an effort to overcome the picture being subordinated to mere wall decoration, Rothko dramatically increased the scale of his pictures, and when he had the choice he preferred to hang them in small rooms where they would move from the floor to the ceiling and even extend out beyond the edges of the wall.[12]

Emphasizing the painting as an object in and of itself, over and above that of the Renaissance idea of the painting being a window unto the world, Rothko's translucent rectangular forms exist purely as blocks of color. By the late 1940s the visual elements making up the formal composition of his pictures became increasingly simplified, from a multiplicity of washed-out geometric forms floating on the surface, as in *Multiform* (1948) where we see approximately ten rectangular forms of varying size, color, and dimension, that eventually were reduced as in *Number 7* (1951) where we are presented with three blocks of color in purple, yellow, and orange. Rothko again simplified these so that by the late 1960s compositional elements of his pictures had been scaled back to a single division through the middle of the canvas. As Rothko softened the edges of the planes making up the picture during the height of his color field days, he abandoned illusionist space. The result was, a luminous floating space that has now become the signature of Rothkoesque aesthetics. However, one implication of the softening of the edges of these works during the 1940s to mid-1960s is that he sacrifices the contour. This means neither the abstract form nor the ground plane has an edge/limit, so that both appear to sit together on the same plane. The obvious result of this gesture for the viewer is illiteracy: we can no longer read the picture as a three-dimensional area nor can we simply flatten the space into two-dimensional form. For example, the geometric elements of earth yellow, bright yellow, and orange rectangles making up *Yellow and Gold* (1956) are suspended and left hovering in a dirty white void. Yet Rothko resolves this largely unintelligible relation when he put composition in the service of representation. This is because the strong horizontality of the dirty yellow block and the white line above and below demarcating two dominant blocks of color in orange and yellow immediately references the tradition of landscape painting, while the vertical composition of rectangular elements nods to portraiture.

More significantly, through the formal combination of squares and rectangles Rothko quite clearly produces a religious subject making reference to Christ on the Cross; this compositional geometry is no different to the vertical arrangement of squares and rectangles in, for example, the floor plans of Gothic and Renaissance European churches. While there is no referential within the structure of these pictures from the late 1950s to the early 1960s that we can use to spatially orient ourselves the formal organization of the picture reveals a pictorial essence (religious subject) and in this way abstraction narrates religious experience (stirring forth a sublime experience in the viewer). Similarly, and revealing a humanist focus on emotion, Rothko understands the process of creation as an 'unknown adventure in an unknown space' so that the picture is 'a revelation, an unexpected and unprecedented resolution' for both artist and viewer.[13] This is sounding a little like the original tragedy Friedrich Nietzsche celebrates in *The Birth of Tragedy* whereby Dionysus, as Deleuze describes it, 'reproduces the contradiction as the pain of individuation but resolves them in a higher pleasure, by making us participate in the superabundance of unique being or universal willing.'[14] In what is commonly used as an example of sublime art, Rothko resolves the impossibility of representing horror and chaos by abandoning mimesis in favor of abstraction, so that life is redeemed through the negativity of horror. In a statement issued by Rothko and two fellow color field painters, the three announce that although the critic may find their pictures confusing they have no intentions of defending what they do because the pictures 'make their own defense' as their explanation comes 'out of a consummated experience between picture and onlooker.'[15] Obviously then, Rothko did not attempt to 'represent' the sublime experience of horror in all its alienation, for instance in the way that the German romantic painter Caspar Friedrich did; rather introducing a humanist edge into abstraction the problem of presenting the unfamiliar becomes one of 'evoking' a sublime experience within the viewer.[16] The criticism here is that his pictures are therefore not abstract enough because they articulate redemptive experience as the condition of possibility for the unfamiliar. Why they present an illegitimate connective synthesis is because aesthetic abstraction is put in the service of an identifiable and determinate organization. To clarify, the libidinal charge of the unfamiliar and the horror of the sublime is connected to a unified subjective ground so that the creative potential of generating other associations is frozen within one interpretation of sublime horror – subjective affect is assigned a place in the consummated experience of the picture and the viewer (as Rothko himself describes it).

If we look to *Number 10* (1958) we are presented with a clear division across the lower middle of the picture. A solid red-black tone defines the upper half of the canvas and a deeper darker red almost fusing with the background hovers in the lower section.[17] The color contrasts of dark and light are relations of value defined by light and dark tones. In this picture the balance struck between weight and weightlessness creates a transitional space as positive and negative forms are laid in opposition to one another, evoking a sense of existential vulnerability: the viewer is irreconcilably poised between the two and pushed into the void presented there. Davis might describe such a work as a 'thanatopic image,' that being an image that works to root out the viewer's experience of inner death that consequently becomes the basis of praxis. This is possible because the 'wound has become the place from which one acts in combating the force of death without and within.'[18] Although Davis argues that at this 'register, to feel is to take upon oneself the burden of the articulation of the world that does not resolve or "tone down" affect but that sustains and deepens its claim upon us,' the logic of ontological affect as subjective that Davis advances runs the risk of Oedipalizing the incoherent in an aesthetic experience of identity formation, whereby the subject coalesces with the object in the sublime chaos of emptiness, as the contour is held to ransom.[19] To return to the above example of *Number 10*, the picture is not simply an experiment in relations of color, the viewer is moved by what these connections represent and symbolize – a redemptive space. The horizon line functions like the eye of God transporting the viewer into an idealistic space defined by mystical experience and the somber landscape such illusion introduces.

Remember, for Rothko, what the picture represents is a nothingness into which all the fantasies of the subject can be read and resolved and in this respect the utopian content of his pictures provides the viewer with a guarantee. It is how this resolution takes place that is of interest here – in the final instance the resolution could be likened in some respects to a repressive structure whereby the problem of tragedy and human existence predetermines the pictorial solution of an indescribable nothingness that the color field dictates. Rothko's fourth dimension is made possible only because of the fundamentally autonomous standing of the picture, an independence that anticipates the self-regulating space of absolute identification with the void. Therefore, the connection between pictorial space and situated subjectivity consists of a move from the messiness of the world into another ideal perfected domain and it is this classical organization that produces an illegitimate connective synthesis – what the picture expresses is an essence, not a connection or an accident.

In effect, it could be argued that Rothko is anxious and even hostile towards the radical possibilities of paint as raw matter, in as much as he averts the violence of manual space (where the body of the artist as much as the materiality of the paint exceed representational organization) and the changes in direction such accidental encounters with the body produces. At times Rothko prefers to literally glaze over the surfaces of his pictures in order produce a visual idealism of translucency as saturated tones turn into transparent ones – what Deleuze might call '*luminous disaggregation*' – undermining the objective qualities of color and the materiality of paint in and of itself as light distributes evenly across the picture plane (and in this regard these works share a formal similarity to the Renaissance technique of modeling in light and shade – *chiaroscuro*).[20] Color is henceforth put in the service of narration as we tell a story about what we think is taking place in the shadows or in the light. The authoritarian implications of this highly regulatory connection between the empirical conditions of the medium and the will to introduce an idealistic space come from aestheticizing the struggle of painting per se. More specifically, this struggle is neutralized once the raw edges of the brushstroke are feathered as in *Yellow Orange Red on Orange* (1954) so that, to borrow from Deleuze, the contour of each color plane is no longer geometric but organic, and as Deleuze says 'the organic contour acts as a mold, in which contact is made to work toward the perfection of the optical form.'[21] Ultimately, what this means is that the 'organic contour remains unchanging and is not affected by the plays of shadow and light, no matter how complex they may be', producing zones of formal indistinction.[22] Or, when color represents the void as a resolution to the chaos of life more than showing us something of the struggle of existence the picture foregoes the initial relations of unintelligibility it incites. Unlike the abrasive use of green in combination with yellow and red in Van Gogh's famous painting of peasant shoes that Jameson found so instructive, Rothko's color combinations up until the late 1960s neutralize the violence of diverging relations of tonality emitted in the contours of Van Gogh's shoes in favor of subtle shifts in color value.[23]

Although Rothko's abstract works, like many other abstract painters of his generation, are a 'radical attempt to institute an optical space of transformation,' one that relies on 'disintegrating factors, on relations of value, of light and shadow, of clarity and obscurity,' his voids up until the late 1960s fix the viewer in sacred time and space so as to foster contemplation of an ideal realm at odds with the misery and harsh realities of the real world.[24] The majority of his color fields produce a series of harmonious connections in proportion, color, painterly texture, and composition, and when combined these are expressive of a harmonious relationship between humanity and the cosmos. The world is presented as constant and yet incomprehensible, more than it is changeable and comprehensible. We are left with a pictorial organization whose utopian content narrates a clearly moral vision of human existence. It is at this level, one that Deleuze and Guattari might describe as an illegitimate connective synthesis, where the utopian content of the pictures connects the ideal space of the void to a utopian interpretation of that space viewed as redemptive. Here the transcendent interpretation of utopia is created by the apparent entrapment of the subject, who succumbs to the authority of the picture. Further, the reinforcement of this connection between utopia and content produces a balanced and proportionate structure (a fixed interpretation in space) neutralizing the very line that separates utopia from the present condition. Briefly, what constitutes utopian praxis is the very struggle over the temporal condition of that line between the utopian and present condition. When we therefore speak of the form of utopia (as opposed to utopian content) we are referring explicitly to this struggle. As such, Rothko's redemptive space is also where the utopian demand of art is expelled.

In addition, we cannot forget the connection Rothko makes between morality and his pictures. His work sets out to judge life in terms of aesthetics, proposing that human life can be validated and atoned for aesthetically. Tragedy is not an aesthetic phenomenon for Rothko; it is aesthetically judged and in this regard his pictures are implicitly religious and didactic. He himself noted: 'I think I can say with some degree of truth that in the presence of the pictures my preoccupations are primarily moral and there is nothing in which they seem involved less than aesthetics, history or technology.'[25] The Oedipal structure of self-referentiality is now disclosed: the raw and 'meaningless materiality of the body and nature,' as Jameson was to describe it, is infused with moral value – haptic (from the Greek, *apto*, to touch) space is no longer presentable, as a visual organization structured around representation and signification is kindled.[26] The visual void concomitantly represents and resolves the 'lack' that the nothingness of the color field unmistakably expresses, and like Adorno's insistent rejection of societal rationalization, this resolution, to borrow from Jameson, is the effect of a narcissistic obsession 'with the self as the vehicle of anxiety, rather than with the free acts that generate anxiety.'[27] Trauma is formally represented and experientially resolved as the key ingredient of aesthetic experience and in this way the color field void never fully realizes its utopian potential as a dialectical tool.[28] Deleuze and Guattari were absolutely spot on when they noted in *Anti-Oedipus* the neurotic tendencies of abstraction:

> A paranoiac *form of expression* that no longer even needs to 'signify' its reactionary libidinal investments, since these investments function on the contrary as its signifier; an Oedipal *form of content* that no longer even needs to represent Oedipus, since the 'structure' suffices.[29]

In many respects the challenge to de-aestheticize that Adorno confronts us with is one of how culture can authentically affect and be affected by life. Here, Deleuze provides us with an interesting point of departure. In *Difference and Repetition* he distinguishes between the criterion of accuracy and that of authenticity. A representation he states is 'a false movement of the abstract' whereas a-presentation is the singular subject that persists in the abstract effect of negative bare repetition.[30] Using the criterion of accuracy leads to a repetition of the Same, whereas the criterion of authenticity produces a repetition of heterogeneity, a dynamic connection unfolding as the pure movement of difference. The latter he describes as affirmative, the very excess of the Idea; it is categorical not conjectural, dynamic rather than static.

Rothko's pursuit of the incommensurable, one that harbors a definitively negative traumatic experience, turns the problem of representation into a repressive strategy and this is one of the central insights of Deleuze and Guattari's critique of psychoanalysis raised in the previous chapter. They note this situation doesn't just domesticate, it also silences a subject. Using the Oedipal framework in a manner that convinces the viewer they are producing 'individual, personal statements,' what in fact happens is that we are stripped of our capacity to speak freely and openly.[31] In their view, schizoanalysis works to de-Oedipalize us by introducing a 'malevolent activity' into the equation.[32] Rather than engage in a moralizing discourse to do with the fundamental good of humanity, schizoanalysis challenges the Platonist vision of reality divided between the ideal order of the True and the mere copies of this as they appear in tainted form in the real world. For Deleuze and Guattari there is no finite structure representative of identity, the self, psyche, or the world as a whole. Advocating for a concept of difference in and of itself, they prefer to celebrate simulacrum. Deleuze says:

> The simulacrum is the instance which includes a difference within itself, such as (at least) two divergent series on which it plays, all resemblance abolished so that one can no longer point to the existence of an original and a copy.[33]

The connective synthesis becomes an illegitimate connection when self-referentiality fails to produce difference. What we are left with is an exhausted force emptied of all affirmation, joy, lightness, and positivity. Meanwhile, a legitimate connective synthesis is an affirmative transmutation, a process of repetition that produces simulacrum: creative differences.

It is in his study of Nietzsche where Deleuze puts the practical and affirmative character of the eternal return to work, extracting from the concept the following important lesson: 'The lesson of the eternal return is that there is no return of the negative. The eternal return means that being is selection. Only that which affirms or is affirmed returns.'[34] Repetition does not make the same return, rather it is difference that is selected through the return and as such eternal repetition is intrinsically creative. Without this difference a dominating force emerges, denying everything in its wake that it is not, to the point where this negative dialectic turns into the very essence of the force itself (this could also be understood as an illegitimate use of the connective synthesis). Deleuze uses this distinction between affirmative and negative forces of difference in his work with Guattari. Essentially, a schizoid investment of desire can also be construed as an affirmative and open connection, while a fascistic or paranoiac investment is filled with the negativity of religious moralizing and disgust, the pathos of contradiction, along with the nostalgia for a vanished past setting out to 'justify life and submit it to the labour of the negative.'[35] It is in this latter sense that the illegitimate connective synthesis is made simply because the utopian demand of the connection to transmute as it affirms is ossified. Here a detour through the works Rothko produced in the final years of his life can be instructive when clarifying what a legitimate connective synthesis may look like.

In 1968 Rothko suffered from an aneurysm of the aorta and was unable to endure the physical demands of working on canvas. As such he began using acrylic and paper. After initially stapling the sheets to plywood he moved to taping them down with masking tape. This made it easier for him to remove the sheets without damaging them. Consequently, after the masking tape was detached from the paper a border emerged and a partial pictorial object that could be detached from the white wall ensued. The effect of this accidental marking was remarkable because a forcefield contour came into play working to ground the geometric elements dividing the picture plane that had up until this point hovered in space. Contour is understood as an isolator, even a 'line that delimits nothing still has a contour,' because a contour has a 'power of vibration and nonlocalization.'[36] Working with this accidental manual marking, Rothko uses the contour to connect the form and ground, delimiting the limits of each and flattening both onto a single plane. In this way, the contour works to give this flattened area a visual tangibility otherwise not evident in the more luminous works of the late 1950s and early 1960s. In this series color moves 'closer to the pure state of a pictorial "fact" that has nothing left to narrate.'[37] The temperature of color is gauged as browns are cooled and blues are warmed. Tones begin to fracture, as black tends towards blue, green, or even pink; these tones include within themselves other pure monochrome tones defining either the upper or lower region of the picture so that no one element transcends the other. Here the contour of the masked edges deterritorializes the void, deforming the monochromatic purity constituting one half of the picture, partially attaching this half to the brushed regions of the other half. Continuing on from here, Deleuze is instructive in his clarification that this 'fact is the constitution or reconstitution of a haptic function of sight,' whereby the 'accident . . . has itself become durable.'[38] More importantly, the elements of the picture are detachable from the ground unlike the floating rectangular forms of his earlier work. Second, they are partial voids, for what had once been a far off world that we succumbed to has now been zoomed in on. We are now presented with a close-up. Interestingly, it is only during the latter part of his life work that the complete transcendent object of aesthetic experience (illegitimate connective synthesis) turns into a partially detachable object (legitimate connective synthesis).

We are now left asking: does the color field picture invoke an aesthetic of terrorism? The short answer is prior to the last few years of Rothko's life it does, in so far as the formal organization of the picture narrates a religious subject – absolute, ideal, and separate – and also in the way the sublime experience of human tragedy and the horror of existence is abstracted to signify a religious experience of redemption. In these works aesthetic experience descends from the despotic signifier of the sublime object. In the spirit of Heidegger a happening of this kind harnesses the unintelligible power of anxiety by throwing Being into ontological crisis and despair, as all the guarantees of the humanist subject are put out to pasture. In this manner, the privilege Rothko gave to subjective affect means that his pictures end up participating in the very problem they set out to avoid. All in all, the irony is that up until the late 1960s Rothko produced representational images and remained firmly rooted in a sentimental, albeit morbid, version of humanism. This is because the works prior to 1968 summon forth an encounter with nothingness that doesn't just represent the human condition they also inaugurate a complete connection between viewer and art object, in so far as these works resolve any unmanageable experiences the viewer may have through their identification with the picture. And were we to follow the narrative definition of ideology Jameson gives in *Fables of Agression* they could be described as being completely ideological. That is, the pictures involve a 'mapping of the real, but also the essentially narrative or fantasy attempt of the subject to invent a place for himself/herself in a collective and historical process which excludes him or her and which is itself basically nonrepresentable and non-narrative.'[39] Adding to this, the terrorism comes from the idea that art can produce a kind of autism in the subject, in the same way as Deleuze and Guattari accuse the analyst of doing with the schizophrenic, whereby the subject succumbs to the fantastical authority the picture poses. Furthermore, although it may be an object without purpose, and in this regard it is radically autonomous as Adorno suggests, it is a far cry from being a socially conditioned entity.

To return to Adorno once more, in his estimation the criticality of self-referentiality is the effect of a dialectic taking place between independence and sociality and when it is erased culture quite simply looses its integrity and utopian demand altogether. He announces 'no authentic work of art and no true philosophy, according to their very meaning, has ever exhausted itself in itself alone, in its being-in-itself. They have always stood in relation to the actual life-process of society from which they distinguished themselves.'[40] Having exorcized the figure Rothko's abstract canvases may on first appearances be conceived of as responding to Adorno's call to de-aestheticize, clearly meeting the challenge Adorno put forward that art discover its utopian potential. Yet it is only when we are too hasty that we collapse this appeal of Adorno's with a call to abstract expressionism of the kind Rothko produces up until the latter part of his life. The point Adorno tried to make is that when we take the utopian content of a cultural object as our point of departure we only ever focus on the object rather than the dialectical condition of utopia. Instead, utopia is a structural contradiction that constitutes the machine of history, as Jameson was to argue.

For Jameson, utopia is a dialectical process, working to defuse everything that gets in the way of realizing freedom. That is, utopia is not the synthesis of a series of idyllic social principles epitomized by a free social collective existing in another space and time as advanced by both Plato in the *Republic* and Thomas More in *Utopia*, this being a topological vision of utopian places that remain totally unrelated to the realities of the contemporary world.[41] Although he condemns the fantasy mechanism of utopia for bearing all the 'earmarks of compensation and denial' Jameson salvages the truth value of the fantasy, arguing it can be a useful instrument of philosophical speculation when it is used to confront the reality principle.[42] He goes on to say:

> The daydream can succeed as narrative, not by successfully eluding or outwitting the reality principle but rather by grappling with it, like Jacob's angel, and by triumphantly wresting from it what can precisely in our or its own time be dreamt and fantasied as such.[43]

Instead of focusing on the content of utopia, or the representation of the idea of utopian life styles, Jameson concentrates on what Ian Buchanan helpfully describes as the machine of utopian praxis, whereby the failure of utopia is considered to be useful. The optimism of utopian failure arises from how utopia can be dialectically put to work, and in Jameson's thinking, its significance comes from this failure – the failure of utopia to present itself in reality.[44] The failure utopia presents effectively brings reality into sharp relief; in so doing it forces us to meet head-on the challenge unfreedom poses in the context of our current situation. In this way, the machine of utopia is inherently performative because, as Buchanan explains, it presents what it in fact represents by paradoxically not presenting it.

Using Derrida for guidance, the example Buchanan gives is that of the promising-machine: a voluntary act undertaken without expectation. The promise, he says, may create an expectation but it can only be said to be a promise in so far as it remains unfulfilled – were it to be realized the promise itself would rapidly come to an abrupt end. Further, promises are made without any guarantees for we never really know in advance which promises will come to fruition and which ones will expire completely. What is interesting about Buchanan's use of Jameson and the concept of utopia is that he insists the logic of the promise doesn't provide us with any guarantees; its utopian work comes from how it keeps the window of opportunity open onto the future. In effect, this open expectation spurs us on to actively engage with our current conditions and improve these in a future-oriented way. Hence, utopia is a history machine, as it puts history in the service of freedom and this is an idea that shares sympathies with the concept of utopia Deleuze and Guattari advance.

In *What Is Philosophy?* Deleuze and Guattari outline their rather idiosyncratic concept of utopian thinking. They clearly state the similarity between their concept of utopia and that of Adorno's negative dialectic, because like Adorno what makes the activity of philosophy political is their shared belief in a utopian principle central to thought itself.[45] However, contrary to the model of conflict espoused by Adorno, they claim it is not resistance or conflict that defines utopian thinking, because this implies a dualistic way of thinking (where the outside is the antithesis of the inside). On the contrary, philosophical praxis for Deleuze and Guattari is inherently utopian in so far as it produces new concepts. In turn, these create new peoples and new earths. Utopian thought consists of an experimental struggle with the past taking place in the context of the present, all for the sake of the future. That is, philosophical thinking works to create a future that is different, yet informed by the past and present. In this way, the concept of utopia is associated with another concept of theirs – absolute deterritorialization.

Briefly, the concept of deterritorialization points to a line of escape, or a decoding movement. Expressive of the mobility of the whole, absolute deterritorialization is a temporal movement and one that is immanent to relative deterritorialization. For this reason it can be described as a virtual movement animated by the movements of relative deterritorialization taking place within actual life. Relative deterritorialization brings the parts of a set into relation, producing changes within and among the parts in question. For instance, in a Rothko color field painting the composition of the picture (floating geometric forms organized as a landscape composition and yet framed by a portrait layout) formally produces a relative deterritorialization. Meanwhile, the varying intensities of hue and color effected through the gradations of his bleeding lines and the zones of washed color invoke an absolute deterritorialization of portraiture and landscape. Yet, the point of view implied by the portrait layout is another way of reterritorializing these movements, working to generate a unitary movement, and as we have already articulated above this topological definition of trauma as a utopian space into which all the fantasizes and contradictions of the subject are resolved and subsumed could testify to a more authoritarian tendency within the color field works. As such, relative deterritorialization involves the movement of immobile spatial segments and the parts (lines, planes, volumes) these consist of, tending overall towards the closure of a set.

Deleuzian utopia neither refers to an ideal social organization nor does it posit an Other time unrelated to the real. Utopia for Deleuze and Guattari is absolutely real; it entails an untimely mode of thinking that involves a time to come and the becoming of unforeseeable futures.[46] What this means for our broader discussion of traumatic memory in the context of this book is that the utopian potential of memory does not come from what memory guarantees; instead it surfaces in the demand memory makes on the future. Further, if the deterritorializing and liberating movement of culture comes from its capacity to effect change through lines of escape as opposed to contradiction in the way that Adorno advocates.[47] As we will see in Chapter 4, for this demand to retain its utopian potential it still needs to be dialectically engaged and in this way the demand we speak of also entails the ability to forget. Now we are faced with a choice between a nostalgic turn to the past whereby memory is defined by temporal inertia (a finite regulating past) and a nonmoralizing future-oriented conception of memory in the service of an indeterminate existence. Essentially, the dilemma of representing trauma that Adorno noted now marks a moment of temporal complexity rather than spatial impossibility (such as in the color field void).

At this point we return to our opening problem of how culture can extract the sense of trauma in all its complexity, especially its inhuman dimension. Davis suggests a combination of objective and subjective historiography, one that looks to art for guidance. But as already noted the sublime experience of the void does not necessarily invoke the utopian demand of the inhuman; instead it can produce an authoritarian limit of identification. For Adorno it is only in so far as culture 'withdraws from Man' that it 'can be faithful to man.'[48] Libeskind's response to Adorno is that 'anyone who takes a neutral viewer of the Holocaust, who is able and willing to discuss it in statistical terms, is taking the position of the Nazis.'[49] He agrees with Adorno and extracts the implications this position has for architecture: 'If in architecture, you neutralize the issue, if you find yourself focusing on numbers and "good taste," then you are no longer participating in the truth of it.'[50] But what might the 'truth' of traumatic memory entail? Following Nietzsche, for Deleuze this means 'bringing of power into effect, raising to the highest power' and creating new possibilities in life, all the while using the criterion of authenticity over and above that of accuracy.[51] Deleuze vehemently retaliates against the binary logic of true/false on the basis that it is exclusionary. That said, he also insists in *Negotiations* that 'the idea of truth isn't something already out there we have to discover, but has to be created in every domain,' by which he means we invent truths through a process of falsification: we falsify established positions.[52] However, quite different to the principle of negation underpinning Adorno's understanding of the dialectic, Deleuze maintains that the process of falsification amounts to understanding the ideas of another in an operation similar to what Bergson might describe as an act of 'fabulation': through the reflective series a variety of terms take shape, and out of which a people is constituted. And it is precisely the authentic condition of truth that is experimental, as this gives rise to excess and affirmation where we pragmatically engage with the problem of representation that traumatic memory poses.

On the whole, the sense of trauma can never be reduced to a problem of perspective because all this does is either posit the authority of one perspective over others (on the basis of accuracy), or completely strip trauma of its affective impact through a multiplicity of perspectives. Thus far there is not much difference here between Davis and Deleuze. However, where they do part company is over how affect is apprehended. Davis chooses the binary logic of a subject and object arguing in favor of a situated subjectivity. Yet, in situating the subject, affect is ensnared in a determinate structure (subject). For instance, to state that the holocaust happened during World War Two is to concomitantly determine a fixed point in space and time; however, the sense of trauma lingers on, occupying many different points in space – Germany, a survivor, art, Israel, holocaust museums – and many points in time – now, then, between, again, and soon. It becomes clear that were we to posit a situated subjectivity in the context of trauma, the affect of trauma (beyond spatial and temporal coordination) that arises out of the compossibility of human and inhuman (pre-individual) affect is completely negated when it is identified solely in terms of subjective affect. It is compossibility that trauma invokes and this compossibility destabilizes the very ground of subjectivity Davis attempts to construct. Using Deleuze, the task becomes one of how memory and trauma connect: whether this is an illegitimate (habitual and subjective) or legitimate connective synthesis (productive and affective).

After considering the connection between trauma and remembrance it becomes apparent that it is not so much a matter of deciding upon whether or not one memory is more accurate than another; rather we need to begin to address the authenticity conditioning the truth of memory and it is this authenticity wherein lies the utopian force of traumatic memory. This chapter has argued that the work of memory is implicitly utopian but this is only if we use it as a utopian promise-machine (to borrow from Buchanan); only then are we better equipped to meet the challenge to de-aestheticize that Adorno poses in the wake of the holocaust and engage the affectivity of trauma with what Deleuze describes as the 'intensive fact of the body.'[53]

Notes

1. Adorno, Theodor W. *Negative Dialectics*, trans. E. B. Ashton (London: Routledge, 1973), 363.

2. The essay was written in 1949 and first published in 1951. See Adorno, Theodor W. 'Cultural Criticism and Society,' in *Can One Live after Auschwitz?*, ed. Rolf Tiedemann (Stanford, CA: Stanford University Press, 2003), 162.
3. Adorno, *Negative Dialectics*, 366.
4. Adorno, Theodor W. and Max Horkheimer. *Dialectic of Enlightenment: Philosophical Fragments*, trans. Edmund Jephcott (Stanford, CA: Stanford University Press, 2002).
5. Adorno, 'Cultural Criticism and Society,' 149.
6. Felman, Shoshana. 'Education and Crisis, or the Vicissitudes of Teaching,' in Caruth, Cathy (ed.). *Trauma: Explorations in Memory* (Baltimore, MD: Johns Hopkins University Press, 1995), 39.
7. Davis, Walter. *Deracination: Historicity, Hiroshima and the Tragic Imperative* (New York: SUNY, 2001), 7.
8. Ibid.
9. Adorno, *Negative Dialectics*, 365.
10. Born in Dvinsk, Russia in 1903 Rothko (originally Marcus Rothkowitz) emigrated with his family to the United States in 1913.
11. Rothko, Mark. *Writings on Art* (New Haven, CT: Yale University Press, 2005), 99.
12. His dealer Sidney Janis describes Rothko's hanging instructions during the mid-1950s in this way. See Compton, Michael. 'Mark Rothko, the Subjects of the Artist,' in *Mark Rothko 1903–1970* (London: Tate Gallery, 1987), 56.
13. Rothko, Mark. 'The Romantics were Prompted . . .,' in Harrison, Charles and Paul Wood (eds). *Art in Theory 1900–2000: An Anthology of Changing Ideas* (Oxford: Blackwell, 2003), 574.
14. Deleuze, Gilles. *Nietzsche and Philosophy*, trans. Hugh Tomlinson (New York: Columbia University Press, 1986), 12.
15. Gottlieb, Adolph, Mark Rothko and Barnett Newman. 'Statement,' in Harrison, Charles and Paul Wood (eds). *Art in Theory 1900–2000: An Anthology of Changing Ideas* (Oxford: Blackwell, 2003), 568–9.
16. In seeking out the tragedy of human experience the existentialist focus of Rothko means with his large-scale color fields subjective affect becomes the site of emancipation, or what Davis might term in the context of deracination as situated subjectivity.
17. The softness of the brushstrokes defining the lower half of this picture are reminiscent of Rothko's earlier experimentation with watercolors.
18. Davis, *Deracination*, 226.
19. Ibid., 227.
20. Deleuze, Gilles. *Francis Bacon: The Logic of Sensation*, trans. Daniel W. Smith (Minneapolis, MN: University of Minnesota Press, 2003), 105.
21. Ibid., 102.
22. Ibid.

23. Jameson, Fredric. *Postmodernism: Or, the Cultural Logic of Late Capitalism* (Durham, NC: Duke University Press, 1991), 7.
24. Deleuze, *Francis Bacon*, 104.
25. Cited in Compton, Michael. 'Mark Rothko, the Subjects of the Artist,' *Mark Rothko 1903–1970* (London: Tate Gallery, 1987), 58.
26. Jameson, *Postmodernism: Or, the Cultural Logic of Late Capitalism*, 7.
27. Jameson, Fredric. *The Seeds of Time* (New York: Columbia University Press, 1994), 77.
28. This is not dissimilar to Jameson's observations of Walter Benjamin: 'So the melancholy that speaks from the pages of Benjamin's essay – private depressions, professional discouragement, the dejection of the outsider, distress in the face of a political and historical nightmare – searches the past for an adequate object, for some emblem or image at which, as in religious meditation, the mind can stare itself out, in which it can find momentary, if only aesthetic, relief.' See, Jameson, Fredric. *Marxism and Form* (Princeton, NJ: Princeton University Press, 1971), 60.
29. Deleuze, Gilles and Félix Guattari. *Anti-Oedipus: Capitalism and Schizophrenia*, trans. R. Hurley, M. Seem, and H. R. Lane (Minneapolis, MN: University of Minnesota Press, 1977), 370.
30. Deleuze, Gilles. *Difference and Repetition*, trans. Paul Patton (New York: Columbia University Press, 1994), 23.
31. Deleuze, Gilles and Félix Guattari. *A Thousand Plateaus: Capitalism and Schizophrenia*, trans. Brian Massumi (London: Athlone Press, 1988), 38.
32. Ibid., 112.
32. Davis, *Deracination*, 131.
33. Deleuze, *Difference and Repetition*, 69.
34. Deleuze, *Nietzsche and Philosophy*, 189.
35. Ibid., 18.
36. Deleuze, *Francis Bacon*, 89–90.
37. Ibid., 108.
38. Ibid.
39. Jameson, Fredric. *Fables of Aggression: Wyndham Lewis, the Modernist as Fascist* (Berkeley, CA: University of California Press, 1979), 12.
40. Adorno, 'Cultural Criticism and Society,' 151.
41. Plato, *Republic*, trans. Desmond Lee (London: Penguin Books, 1987); More, Thomas. *Utopia* (Cambridge: Cambridge University Press, 1975).
42. Jameson, *The Seeds of Time*, 74.
43. Ibid., 74–5.
44. Buchanan, Ian. 'Metacommentary on Utopia, or Jameson's dialectic of hope,' *Utopian Studies*, Vol. 9, No. 2, 1998, 18–30.
45. Deleuze, Gilles and Félix Guattari. *What Is Philosophy?*, trans. Graham Burchell and Hugh Tomlinson (London and New York: Verso), 99.

46. What makes philosophy political is how a concept connects with a present milieu, 'with what is real here and now in the struggle against capitalism, relaunching new struggles whenever the earlier one is betrayed.' See ibid., 100.
47. To recapitulate, Deleuze and Guattari were quoted in Chapter 5 as saying: 'A social field is always animated by all kinds of movements of decoding and deterritorialization affecting "masses" and operating at different speeds and paces.' Continuing on from here they state: 'These are not contradictions but escapes.' See Deleuze and Guattari, *A Thousand Plateaus*, 220.
48. Adorno, 'Cultural Criticism and Society,' 151.
49. Libeskind, Daniel. *Breaking Ground* (New York: Riverhead Books, 2004), 82.
50. Ibid.
51. Deleuze, *Nietzsche and Philosophy*, 103.
52. Deleuze, Gilles. *Negotiations: 1972–1900*, trans. Martin Joughin (New York: Columbia University Press, 1995), 126.
53. Deleuze, *Francis Bacon*, 40.

CHAPTER 3

The Vietnam Veterans Memorial

> At the very least, my brother and all the others like him deserve their self-respect, a job, and the right to live out the rest of their lives with the nightmares that war brings in some kind of secure peace.
>
> I can't tell Donnie about this letter because what if that veteran is right! What if no one cares? (Sister of Vietnam veteran Donnie)[1]

> Coming back to the world was a bitch! Years of foul accusations, stereotyping, lack of respect and not being accepted back into the mainstream society. However, I dealt with it by using something I had learned in Viet fucking Nam. I just turned on the ol 'fuck it' attitude. (Vietnam veteran Rick Rogers, Wichita, Kansas)[2]

Fought between 1956 and 1975 American involvement in the Vietnam War saw over two million US citizens serve and some 58,000 die or be declared missing in action. Michal Belknap in his study of the war cites that during the period August 1965 to October 1967 those who felt it was not a mistake to send troops to Vietnam fell from 61 percent to 44 percent, not to mention that by 1967 a total of seven people had set themselves alight in protest, and the antiwar movement had expanded to become a serious force within American social and political life, including not just students and professors but also members of the clergy and business executives.[3] It is obvious to say that the war divided the nation and that many of the veterans who returned home were faced not only with the nightmares of combat but also the brutal fact that they were unwelcome.[4] It is important to remember that because of the system of Selective Service many of those from privileged socioeconomic backgrounds were able to avoid the draft and the figures for the period 1965–6 show that only 2 percent of college graduates made up 2 percent of the draftees. Furthermore, college graduates who did serve in the military only had a 42 percent chance of being deployed to Vietnam as compared with high school graduates who had a 64 percent chance and high school dropouts who had a 70 percent chance.[5] Needless to say, the sense of injustice that American Vietnam veterans felt when they returned home was not just because the community had abandoned them after the war but the very system that drafted them into service in the first place was skewed against them from the outset. This sense of national abandonment along with the horrors of the war produced long-lasting personal and national scars.[6]

It is important to remember the veterans returned home at a time when American society defined the world stage using the monolithic interpretation of a Cold War America. Events such as the Soviet Union testing its first atomic bomb in 1949, the instigation of communism throughout China in the hands of Mao Zedong, interpreting the French colonialist struggle in Indochina and the fighting in Vietnam as an ideological struggle against communism, and American efforts to contain Korean communism as equal to the situation in Vietnam, all combined to produce a dominant historical narrative.[7] The United States had clearly asserted its global control in the wake of World War Two by fashioning itself into a world superpower and guardian against the threat of communism.

The Cold War narrative was one way to police the world and the challenges of a different political system. The failure of the war in Vietnam was therefore tantamount to the inability to contain the communist menace; as such it threatened to decode the dominant Cold War narrative putting elements of it to work differently by dismantling the overcoded connections between post-World War Two national American heroism, victorious America, and the communist threat. On another level, a violent, albeit distorted, collective memory was activated when the Vietnam veteran was represented as a person who threatened to destabilize the effect of the Cold War narrative (America as a virtuous guardian and world superpower). For instance, the uncomfortable and brutal events making up the war were swiftly repressed, such that the My Lai massacre which saw over 300 Vietnamese civilians brutally slaughtered had all but been erased from American memory by the 1980s, leading renowned Vietnam War historian Christian Appy to exclaim that few of his students barely even knew the name 'My Lai' anymore.[8]

The Vietnam War did not end the day America began withdrawing from Vietnam. The violence persisted on the home front as veterans were either demonized or simply rendered invisible. For a long time it was not just their experiences but also their very presence in American society that was quite literally obliterated. An enraged Vietnam veteran Tom Carhart publicly declared:

> When I came home from Vietnam in the December of 1968 I was literally spat upon in the Chicago airport as I walked through in my uniform. That spit hurt; it went through me like a spear. Welcome home![9]

The anger veterans such as Carhart felt was not simply that nobody cared; rather others didn't feel implicated in the very memory engaging the social field they all shared in common. It was this painful situation along with the desire to heal the emptiness it fostered that provided the impetus to build a Vietnam Veterans Memorial. On 27 April 1979 the Vietnam Veterans Memorial Fund was founded by three veterans – Jan Scruggs, John Wheeler, and Robert Doubek – with the mission to raise funds, commission a design, and secure a well-known federal site for the location of it. Approximately 275,000 people donated money and on 1 July 1980 US President Jimmy Carter signed a bill (PL 96-297) endorsing the building of the memorial on the National Mall in Washington, DC.[10] A national design competition was announced with four criteria: to include the names of the dead and missing, to be reflective and contemplative, not to be a political statement about the war, and to blend with the site.

When Chinese American Maya Ying Lin was announced as the winner of the memorial design competition she was only twenty-one years old and still a student of architecture at Yale University.[11] Lin went on to meet the staggering task of creating a place where everyone would be welcome not just to remember the past and grieve, but also to reflect upon the difficult place the war continued to occupy within American society. Her competition entry proposed a 500-foot wedge-shaped black granite wall, polished to form a mirror-like surface.[12] In her submission she describes her idea in the following manner:

> Walking through this park-like area, the memorial appears as a rift in the earth – a long, polished black stone wall, emerging from and receding into the earth. Approaching the memorial, the ground slopes gently downward, and the low walls emerging on either side, growing out of the earth, extend and converge at a point below and ahead. Walking into the grassy site contained by the walls of this memorial we can barely make out the carved names upon the memorial's walls. These names, seemingly infinite in number, convey the sense of overwhelming numbers, while unifying those individuals into a whole. For this memorial is meant not as a monument to the individual, but rather as a memorial to the men and women who died during this war, as a whole.[13]

As chief designer, Lin was immediately thrust into a position of power as the representative of a silenced minority. However, as a young Asian woman still studying architecture she quickly became the vehicle through which some veterans made their own anger, frustrations, and hurt appear. Lin explains: 'It took me months to realize obviously a lot of people are going to be extremely offended that the creation of the "American" Vietnam Veterans Memorial is not only not a veteran but she is a "she," she is "Asian." '[14] For instance, members of the Memorial Fund committee received letters demanding, how they could 'let a Gook design the memorial?'[15] Cartoons were publicly released and disseminated accentuating Lin's Asian features holding a sign with 'designer' written on it and a group of veterans looking down on her saying 'Hi Mama San.'[16] One way to comprehend the sexist and racist accusations leveled against her by many of the veterans is to invoke the conceptual apparatus of minoritarian and majoritarian.[17] Although spoken by a supposed minority – not in the Deleuzian sense but according to more common political usages of the term as a definable numerical group, small in number as compared to the dominant social group of a majority – the slurs constitute, to borrow from Deleuze and Guattari, a majoritarian language (exercise of power and the instigation of an order-word). This is a language that operates according to a principle of subjectification and for Lin this meant focus was given to her not having American roots, being a nonveteran, an Asian, a woman, and a student. For a while the intolerance and animosity many veterans felt toward her seemed to doom the whole project to failure. However, the position she held as a young Asian woman began to function like a deterritorializing movement, decoding the very order-words that the veteran's majoritarian language established. That is, the subjectifying slurs and the identity formation of the veterans as a homogenous group began to splinter.

The hostility some veterans expressed towards Lin and her design took place amid angry cries to build a more traditional monument. Veteran Carhart angrily declared:

> When I saw the winning design I was truly stunned, I thought that the most insulting and demeaning memorial to our Vietnam experience that was possible. I don't care about artistic perceptions. I don't care about the rationalizations that abound. One needs no artistic education to see this memorial design for what it is: A BLACK SCAR! Black: the universal color of sorrow and shame and degradation in all races and societies worldwide. In a hole, hidden as if out of shame.[18]

The memorial was seen by many veterans as a way to neatly transfer them from a subjugated to a dominant subject position. They clearly expressed the desire to have a memorial that used the standard visual vocabulary common to most monuments constructed in memory of war (bronze, marble, figurative, a strong vertical structure on a pedestal, with an indisputable representation of the veteran as a national war hero). One solution that was proposed entailed changing the wall from black to white, raising the wall to sit above ground and to add a flagpole at the vertex with an American flag, in effect turning the wall into a classical pedestal base lending support to a more nationalistically defined gesture waving the stars and stripes. The aim of this suggestion was to organize trauma into more manageable form by building a structure that would objectively predetermine the social and symbolic value of public remembrance using a traditional memorial vernacular familiar to all. To summarize, using the majoritarian language of bravery and national pride, the visual vocabulary of a classical monument would simply neutralize the chaotic affect of the Vietnam trauma.

The definition Deleuze and Guattari give for minoritarian is not intended to refer to a numerical majority or minority (this is how it is commonly used in politics and social theory), and in the context of memorial culture it is a creative power (*puissance*) that comes from a new way of using memory and the sensation of violence trauma gives rise to. Meanwhile, minoritarian indicates a mutation or variation of the dominant majoritarian mode (*pouvoir*). All majoritarian languages carry within them the capacity to change, or as Deleuze and Guattari characterize it: to become minoritarian. They write: a majority 'implies a constant, or expression or content, serving as a standard measure by which to evaluate it.'[19] Appearing twice, both in the 'constant and the variable from which the constant is extracted,' is what makes an adult white heterosexual European male majoritarian.[20] In this way, the concept of majoritarian presupposes a dominant standard and a situation of power. Meanwhile, minoritarian is not inferior to the majority; it is simply a different usage or function. It transforms the majoritarian language by using it creatively and making it work differently. What we will now discuss are the ways in which the memorial dislodges majoritarian language by working with the general affect of trauma.

To begin with, the memorial's relevance comes from demolishing what Deleuze might describe as the 'great epical heredity' of history without discrediting the historical enormity of the event.[21] As Cathy

Caruth claims we do not own history because 'we are implicated in each other's traumas' or because we author it, we own history only in so far as history is turned into a majoritarian language that functions to subject us to the security of a determinate subject position (Cold War, America as a world superpower and guardian against communism).[22] Lin's response to the competition brief suggests that the question of social relevance in respect to memorial design is not primarily a problem of ownership; rather it is how to create what Deleuze might call a 'sensory aggregate,' that is trauma cannot be represented (idealism) nor identified as a distinct thing in space or an instant in time (realism).[23] Trauma is a temporal movement producing affects and energies that, as these combine in a body, shock and stimulate traumatic memory thinking throughout the body. The aggregate that occurs happens as invisible forces begin to braid one another and what we end up with is both a subjective and collective movement. However, it is habitual memory that then organizes these movements according to one's interests and here ownership over the dynamic and chaotic circulation of traumatic memory occurs, concomitantly inaugurating subjective perception. For example, Americans worked hard to render the distressed Vietnam War subject (the individual veteran and the whole national experience of the war itself) invisible. The effect of this was that the trauma of the war never took place in *chronos* (chronological time) and only in *aion* as pure affect (nonchronological time). This meant temporal continuity was 'split, divested, turned in on itself, coiled up, or even extended beyond its natural limits.'[24] Caruth explains this situation in terms of the 'shock of the mind's relation to the threat of death is thus not the direct experience of the threat, but precisely the *missing* of this experience, the fact that, not being experienced *in time*, it has not yet been fully known.'[25]

When Caruth speaks of a 'lack of experience' and its return as an 'attempt to overcome the fact that it was *not* direct' she, like Freud, posits an Oedipal trauma whose return marks an attempt to conquer what was not originally grasped.[26] What returns for Caruth, as for Freud, is the repressed material of the past, the origin of which is not available as an object of knowledge. Using Deleuze we will add to Caruth and suggest that what returns is the nonhuman force of *aion*; a sensation of violence appears when we try to integrate this largely irruptive combination of traumatic affects (a choking throat, a body overcome by a sudden bout of sweat, a shaking hand, or a twitching eye) and percepts (nonhuman forces emitted through the pulse and stammer of a shattered and anxious landscape) into the logic of chronological time (a majoritarian movement), forming a clear movement from the content of *aion* to the representative expression of it. To relate this to the utopian memory thinking outlined in the previous chapter, the utopianism of the Vietnam Veterans Memorial comes from the way in which the memorial entails a struggle over this separation of *chronos* and *aion*, the level of form as opposed to content, and the struggle over how these tension each other is where the politics of the memorial lie.

Given the violent erasure of the veteran experience from American memory how could the Vietnam Veterans Memorial connect with the full force of social violence without taking it over? The challenge here is one of relevance. How can a designer extract something from the tone, timbre, color, sound, and texture of the whole of violence without reducing this to an abstract interpretation summarized by the statistic of 58,132 dead and missing?[27] Under such circumstances a designer could either look at the violence for what it signifies or he/she could take it to be a nonsignifying element preferring to ask how that violence works. Most of the 1,421 submissions took the former route; examples include a forty-foot rocking chair, a two-storey high pair of military boots, and a US flag spread over two acres. Meanwhile, the winning entry by Lin could be described as using an intensive design method, one that did not try to interpret or explain the violent legacy of the war; instead, the strength of her response came from how she put the violent affect of trauma to work using a minoritarian language.

Rather than move from content to expression Lin's design concept of a wounded landscape suggests she started from the position of a nonsignifying break (a cut into the National Mall). She then combined this with a series of heterogeneous affects (the power to affect and be affected) and percepts (not a perception but a field of forces that seize the solemnity and the shrilled shockwaves traumatic silence emits). What becomes apparent here is that the memorial design is the effect of a manual mark, and as Deleuze was to say of Irish-English painter Francis Bacon:

> 'Free marks' will have to be made rather quickly on the image being painted so as to destroy the nascent figuration in it and to give the Figure a chance, which is the *improbable itself*. These marks are accidental, 'by chance'; but clearly the same word 'chance,' no longer designates probabilities, but now designates a type of choice or action without probability. These marks can be called 'nonrepresentative,'

> precisely because they depend on the act of chance and express nothing regarding the visual image: they only concern the hand of the painter.[28]

Like the free marks Deleuze identified in Bacon, as Lin cut into the earth she too shattered the hidden force of figuration that had up until that point defined the memorials and monuments lining the Mall. Her cut into the land productively connected the land to her own body in order to wrench the memorial away from 'nascent illustration and narration' so that the Figure – the wound and the latent scream – could emerge out of the temporal struggle between *chronos* and *aion* that trauma incites.[29]

Instead of moving clearly from the position of the present back into the past attempting to represent that past in its entirety, the memorial presents the indiscernible pre-personal affect of the war sustaining that affect through a block of violent sensation as opposed to narrative meaning.[30] For Deleuze the pre-personal is not the antithesis of the human, a proposition that would in effect presuppose the human, nor is it an extension of Nietzsche's proclamation that God is dead (the moment when human history and identity were no longer a matter of genealogy originating in the Judeo-Christian notion of Genesis). Concomitantly, affects cannot be collapsed into feelings for they are 'becomings that spill over beyond whoever lives through them.'[31] This is what leads him to conclude, with Guattari, that the 'affect is not the passage from one lived state to another but man's nonhuman becoming.'[32] When Deleuze and Guattari state the 'work of art is a being of sensation and nothing else: it exists in itself' they announce an important quality all art shares.[33] That is, art creates affects and percepts as pre-personal singularities. For this reason Lin describes her initial impulse to slice into the earth, whereby she 'imagined taking a knife and cutting into the earth, opening it up, an initial violence and pain that in time would heal.'[34]

Percepts are not to be confused with the perceptions of a subject, which subsumes the power of a percept under a representational rubric of a person who organizes their experiences independently of the percepts themselves. Deleuze explains that percepts 'live on independently of whoever experiences them.'[35] Percepts are forces such as pulsating heat or a dull throb; they are pre-personal and insensible forces that define landscapes, such as the shimmering landscapes of Cézanne who says: 'Man absent from but entirely within the landscape'[36] Hence, when we describe Lin's memorial as working with the wall as percept, we are looking to the way the design expresses the specificity of division, the psychic violence dividing the nation, a wall that abstracts the quality and the power of that violence without trying to signify it (the war hero, a grand master narrative, a clear separation between victims and the guilty, and so on). Such forces emerge between the grass and the granite that forms a lesion in the earth; the falling path that sinks the memorial into the grassy slopes of the National Mall; and it comes from the shadow of names destined to stone, along with the trembling remnants of traumatic silence that gathers there.

Likewise, an affect is not to be mistaken as a feeling we experience; for affects move 'beyond the strength of those who undergo them,' or, to put it differently, affects are pre-personal modes of transformation.[37] Affects are not organized spatially or temporally; the affective register comes from the designer creating a landscape of percepts that make invisible forces visible, such as when we see ourselves before the invisible in the polished surface of the granite wall: it is not so much that the black void infers violence, it is more that through this affective encounter with the erasure of existence the violent force of trauma appears. In so doing, the memorial stirs forth a connection between the visitor and the site. On a simple level, we cannot distinguish between where the landscape ends and the wall begins, in effect the point of their contact is indiscernible. In this regard, the memorial constitutes a landscape-becoming-wall. It is this compound of affects and percepts that characterize what Deleuze and Guattari call a block of sensation. That is, for them a designer or artist can be described as designing sensations through the language of sensation, whereby sensation points to an asignifying force that opens us up to unconventional perceptions and feelings (affections). The only representation that is apparent at the level of sensation is in reference to the materiality of sensation and if we look to Lin's initial watercolor designs for the project we can see how she works with this.

Lin's competition submission consisted of a handwritten essay and painted images. Examining the small paintings of her submission, what is now the black granite of the wall once seemed like a tear in the paper, even a gaping wound, a shadow, a moment of emptiness, or a pause in time. The edges of the blue horizon line are softened in the manner of a Rothko producing a nonillusionist space. Like Rothko's later work, her use of a solid black geometric form amid soft washes of blue tones modulates these colors in opposition to each other, so that relations of tonality define the cool tone of the image. Lin's use of color carries a '*haptic* function, in which the juxtaposition of pure tones arranged gradually on the flat surface forms a progression and regression that culminates in a close vision.'[38] In this way she decodes the perspective grid leaving us with a space that refuses to be read as a three-dimensional area. Like the paintings the edges of the two black walls are finite, producing a solid shape that orients the site. We are left asking whether it is the landscape that *contains* the black gash or whether the gash is the land straining to give birth to the wound that shapes its supposedly tranquil grassy slopes. This form seems suspended there in time, motionless, a bristling memory that issues forth a piercing scream no different to Bacon's pope in *Study after Velázquez's Portrait of Pope Innocent X* (1953). A sensation of violence is effected through the push and pull rhythms of a sharp V-like structure overlaid onto a circular path, dragging the site in different directions. The memorial is a physical mark – the landscape-as-memory – that pries open the ground, producing a nonrepresentational Figure (or what Deleuze elsewhere describes as an orgiastic representation of the monstrous). Hence, the nonillusionist space of these paintings produce a work without perspective markers or a definitive homogenizing point of orientation that would leave us with a sense of near and far. We are presented quite simply with a wounded body consisting of an incision that swells through the land, a path that emigrates into the earth defenselessly awaiting the footsteps of a solitary traveler.

When Lin speaks of wounding the landscape it is not a question of designing a symbolic metaphor in that she herself explains: 'I cannot force a design; I do not see this process as being under my conscious control. It is a process of percolation, with the form eventually finding its way to the surface.'[39] Her design process takes shape in different forms; sometimes it starts out as an essay, other times as a sketch or as a model, and it is interesting to note when it comes time to make a model (she also refers to the model as a sketch) she thinks with her hands. Models provide her with 'clues' and for 'most who are used to looking at models as finished miniature representations of actual work, they are sometimes indecipherable.'[40] It is here where we first glimpse the indiscernible zone that eventually comes to characterize the memorial. The final work is an intuitive aggregate of relations between idea, sketch, model, and site. The simplicity and formal clarity that this aggregate produces is, however, quite unlike the blank slate of a purely minimalist aesthetic. Generally speaking, the minimalist object is entirely self-sufficient whereas Lin's memorial is not, although it could be described as being self-referential in the dialectical sense of the term.

Consider Judd's *Untitled* (*c.*1975) concrete blocks in Marfa, Texas. Taken together they form a wall across the landscape. The minimalism lies in his use of pure, simple, and elegant forms that in their regular dimensions and spacing combine to produce a sense of balance and proportion. Judd's blocks are nonfigurative and yet they still carry a powerful sense of materiality (concrete and weight), one that draws attention to their structure. However, as a work of art they are completely self-justifying and immune to history in every sense. Put differently, Judd's objects refer to nothing other than themselves.[41]

While the Vietnam memorial shares many of the formal aesthetic qualities found in Judd's work it incorporates a surrealist edge, combining familiar architectural elements (wall, corner, window, path) in unfamiliar ways (what Freud was to describe as *condensation*). As Norwegian architect and theorist Thomas Thiis-Evensen defines it, 'the main purpose of the wall is to *delimit* a space and to *support* the roof.'[42] He adds, the 'wall's architecture, in other words is a concrete realization of the existential struggle between an "attacking" exterior and a "secure" interior and thereby acquires expressive importance.'[43] Thiis-Evensen understands the wall in terms of demarcation, an architectural element that either closes off or opens a space up, mediating between spaces and indicating positions in space (in front of, behind, above, below, right or left). Responding to the varying degrees of accessibility that a wall produces depends upon the materials used, degrees of weight and motion, the reflection of light, and the silence of shadow. For instance, hardness, softness, lightness, and heaviness, all generate different sensations. That is, a soft wooden wall emits warmth, whereas a wall made of stone can be alienating, hard, and cold. This now brings us to the third element in the being of sensation composite that Deleuze and Guattari insist all art shares: the house. Trying to move beyond the human-centric focus of Maurice Merleau-Ponty's concept of the 'flesh' as it is propounded in *The Visible and the Invisible*, the house is a pre-personal concept of mediation between the outside and inside. Unlike the tenderness and pliability of Ponty's porous flesh, the house is a structure (of forces) that provides an armature for affects to take place. A house orients a body with its planes (front, back, left, right, up, and down), founding the ground with the floor, with the roof and walls it creates separations between the inside and outside. Yet, as it frames the world, its doors and windows provide openings that concomitantly engage inside and outside spaces.

The problem of national division that the Vietnam War incited is implied by the memorial's wall structure. One might also argue though that the memorial is much more than a single wall, or simply two walls joined together. Using the architectural element of a wall that commonly produces a sense of inside and outside, division and exclusion, protection and safety, Lin combines this with a variety of other architectural elements. It is at once a wall (enclosing structure) and a window (an opening) as the polished granite surface emits reflections that expose the viewer to spaces beyond the wall itself, such as the surrounding trees and lawn reflected in its surface. The memorial is a wall-becoming-path, inviting us to embark on a journey, not just forcing us to a standstill; we move ten-feet below the earth's surface and slowly rise again; we follow our own reflection as it connects with the reflections of the park and the names of the dead and missing. A wall-becoming-window presents itself as another world is reflected in the surface of polished granite; a wall that we cannot penetrate but from which we glimpse the slippery images of the world around us in reflected form. Engaging the temporality of the journey the memorial decodes the functional definition of the wall-corner (termination of a surface and the creation of a space); inverting the solid connection between a vertical and horizontal line (this being the dominant connection traditional monuments articulate) it creates a circular tapestry instead of a V-shaped structure. The circle connects the surrounding field producing an invisible path through the grass as we follow the time-line off into the distance. The chronological listing of the dead and missing move the visitor through time up one path at which point they cross the lawn to chronologically meet up with the list of names at the end of the wall on the opposite side.

Working with everyday architectural elements in unconventional ways infuses an affective intensity into the memorial, one that turns the self-justifying aesthetic of minimalism on its head, releasing a self-referential aesthetic in its place. Put differently, the affective intensity of the Vietnam Veterans Memorial emerges from using architectural elements against the grain, while concomitantly making reference to the environment in which the memorial appears, so as to subvert the dominant language of nationalism defining that landscape. Contrary to minimalism though, bodies are neither reduced to a series of formal qualities that combine into a coherent and self-justifying body as minimalism tends to do, nor is the body characterized by the subjective time of the unconscious as psychoanalysis defines it. What this means is that Lin starts out with the affective mode of desiring bodies prior to their signification and representation. To borrow from Deleuze and

Guattari, through her use of materials Lin wrests the 'percept from perceptions of objects and the states of a perceiving subject' along with the 'affect from affections as the transition from one state to another' working to 'extract a bloc of sensations, a pure being of sensations.'[44] We are presented with the impersonal general affect of trauma instead of subjective opinions or the feelings of a fully coherent subject (as phenomenology advances). Lin states:

> The Vietnam Veterans Memorial is a geode. I envisioned it not as an object inserted into the earth but as part of the earth, a work formed from the act of cutting open the earth and polishing the earth's surface, dematerializing the stone to pure surface, creating an interface between the world of the light and the quieter world beyond the names.[45]

Lin decodes the symbolic significance of a wall (a space we can conquer) to produce a historically contingent structure through which visitors communicate, exemplified by the spontaneous memorials consisting of thousands of letters, poems, teddy bears, flowers, war medals, rifle casings, arm bands, toys, marijuana joints, cigarettes, IV bags, letters, army boots, photographs, knives, army hats, and the like that visitors have left there. These elements form a shared sense of trauma that infuses the overall tone and timbre of the site. Working with affect and percept Lin creates new feelings and perceptions that accordingly generate a healthy distance on the past. What did the war leave behind? Dog tags, unidentifiable bodies, and memories. Herein lies the importance of listing all 58,132 names chronologically, not alphabetically – to avoid turning each name into an abstraction, just another 'Smith' amid a sea of 'Smiths.' She announces in her competition entry essay that 'it is up to each individual to resolve or come to terms with this loss.'[46] Here the time-line of a list of names in chronological sequence according to date of death is used as affect.[47] There is a combined sense of stillness, ruin, injury, and disturbance that the wall of names stirs forth and this is what constitutes the affective dimension of memory that Lin taps into. Visitors to the site have to look up an individual name in a book then locate it on the wall. What this does is encourage a lived-time experience as one looks up the name and travels down to the wall to find it. One visitor remarked that she 'was stricken with, well, grief, when [she] saw name after name,' this is because she 'realized that behind each name there was a sad story, a sad home, brokenhearted parents, children and wives.'[48]

But does the memorial engage in another majoritarian language – one that marginalizes the Vietnamese experience so as to bolster the

American viewpoint? Put differently, does it participate in a deeper operation of repression of American cultural memory, leaving the unsavory effects of the American combat on the Vietnamese landscape unaddressed? In other words, is the memorial ethnocentric? As an expression machine, the Vietnamese claim on American remembrance of the war formally makes its appearance throughout the memorial at the level of an Asian aesthetic sensibility common to the poise and equilibrium of a Japanese garden: the balanced combination of an implied circular path that quietly meets at either end of the wall, the gentle scale of the wall in relation to the site, and in Lin's use of minimal materials for maximum affect. The crack of unfamiliarity then occurs when Eastern and Western (minimalism) aesthetics formally engage one another and it is this crack that transcends majoritarian relations of domination. If we are to follow Deleuze's conceptual lead here, the memorial could be described as invoking a pre-personal dimension in the sense that it does not interpret or represent the experience or perceptions felt by different individuals or ethnic groups.

The memorial presents the sensible affect of trauma without situating it in a representative narrative. The politics of this gesture needs to be noted here: this comes from the memorial's refusal to engage with a historical interpretation of the war, especially since it was majoritarian history in the first instance that rendered the veteran invisible in American society. It is majoritarian history and language that translated the affect of trauma into a manageable narative (the US fight against the threat of communism), the content of which is then used to communicate a summarized and deeply censored narrative (majoritarian history) of the veteran experience to society. Focusing on affect and not content, the memorial quite simply does not engage with this power play. By not narrating that trauma, visitors to the site get a sense of it through the long list of names presented to them. Lin writes:

> This memorial acknowledged those lives without focusing on the war or on creating a political statement of victory or loss. This apolitical approach became the essential aim of my design; I did not want to civilize war by glorifying it or by forgetting the sacrifices involved. The price of human life in war should always be clearly remembered.[49]

Actually the memorial produces a new context for national remembrance, one that is not heroic yet all the while dignifies the veterans. In addition, the memorial actively draws attention to its participation in and difference from the creation of national history. One wall is directed towards the Lincoln Memorial (a signifier of liberal freedom) the other towards the Washington Monument (a signifier of democracy). Taken together the walls recreate the symbolism of this context, decoding these dominant points of signification by producing connections to other landmarks across the Mall. In this way Lin fashions a foreign history using the historical vocabulary specific to America; in effect collective remembrance is made to stammer as memories produce the wound as a struggle of a fundamental temporal split (*chronos* and *aion*). The result is that the veteran cannot be defined by the majoritarian history characterizing other monuments and memorials throughout the Mall.

As already noted many veterans had an adverse reaction to the design because they wanted a structure that would represent their trauma and re-author that experience along the lines of the celebrated war hero, a monument that would recast the history of the war away from national failure to that of individual victory, one that would represent their contribution to the forging of national identity in a positive light. Over time, the security some veterans found in an unambiguous identification with not being an Asian, a woman, nor a person who had lost their youth during the war was no longer prioritized, as it began to give way to an '*expression machine* capable of disorganizing its own forms, and of disorganizing its forms of contents, in order to liberate pure contents that mix with expressions in a single intense matter.'[50] It was because of this social transformation that a minoritarian memorial could come into existence.

Lin preferred to overturn the symbolic vocabulary common to most war memorials and monuments constructed until then, these being: wars produce heroes; courageous suffering defines the hero; trauma is the unfortunate consequence of war and heroism; and violence ends once the conflict comes to a close. The minimalist visual vocabulary she uses resists a monumental language that inevitably commemorates rather than conserves the affective dimension of violence and trauma. She achieves this in her use of a semiotics of affect: through a structure that configures (house) the pre-personal forces of injury (percept) that war gives rise to in connection with the affectivity of public remembrance (becoming-other). For instance, the form of the memorial does not resemble a Vietnam veteran or even attempt to represent their experience in its entirety; rather it presents a landscape imbued with trauma and constituted through an affective wounding of the site, a landscape whose guts have quite literally been cut open for all to see, feel, and listen to. Maximizing the sociality of memorialization instead of the tragic dimension of mourning Lin engages the majoritarian language of architecture – the wall as dividor – infusing it with a minoritarian edge – division turned crack, and a wound understood to be a temporal lesion. In this way, she sets architectural codes and language in motion in defiance against the proscribed context of that language to liberate and decode it.

Herein lies the weakness of the nearby fifty-foot US flag and the Three Servicemen monument by Frederick Hart.[51] It depicts three Vietnam soldiers, one of whom is an African American. It is in the style of a classical monument consisting of figures firmly situated on a pedestal. The figures are slightly larger than life and are cast in bronze. In this way, the artist invokes a language of fixity that is further accentuated by the verticality of the monument design. Hart clearly communicates a specific position to the viewer: the heroism of the Vietnam veteran. In other words, the monument provides a distinct interpretation for the affections violence lets loose. Hart clearly chose to narrate an untainted historical version of events, visually describing the heroic dimension of the soldier in combat in a vernacular familiar to all. There is no sensation, only matter, no affect and all content. Hence, the artist fails to unleash the invisible force of trauma in the way that Lin's memorial does. Why this work sits uncomfortably and unsympathetically in relation to Lin's memorial is because it sets out to glorify and civilize the loss of life and the nationally contentious aspects of the war.[52]

The Vietnam memorial does not try to replicate the past, or call upon old perceptions, or reminisce over the past in the context of the present. It is not a stereotypical perception of warfare or the war hero that are Lin's design tools. She works with the social anxieties that the war produced, starting out with the landscape as percept, putting the affective dimension of stillness, the throb of injury, and the scream of a crack in the earth to work, not as a political statement but in order to combine the softness of grass, the hardness of stone, the somberness of shadow, the darkness of earth, and the rhythms of intertwining visible and invisible pathways to maximum effect. Unlike Hart's classical monument standing tall and firm, the power of Lin's memorial lies elsewhere in an unrecognizable and indeterminate block of sensation. In Deleuze and Guattari's words: 'The monument does not actualize the virtual event but incorporates or embodies it: it gives it a body, a life, a universe.'[53] The Deleuzian monument, or what we will call the minor memorial, denotes the creation of a zone of indetermination whereby the materiality of the wall becomes sensation. Here the form of the wall actually disappears leaving us with a sensory becoming, 'otherness caught in a matter of expression.'[54] The monument that emerges, in the way that Deleuze and Guattari use the word, is this indeterminate zone of affect. In effect, we pass into the wall as our own independent 'self' becomes imperceptible. For this reason the design works not with specific memories lifted from the past but with a combination of sensations that allow the force of a past trauma to appear in and affect the present. As such, we do not ask the humanist question: what does it mean to be human? Nor do we ask the ontological question: what is the nature of being? At the wall the 'human in us is now indistinct.'[55] This may explain where the continued power of the memorial lies: it is through the semiotics of affect that makes the preceding causes of the memorial simultaneous with its effects.

Lin diffused the dominant representation of the Vietnam veteran (a brutal, contemptible, and unwanted figure in national consciousness) while producing a new politically charged representation – a platform from which the veterans and their families could resituate themselves within American society on their own terms. In this regard, the memorial neither resolves nor defuses the affectivity of trauma. This is because it is no longer a utopian representation but, to borrow from Jameson's discussion of literary utopias addressed in the previous chapter, it could be considered as a type of utopian praxis producing an alternative way to remember and engage the past. And as Jameson was to describe the utopianism in the novelist Joseph Conrad's writing as an '*aestheticizing strategy*,' this being a term that is 'not meant as moral or political castigation, but is rather to be taken literally, as the designation of a strategy which for whatever reason seeks to recode or rewrite the world and its own data in terms of perception as a semi-autonomous activity,' so too does Lin's memorial entail an aestheticizing strategy, one that comes from putting the utopian memory machine to work so as to enable the praxis of real politics to take place, not just the aesthetic representation of an ideal and neutral memory.[56]

Using the traumatic impact of the war as her starting point, Lin produces the conditions for affectivity to take place, never succumbing to simply creating an objective rendition of that impact. However, contrary to Davis's theory of deracination, as outlined in the previous chapter, Lin does not reduce traumatic impact to subjective affect. Instead of giving priority to subjective perception the memorial is a milieu that is both subjective and collective, it is one that testifies to a nonhuman affectivity (landscape-becoming-wall). Here different bodies (not just the body of an individual) connect, affect, and transform one other. Sociologically, the Vietnam Veterans Memorial project insisted upon a connective synthesis between invisible forces, the movement of memory and the act of public remembrance; it is this connection that has the potential to create something radically new and utopian (what could otherwise be described as a legitimate connective synthesis).

In the final instance, the memorial is opposed to memorialization in that it doesn't attempt to look back and pass judgement or lay blame. Speaking powerfully to Deleuze's concept of sensation and affect, it presents a nonhuman wound: a landscape that has been sliced open (a nationally significant piece of land at that) to produce a 'coloring void,' a landscape section that emits 'subtle imperceptible variations' in hue, tone, reflection, and texture.[57] Her design opened up the American social imaginary to the veteran experience by bringing it into contact with the affect of trauma. More precisely, the design consists of an indeterminate wounded line that lies beyond representation and is without organization, working to produce a geometry of affects and percepts that occur prior to the management and organization of a perceiving subject. As one visitor noted: 'There is an energy there that is unreal.'[58] It is this combination that generates an amplified milieu of sensation in connection with the body.

The strength of this design comes from the way in which it came to create a whole new set of local values, inventing a variety of violent conditions that were then tossed out into the social field and improvised upon. Although at the time of the memorial's design and development phases the veteran and the Cold War narrative coexisted with each other, Lin's design acknowledged that they did so as diverging consistencies – hence the importance of bringing two walls together at a point that then took on an invisible circular path, connecting the separate ends of each wall/path. Interestingly, it was not just the design that represented the violent trauma of warfare, nor did it subjectify the veteran experience by using it to define a unified group that could be clearly identified as the 'Vietnam Veteran.' Instead, the wall 'makes existence an *aesthetic phenomenon* rather than a moral or religious one' and in this regard it entails the partial use of the connective synthesis of desire Deleuze and Guattari advance in *Anti-Oedipus*.[59] It is not the wall that is sensation here; rather, as this chapter has shown, the wall produces particular blocks of sensation that together present a zone of indiscernibility between American loss and ownership, between Asian and Western aesthetics, in what might otherwise be described as a minor memorial.

Notes

1. Palmer, Laura. *Shrapnel in the Heart: Letters and Remembrance from the Vietnam Veterans Memorial* (New York: Random House, 1987), 218.
2. Ibid., 212.
3. Belknap, Michal R. *The Vietnam War on Trial: The My Lai Massacre and the Court-Martial of Lieutenant Calley* (Lawrence, KS: University Press of Kansas, 2002), 21–2.
4. Marine Lieutenant Philip Caputo recalls: 'No enemy soldiers entered the ambush, but thousands of insects did. We lay awake eight hours, enduring bites of mosquitos and stinging fire ants,' lying in foxholes 'picking off the leeches that sucked our veins' (cited in Belknap, *The Vietnam War on Trial*, 44).
5. Belknap notes: 'poorly educated, low-income whites and poorly educated low-income blacks together bore a vastly disproportionate share of the burdens in Vietnam' (ibid., 26–7). See also, Appy, Christian. *Working Class War: American Combat Soldiers and Vietnam* (Chapel Hill, NC: University of North Carolina Press, 1993).
6. One of the primary horrors of battle was that the distinction between civilian and enemy was corroded. As one former navy SEAL and US Senator Boby Kerrey cynically announced, the Vietnam Veterans Memorial Wall in Washington listed the names of all those died 'because they didn't realize a woman or a child could be carrying a gun' (cited in Belknap, *The Vietnam War on Trial*, 47). Jan Scruggs (president of the fund) was inspired by the film *The Deer Hunter* (1978) to establish the memorial fund. Starring Robert de Niro and Meryl Streep the film examines the psychological damage of war by focusing on a group of blue-collar workers from Pennsylvania – Michael, Nick, and Steven – who were drafted to serve in Vietnam. After being captured by the Vietcong they are taken to a prison camp where they are forced to play Russian roulette against one another. The trauma of these experiences in captivity continued to haunt them even once they returned home. Unable to reintegrate back into society the film exposes the darker side of American history, as the veterans became outcasts whose war experiences lurked in the shadows of the national unconscious.
7. Within the scope of this book we do not have the space or time to fully discuss the history of the Vietnam wars. For a detailed scholarly study see Young, Marilyn. *The Vietnam Wars 1945–1990* (New York: Harper, 1991).
8. Appy, *Working Class War*, 277.

9. Mock, Freida Lee (dir.). *Maya Lin: A Strong Clear Vision* (New York: American Film Foundation, 1994).
10. Nearly $9,000,000 was raised. It was not only individuals who donated to the fund but also corporations, unions, and other civic organizations.
11. Palmer, *Shrapnel in the Heart*, xviii.
12. On 16 March 1982 the ground was broken at the site and the memorial was dedicated on 13 November 1982.
13. Lin, Maya. *Boundaries* (New York: Simon & Schuster, 2000), 4:05.
14. Mock, *Maya Lin: A Strong Clear Vision.*
15. Ibid.
16. Ibid.
17. These are well documented in Mock, *Maya Lin: A Strong Clear Vision.*
18. Ibid.
19. Deleuze, Gilles and Félix Guattari. *A Thousand Plateaus: Capitalism and Schizophrenia*, trans. Brian Massumi (London: Athlone, 1988), 105.
20. Ibid.
21. Deleuze, Gilles. *The Logic of Sensation*, trans. Mark Lester with Charles Stivale (New York: Columbia University Press, 1990), 324.
22. Caruth, Cathy. *Unclaimed Experience: Trauma, Narrative and History* (Baltimore, MD: Johns Hopkins University Press, 1996), 24.
23. Deleuze, Gilles. *Negotiations: 1972–1900*, trans. Martin Joughin (New York: Columbia University Press, 1995), 123.
24. Deleuze, Gilles, *Francis Bacon: The Logic of Sensation*, trans. Daniel W. Smith (Minneapolis, MN: University of Minnesota Press, 2003), 40.
25. Caruth, *Unclaimed Experience*, 62.
26. Ibid., 62.
27. Palmer, *Shrapnel in the Heart*, xii.
28. Deleuze, *Francis Bacon*, 76–7.
29. Ibid.
30. Although Lin's memorial has carried enormous influence in the art of contemporary memorial design such as the Oklahoma City National Memorial (2000) and the World War Two Memorial (2005) just to mention a few, none carry the same social performative weight as the National Vietnam Veterans Memorial.
31. Deleuze, *Negotiations*, 137.
32. Deleuze, Gilles and Félix Guattari. *What is Philosophy?*, trans. Graham Burchell and Hugh Tomlinson (London: Verso, 1994), 173.
33. Ibid., 164.
34. Lin, *Boundaries*, 4:10.
35. Deleuze, *Negotiations*, 137.
36. Deleuze and Guattari, *What is Philosophy?*, 169.
37. Ibid., 164.
38. Deleuze, *Francis Bacon*, 107.

39. Lin, *Boundaries*, 3:07.
40. Ibid., 3:09.
41. Minimalism uses the phenomenological principle of being *in* the world as its starting point. For instance, Judd's *Untitled* Douglas fir plywood boxes (1976) consist of fifteen variations of the same box. Judd simply presents us with an object and doesn't aspire to any illusionism whatsoever embracing the materiality of the object. And yet minimalism, too, continues to endorse the same self-justificatory characteristics as pop art. Although intensely critical of pop art for the way it exploits history Judd's own work doesn't stand for anything outside of itself and suffers from the same invulnerability as the pop predecessors he critiques. The sparse abstract orderly nature of Judd's aesthetic has obvious connections to modernism, in particular the work of Kasimir Malevich, but whereas the nonobjective paintings and the invisible geometry coordinating Malevich's picture plane invoke a transcendent realm (much like Rothko), Judd's work is factual and quite literally anchored in space. Reducing art to its purest elements and form, as Malevich did, Judd may have denied metaphysical metaphors but in referring only to itself minimalism is resistant to the social environment in which it appears and is therefore explicitly protectionist. In this regard, we experience the minimalist object as radically autonomous, one whose historical immunity creates an uncritical distance between the object and its context.
42. Thiis-Evensen, Thomas. *Archetypes in Architecture* (Oslo: Norwegian University Press, 1987), 116.
43. Ibid., 116.
44. Deleuze and Guattari, *What is Philosophy?*, 167.
45. Lin, *Boundaries*, 2:07.
46. Ibid., 4:05.
47. Lin decided to use the names prior to reading the competition brief that also stipulated all the names of the dead and missing needed to be included in the memorial design. Further, her directions required the following symbolic visual queues to distinguish between a confirmed death – a diamond follows the name – or a cross – symbolizing missing in action – a diamond superimposed over a cross – a serviceperson's remains were returned – or when a serviceperson returns alive – a circle inscribed around a cross. See Lin, *Boundaries*, 4:10, 4:14, and Palmer, *Shrapnel in the Heart*, xii.
48. Palmer, *Shrapnel in the Heart*, 200.
49. Lin, *Boundaries*, 4:09.
50. Deleuze, Gilles and Félix Guattari. *Kafka: Toward a Minor Literature*, trans. Dana Polan (Minneapolis, MN: University of Minnesota Press, 1986), 28.
51. This was the first time an African American was depicted in a national monument.

52. There are similar problems with Glenna Goodacre's memorial design for the Vietnam Women's Memorial installed nearby and dedicated in 1993. It too is a bronze sculpture, depicting three Vietnam servicewomen caring for a wounded male GI.
53. Deleuze and Guattari, *What is Philosophy?*, 177.
54. Ibid.
55. Ibid., 174.
56. Jameson, Fredric. *The Political Unconscious: Narrative as a Socially Symbolic Act* (Ithaca, NY: Cornell University Press, 1981), 230.
57. Deleuze and Guattari, *What is Philosophy?*, 181.
58. Palmer, *Shrapnel in the Heart*, 49.
59. Deleuze, Gilles. *Nietzsche and Philosophy*, trans. Hugh Tomlinson (New York: Columbia University Press, 1986), 23.

CHAPTER 4

9/11 News Coverage

In his address to the nation on 11 September 2001, American President George W. Bush declared that no American will ever forget the terrorist attacks of 9/11, going on to announce that the country would 'go forward to defend freedom and all that is good and just' in the world.[1] This chapter will look to the social reality and function of remembering traumatic events such as 9/11 asking: at what point can we declare that we are remembering too much? Or more significantly, when does the trauma of a past event turn despotic? It will be argued that the mass media's appropriation and repetition of 9/11 images along with the public's will to consume these constitutes a repressive and authoritarian social organization, one that comes from converting the libidinal affects and energies of memory labor into a habitual, albeit paranoid Memory. In this way, the postmodern logic of memorial culture is understood not just as a periodizing concept exemplary of late capitalism, as Jameson proposes, it is also symptomatic of culture's complicity with a broader problem of social repression operating at the level of desire: seamlessly turning the creative and disruptive energies of a little forgetting into a repressing force of Memory signification.

Notwithstanding the fact that for the first five days after the 9/11 attacks the media covered the event around the clock in the absence of commercial breaks (even sports channels turned to disaster coverage), the majority of Americans persistently watched the pastiche of images repeat on their television screens despite the fact that viewing the material made them depressed. The Pew Research Center for People and the Press reported 63 percent of Americans admitted to being addicted to news coverage of 9/11, as opposed to the 50 percent who watched the Gulf War; yet, what is interesting is that the former also admitted they were sadder, more frightened, and fatigued by the 9/11 coverage than that of the Gulf War.[2] The Pew Center also reported on 19 September 2001, that 71 percent of Americans polled had become depressed post 9/11 and nearly half were encountering difficulties in concentration, while one in three were experiencing difficulties sleeping.[3] Although the terrorists had deterritorialized the landscape the repetitive pastiche of disaster images that made up the breaking news of 9/11 worked to reterritorialize the landscape of the American psyche with the terror of Memory. Put differently, the terrorists instigated an act of terror not just restricted to the date – 9/11 – but they used the labor of Memory as a weapon of terrorism, relying upon a media spectacle that would circulate the memory of the event ad nauseam. That said, the media in its coverage of the event was not merely an ideological weapon wielded by a group of unruly terrorists. The bottom line is the population chose to remain glued to the television, suggesting perhaps the repetition of the traumatic memory of 9/11 in psychic life was in fact pleasurable.

Therefore it is not the spectacular character of media coverage that is so intriguing; it is more the fact that traumatic events are popular that is of interest here. Let's face it, people can always turn the television off! The Pew Research Center noted that, much like the Persian Gulf War, over eight in ten (81 percent to be exact) people polled chose to engage with the news coverage of 9/11 leading the reporters to conclude that there was 'near universal public engagement in the crisis.'[4] In fact, in another report, the conclusion was that since 9/11, 66 percent of respondents agreed they watch more news than they did before.[5] It seems that while the pastiche of 9/11 images spewed across television screens worldwide the tragic gave way to the grotesque and the repeated coverage of 9/11 in the media slowly became reactive, if not because, as Davis was to say in the context of his discussion on death, as 'long as desire remains the search for the lost object, the pristine origin, it is in love with its own death.'[6] Davis is largely concerned with maintaining and articulating the uniqueness of the image, that being its especially unique affect as it exposes the creative aspect of the psyche. Why this is important is because the affective power of the image, which cannot be confused with how accurately an image represents reality, nor how effective it is in instigating abstract thought, stimulates an internal reality that doesn't allow for any kind of complacency in the face of reality. Davis claims the image is how the 'mind as psyche apprehends experience at the affective register' and in order to discover how 'we feel' he recommends we revisit our 'primary and abiding images.'[7] However, as will be argued, it is not the affective power of the image where we take issue with Davis, rather it is with his call to return to our primary reservoir of images. What is important is how this return is put to work: is it the effect of a metaphysical (primary) as opposed to materialist (affective) repetition? To not metaphysically engage the affective register means tapping into how memory disorganizes the very substance of the 'primary' visual field Davis speaks of. In effect, metaphysically engaging memory is what constitutes a reterritorializing Memory.

The concept of reterritorialization refers to a process of movement that subjugates deterritorializing lines of flight. The active connection indicative of the movement of deterritorialization threatens to transform and mutate a territory by virtue of the connections its movement produces. In *A Thousand Plateaus* Deleuze and Guattari insist a 'social field is always animated by all kinds of movements of decoding and deterritorialization affecting "masses" and operating at different speeds and paces.'[8] That is, when the lines of connection work to accelerate lines of flight, deterritorialization is in full force. When the same lines conjugate and block the flow, reterritorialization emerges. Both lines of deterritorialization and reterritorialization exist within a given social field, so that when a new territory is constituted it is not so much that the territory in question returns to what it once was prior to the decoding lines of flight that effected the change in the first instance. They clarify: 'Among regimes of signs, the *signifying regime* certainly attains a high level of D (for deterritorialization); but because it simultaneously sets up a whole system of reterritorializations on the signified, and on the signifier itself, it blocks the lines of flight.'[9]

Deleuze and Guattari outline that although children, women and blacks have memories, the moment we collect these and treat them as either childhood memories or women's memories we in fact reterritorialize zones of proximity and the no-man's land of becoming memory. To describe Memory as reterritorializing is to say that it colonizes the nonlocalizable relation as a relation between two points in time – present as different to the past or even the present as an expression of the past – which inevitably reiterates the difference between past and present. Instead, Deleuze and Guattari form a distinction between what could be described as a childhood Memory and a childhood block. They write: ' "a" child coexists with us, in a zone of proximity or a block of becoming, on a line of deterritorialization that carries us both off – as opposed to the child we once were, whom we remember or phantasize, the molar child whose future is the adult.'[10] In effect, the repetition of 9/11 images throughout mass culture generated a transcendent Memory, one that not only remembers the event but also fantasizes over it, so that memory labor feeds into a much deeper repression of the social field epitomized by the US Congress approved Patriot Act (October 2001) and the public's approval to censor the media in the name of security, where eventually, as Baudrillard was to correctly note, there is no difference between the crime and the crack-down.[11] Baudrillard was spot on when he exclaimed: 'There is no "good" use of the media; the media are part of the event, they are part of the terror, and they work in both directions.'[12] However, what he fails to note is that the repetitive news coverage of 9/11 produces a command to never forget. In this regard, Jameson's analysis is useful – the visual nature of postmodern culture is not simply a problem of how the logic of late capitalism is reproduced, it is also responsible for strengthening and intensifying that logic.

In 'Postmodernism and Consumer Culture' Jameson starts out by announcing that postmodernism is not just another style it is a 'periodizing concept whose function is to correlate the emergence of new formal features in culture with the emergence of a new type of social life and a new economic order,' which, borrowing from the economist Ernest Mandel, he describes as 'late capitalism.'[13] Postmodernism, Jameson argues, is the cultural logic of a deeper socioeconomic condition of multinational capitalism and consumer society. Features of this new society include:

> New types of consumption; planned obsolescence; an ever more rapid rhythm of fashion styling changes; the penetration of advertising, television and the media generally to a hitherto unparalleled degree throughout society; the replacement of the old tension between city and country, centre and province, by the suburbs and by universal standardization; the growth of the great networks of superhighways and the arrival of automobile culture . . .[14]

Defined by pastiche (not parody), along with the end of individualism and the subject, as opposed to the paranoid perspective of centered subjectivity that views the rest of the world as a threat, for Jameson postmodern culture produces a nostalgic turn to the past. This is because history is apprehended through 'pop images and stereotypes about the past,' all of which remain beyond our grasp.[15] In other words, the lighthearted meaningless gestures of postmodern culture – pop art, Hollywood, the media, and so on – scramble the signifiers of consumer culture, deferring meaning in an endless play of signifiers, consistently displacing any point of authorial reference. Hence we end up with what minimalist artist Donald Judd once described (in reference to the pop artist Roy Lichtenstein) as the ahistorical 'representation of representation.'[16] And on a more scathing note, Hal Foster notes that the death of the subject is assumed whereby 'often the subject only returns at the level of ideology (for example, the Nazi subject), the nation (now imagined as a psychic entity more than a body politic), and so on.'[17]

Commenting on postmodern culture in general Jameson notes its complicity with multinational capitalism as culture is absorbed so effectively into commodity production that the critical line between cultural production and socioeconomic life is erased.[18] On this note, he leaves us with the question of whether or not postmodernism can ever resist the logic of consumer capitalism given that it emulates, copies, and even reinforces its logic. He insists one implication is that culture is confined to the past, not just because it fails to present the new, but also because it looses a sense of history, condemned to perpetual change and the present.[19] Taking from the past without concern for how the past and present tension each other is the negative side of postmodernism, leaving us with a tautological gesture that produces amnesia. What Jameson does is historicize this amnesia. He insists postmodernism uses a spatial logic (visual culture) more than a temporal one (history) and this situation is what represses historical consciousness. Furthermore, he suggests it is not enough to assume postmodern space is ideological or just a mirage consisting of the movement of simulacrum; it is also historical, meaning it has a social and economic reality. Thus, while on the one hand postmodern global space is totalizing, in the spirit of Marx we need to grasp its dialectical movement.[20] As such, it is important we identify not only the negative features of remembrance but also a complete disregard for its more positive aspects.

Maybe it is not so much that the cultural logic of consumer capitalism produces amnesia where the problem lies, rather it produces too much memory – memory fanaticism? If, as Marx was to posit in the *Manifesto*, the 'bourgeoisie cannot exist without constantly revolutionizing the instruments of production, and thereby the relations of production, and with them the whole relations of society,' then maybe the current cultural fixation on remembrance could be considered as part of the revolution in production that Marx once alerted us to.[21] The problem is not so much in the shift from the material conditions of history to that of the simulacrum, as Jameson suggests; rather, it is the deterritorializing force of the raw material of memory that is turned into common property through the endless repetition of the same images and memory connections that constitutes the work of a reterritorializing Memory. When trauma in all its concrete actuality is unavailable the drives find investment in the image, producing images of gratification. The entire process is what Deleuze and Guattari would otherwise describe as 'recording' (the key characteristic of the second synthesis of desiring-machines: the disjunctive synthesis). Explaining the disjunctive synthesis of desire, Deleuze and Guattari say: 'In a word, a social as a full body forms a surface where all production is recorded, whereupon the entire process appears to emanate from this recording surface.'[22] In the end, the labor power of trauma is never completely freed of erotic investment because in the final instance postmodern culture valorizes the image-as-image, affixing and integrating mnemonic libidinal energies within a reterritorializing movement of signification. Or, as Deleuze and Guattari might describe it, 'society constructs its own delirium by recording the problem of production.'[23] The problem is at the level of the second synthesis – disjunctive – and the Oedipal usage given to traumatic memory. It is a restrictive and exclusive use of traumatic memory as both imaginary and symbolic.

While the physical structures defining the New York skyline may have been removed, the gaping wound they left behind after 9/11 was quickly filled in by an imaginary space. Baudrillard notes that although the 'two towers have disappeared, they have not been annihilated,' because although 'pulverized . . . they have left behind an intense awareness of their presence.'[24] He defines the quality of this imaginary space as the fragility of the American psyche. Although once a symbol of American global economic power, their collapse punctured America's sense of confidence and omnipotence. He argues Americans have been unable to resolve the 'lack' that 9/11 symbolizes and this exemplifies the formation of what Deleuze and Guattari might term a 'territory,' whereby ground zero is related to an unforgettable act of terror that is largely external to the geographic space of ground zero itself (a distinctive moment in time); yet it is this territorial relation that defines the meaning of that space. Consequently, according to Baudrillard, America appears to have fallen into the very 'neurotic night of imaginary identifications' that Deleuze and Guattari warn us of in *Anti-Oedipus*.[25] The Oedipal designation Baudrillard gives ground zero and by implication the date of 9/11, however, 'creates both *the differentiations that it orders and the undifferentiated with which it threatens us*.'[26] For it is not just what the media coverage of 9/11 represents or signifies that is at stake here, it is more a problem of what it *does*. What really happens is that an endless memory labor comes into effect continually opening up new relations that carry within them unforseeable directions and effects. In this way, effecting breaks and connections in what we remember, how we remember, and the particular points of emphasis we give our memories, it could be described as a legitimate disjunctive synthesis. Under such circumstances it could be noted that the terrorists deterritorialized the American psychic and social landscape. However, a reterritorializing Memory is activated as the population compulsively remembers the event, never coming up for air regardless of how this makes it feel. In an act of psychic and social recording this libidinal repetition is strictly reactionary.

In 'Beyond the Pleasure Principle' (1920) Freud explains that pleasure is a principle regulating mental processes and the compulsion to repeat is governed by the wish to return to an earlier inorganic state – 'death instinct.' Feelings of pleasure and displeasure are differentiated in so far as each is a 'quantity of excitation . . . present in the mind,' yet they remain unconnected to anything.[27] What happens when excitation increases is a feeling of discomfort. Inversely when excitation decreases there is a sensation of pleasure. What pleasure does is invest in undifferentiated excitations, correspondingly organizing them into habits. The compulsion to repeat what is pleasurable is like a defensive strategy or 'protective shield' against discomfort and here Freud clarifies that what is traumatic constitutes 'excitations from outside which are powerful enough to break through the protective shield.'[28] Sometimes the compulsion to repeat the unbound stimuli of discomfort – such as trauma – emerges with complete disregard for the regulatory activities of the pleasure principle. Trying to answer to this dilemma Freud concludes

> *an instinct is an urge inherent in organic life to restore an earlier state of things* which the living entity has been obliged to abandon under the pressure of external disturbing forces; that is, it is a kind of organic elasticity, or, to put it another way, the expression of the inertia inherent in organic life.[29]

The death instinct is a regressive operation and can be best explained as the desire to return once more to an inorganic condition and to 'restore an earlier state of things.'[30] Contrary to popular belief, says Freud, the instincts are not revolutionary, they are conservative, that is they propel us to repeat and seek out an earlier inorganic state. The compulsion to repeat is not just the result of external stimuli, it is also an operation of the psyche. The idea runs as follows: 'Two kinds of processes are constantly at work in living substance, operating in contrary directions, one constructive or assimilatory and the other destructive or dissimilatory.'[31]

Four years after writing 'Beyond the Pleasure Principle' Freud explains in 'An Autobiographical Study' that his work has 'contemplated a new solution to the problem of instincts.' He says he 'combined the instincts for self-preservation and for the preservation of the species under the concept of *Eros*' contrasting this with 'an *instinct of death* or *destruction* which works in silence.'[32] He goes on to clarify that the instincts share a conservative character as 'exemplified by the phenomena of the *compulsion to repeat*.'[33] All new life forms are understood as repeating the original form of organic life and it is in the compulsion to repeat that the death instinct reappears. Interestingly, the presence of the death instinct in all life means that life is ultimately contra-life, this being the essence of its conservative character, favoring identity and unity at the expense of difference and multiplicity. Freud puts forward a homogenous view of repetition – Eros (life) is reducible to Thanatos (death) and Thanatos works to return to an inorganic state. Hence, libidinal repetition is emptied of difference. The crux of Freud's thesis is that when external threats to an organism are made the pleasure principle shields the organism from shock. Sometimes, feelings of displeasure repeat and this happens either because the pleasure principle has failed, or the subject wishes to return to a prior ahistorical inorganic unity. The images of 9/11 reinstate the validity of the system of signification that situates traumatic memory as the fantasized 'other' within that system. If traumatic memory is the chaotic point of difference beyond signification, meaning trauma is presupposed within the repetition of images as the Other-than-signified, then this is where its spectacle power lies. As Žižek teaches us in his use of Lacan, we fantasize over the lost object of signification and what cannot be signified is also the prohibited object of our desires.[34] Once the traumatic memory of 9/11 is repeated an increasingly repressed social field and repressing memory labor comes into effect. Memories of 9/11 now become authoritarian, for in their repetition they turn into a repressing force. However, it is not just the endless documentation and the appropriation of that documentation of publicly traumatic events by the mass media that do not allow us to forget, the public also actively participates in the consumption of this material. The public doesn't want to forget.

For instance, in 1985 only 39 percent of those polled believed the government should be allowed to censor the media in the name of national security, with 50 percent believing the media should be able to report on events without government control. After 9/11 this had risen to 53 percent approving government control and 39 percent believing the media should retain the right to freely report news it believes is in the national interest.[35] This is an interesting set of statistics when considered alongside those cited earlier: the public was not only depressed by 9/11 news coverage but it also admitted to watching it more. Whereas, Freud was to argue we repeat as a result of our repression (compulsive repetition), the findings published by the Pew Research Center seem to suggest and support Deleuze's thesis, in Buchanan's words, that 'we repress because we repeat.'[36] If we let go of the idea of repetitive compulsion not only does death no longer have an instinct we are also able to start our analysis by looking to social oppression first and not individual repression. We are now left with what Buchanan describes as the three forms of Oedipalization. These are: 'the displaced image repression gives rise to (and on which it is subsequently enacted, though falsely); it is also the instrument of that repression (it supplants desire); and it is a repressive model for us to conform to.'[37] Although on one level we may really want to forget 9/11, we give up on this in the name of honoring those who died and, on another level, by putting desire in the service of social distortion. Put differently, a repressive social field is fuelled by a paranoid mode of memory labor whereby Western nationalism (liberalism, freedom, and goodness) is pitted against Eastern fundamentalism (terrorism, oppression, and evil), or cultural censorship is advocated in the name of national interests.

It is not just that forgetting is incompatible with remembering those who died on the day four planes were hijacked and turned into missiles, forgetting is, as Buchanan might conclude in his discussion of Oedipus, 'incompatible with the structural needs of collective life.'[38] Allowing room for forgetfulness to make an appearance does not mean creating a fiction but it does acknowledge that we cannot reduce the process of remembrance to a strictly univocal Memory (reterritorializing), nor can we claim that the collective articulation of trauma is responsible for organically representing that memory (managing the unmanageable and chaotic in a rigid organization). All in all, as a repressive model, memorial culture fails to prompt the following question: how can we liberate ourselves from the gratification traumatic remembrance yields? In the long run the paranoid investment of social desire fetishizes the very system that produces memory as spectacle. Using a Marxist avenue of critique here, the trauma memorial culture mistakenly presents as a determinate experience is really a social relation of production. It is not, as Freud was to posit, that recollection puts an end to what unconscious memories safeguard, that being trauma as the original site of subjectivity; rather, the postmodern subject is traumatically formed as Jameson's alienated subject as it submits to the law of memory signification.

At this point we may want to add to Jameson's position and declare that as historical consciousness is repressed it reemerges as a symptom – a displaced and distorted historical consciousness. As a repressing apparatus, distorted historical consciousness over-identifies with traumatic events as compensation for the loss of historical consciousness, centering the subject in an exceptional time in History. Trauma, that is, locates individual temporalities within a universal time – History. This universal time is a symptom of the repressed historical consciousness that Jameson warns against. Obviously, this fulfills a structural need, but it is also authoritarian and repressive because memory is put to work to foster a return to History. Put differently, memory is metaphysically structured around a determinate connective synthesis (individual time coalesces with the transcendent time of History). Once more the line between *chronos* and *aion* is smudged and the utopian charge of memory is neutralized, for if we recall our earlier discussion, it is in the struggle over how *aion* (affective time) and *chronos* (chronological time) tension each other where the politics of memory lies. The effect of this erasure is habitual Memory. Instead of creating an untimely break in Memory where a utopian antiproduction of memory would come into effect, one that would enable new realities to emerge, the alienated experience of postmodern space that Jameson identifies as sublime gives rise to a metaphysical temporal identification.

In order to disorganize the fixation on traumatic meaning of 9/11 we need to suspend Memory and the whole connective synthesis that reproduces the same images and connections to an immanent terrorist threat over and over again (an illegitimate use of the connective synthesis). So, how can the connective synthesis be broken to make way for new connections to be drawn? Here we need to introduce a more productive understanding of death than that offered by Freud. One significant difference between Freud and Deleuze is that Freud posits that death negates life, while for Deleuze death differentiates life. In other words, Deleuze claims that without death there would be no life. For Deleuze death is problematic, revealing a 'demonic power' in between life and death.[39] With Guattari, he develops what he describes as a *schizophrenizing-death* that desiring-machines engage in.[40] Accusing the psychoanalytic death principle of succumbing to a transcendent configuration, Deleuze and Guattari note in *Anti-Oedipus*

> that there is no death instinct because there is both the model and the experience of death in the unconscious. Death then is a part of the desiring-machine, a part that must itself be judged, evaluated in the functioning of the machine and the system of its energetic conversions, and not as an abstract principle.[41]

As Freud noted, we desire a return to an inorganic state, but perhaps it is not a return to the inorganic so much as a return to the unhistorical out of which we discover an Untimely memory, a memory without a point of origin or a primary visual field, a memory that doesn't define who we are and what we will become. As Deleuze explains: 'The unhistorical is like an atmosphere within which alone life can germinate and with the destruction of which it must vanish . . . What deed would man be capable of if he had not first entered into that vaporous region of the unhistorical?'[42] In this regard, the unhistorical is similar to the utopian promise of memory first outlined in Chapter 2.

Thus Deleuze proposes pleasure is not a principle designed to produce satisfaction, it is empirical, meaning the present is a passive flow of affectivity that contracts and folds the outside into the inside of being. Here the key difference between Freud and Deleuze is that the latter insists pleasure is not a pronoun, it is an 'adverb referring to a mobile place.'[43] Hence, what Deleuze calls 'pleasure' is actually a 'field of individuation in which differences in intensity are distributed here and there in the form of excitation.'[44] By attempting to determine the conditions under which pleasure becomes a principle Freud is forced to invest, or bind, excitations and the free movement of difference in the libido. That is, once excitation and differences are integrated libidinal energies are constituted; from here Freud is able to launch a fundamental separation between the original (unconscious and libidinal energies) and the copy (consciousness and the ego) whereby we make sense of consciousness by interpreting the unconscious. Everything can be traced back to the unconscious. The error of Freud as Deleuze understands it is at the level of representation. In his use of the logic of signification Freud argues the unconscious expresses conscious activity, thereby reinforcing their difference. In addition, where Freud understood death as the negation of life, for Deleuze it produces the differentiation and creativity that yields life. As Deleuze sees it, life is differentiated and creative and there is no matter without the connective synthesis. Death is not inanimate matter, it is the pure form of time. Death work is not especially human because the human being is the effect of the particular connections made by the connective synthesis and the disjunctions that force those connections to break with habit and reproduction (death). In his view, death is the qualitative differentiation that the disjunctive synthesis produces.

In *Anti-Oedipus: Capitalism and Schizophrenia* Deleuze and Guattari explain that the body without organs (BwO) introduces into the connective synthesis 'amorphous, undifferentiated fluid' so as to counter 'organ-machines.'[45] This unorganized intensive surface of flow is the second synthesis of desiring-machines, what Deleuze and Guattari otherwise call its disjunctive operation. The disjunctive synthesis interrupts the connections of the connective synthesis preventing the connective mode from turning into reproductive habits. The BwO is a recording surface that breaks connections in order to make new ones. It is worthwhile quoting them at length here:

> Desiring-machines work only when they break down, and by continually breaking down . . . The body without organs is nonproductive; nonetheless it is produced, at a certain place and a certain time in the connective synthesis, as the identity of producing and the product: the schizophrenic table is a body without organs. The body without organs is not the proof of an orginal nothingness, nor is it what remains of a lost totality. Above all, it is not an image of the body. It is the body without an image . . . The full body without organs belongs to the realm of antiproduction; but yet another characteristic of the connective or productive synthesis is the fact that it couples production with antiproduction, with an element of antiproduction.[46]

Although Deleuze and Guattari are clear to avoid an organicist model that organizes organs and life matter to serve a teleological system of production, their concept of the BwO acknowledges that although this body is primarily nonproductive it is involved with the distribution of intensities and libidinal energies that bring about change. Although they speak of a body *without* organs, the critical focus of the concept lies in an anorganic vision at the level of formal organization and not the organs per se.

Later in *A Thousand Plateaus* Deleuze and Guattari clarify that the BwO is a 'field of immanence in which desire lacks nothing and therefore cannot be linked to any external or transcendent criteria.'[47] It is once the BwO is put in the service of signification and subjectification that it turns into an organism. The BwO is therefore always perched between stratification (hierarchical organization, organism, and signifiance) and the experimental plane of consistency that frees it from the 'surfaces of stratification that block it or make it recoil.'[48] Not all disjunctive syntheses produce a BwO though. The disjunctive synthesis can also lead us to the 'same result of the connective synthesis: it too is capable of two uses, the one immanent, the other transcendent.'[49] In its transcendent use the disjunctive synthesis is exclusive, restrictive, and negative. The illegitimate disjunctive synthesis works according to the differentiating function of either/or, whereas the immanent disjunctive synthesis is affirmative, nonrestrictive, and inclusive, deriving from the operation of 'either . . . or . . . or.'[50] With the latter '*everything divides, but into itself*.'[51]

This conceptual apparatus now helps us reconsider the public's commitment to continue watching news coverage of 9/11 despite the fact that it made them depressed. The images of planes flying into skyscrapers and the architectural skeleton of their remains rising up amid the smoke of gray ash and cement dust carry enormous affective weight. Submitting to the power of those images of disaster may leave the public feeling depressed but the affective power and libidinal charge of viewing catastrophe unfold indicates that traumatic remembrance can be pleasurable. Pleasure here is not a principle in the way Freud was to posit, it is an empirical folding of an external reality within the internal life of the subject. This is because an image that is 'deterritorialized in relation to the exterior necessarily reterritorializes on its interior milieu.'[52] For example, as the Pew Research Center concludes: 'Though horrified at the images being broadcast from New York, Washington and Pennsylvania, Americans give the news media higher grades for its reporting than during the Gulf war – an unprecedented 89% give the media a positive rating, with 56% judging it excellent, 33% good.'[53] These findings are important for our discussion because repetition in the service of reproduction converts the libidinal energies of trauma into recording energies (disjunctive synthesis), but unlike the intensive topography of the experimental BwO there is no moment when new connections are drawn. Instead, the internalized system of repetition becomes repressive, conflating mourning, death, and trauma with gratification. Such metaphysical repetition never actually places trauma *in* the world and in this regard it is merely an exercise in transcendence. Thus reproductive repetition holds life and death in stark contrast to one another so that the representation remains immune to the concrete life of reality (what Deleuze would describe as organic representation).

While the comparison Jameson draws between the hegemony of postmodern culture and socioeconomic realities is instructive it has to be expanded to include another thesis that acknowledges the important role of memory production in the context of postmodern culture. The stereotypes Jameson speaks of come from a habitual organization of collective memory, and the repetition of public traumatic events ad nauseam in effect produces a command to not forget the stereotype. This situation impedes the formation of a critical disjunctive; however, it is only through some kind of antiproduction, or as Deleuze and Guattari might argue, through a legitimate use of the disjunctive synthesis, that stereotypical or habitual modes of remembrance are broken. The conflict Adorno spoke of now returns to haunt us once more – mass culture is without conflict, but only in so far as psychic and social libidinal energies of antiproduction have been neutralized. Hence, the episodic dimension of mass culture that Adorno notes is perhaps the effect of too much memory. We can now slightly amend the Freudian discussion of the death-instinct, using Deleuze and Guattari's thesis that death is the disjunctive synthesis that breaks the habitual connections of the connective synthesis and without this break life would come to a standstill.

Once 'reality' is taken to be the lost object of our desires then the present is rendered completely impotent and the future merely becomes a luxury. It is perhaps for this reason that when postmodern culture activates history it deactivates the force of change driving history; by reducing reality to a system of endless quotation, the past turns into a stereotype and as Jameson instructs it is the stereotype we nostalgically mourn over. Whereas for Jameson the postmodern is not paranoid, the implication of our argument here is that the nostalgia he speaks of is in itself a paranoid social libidinal investment of memory because the past functions to recode and reterritorialize the present, imposing upon the present too much remembrance and not enough forgetting. It might be an interesting thought experiment to shift the parameters of Jameson's argument and posit that postmodern culture is in fact symptomatic of a failure to forget: the terror of what Deleuze and Guattari describe as a reterritorializing Memory. The point is that terrorism doesn't come from the actions of a group of fundamentalists; it is the effect of reterritorializing Memory. To be sure, a little forgetting – memory failure – allows the past to inform but not overwhelm the present, so that we can optimistically orient ourselves in the present, looking forward in time with hope and confidence. The issue now becomes one of how to disentangle the idea that the failure of memory is an ideological exercise in historical amnesia from the free act of curbing or disciplining public remembrance, in order to positively embrace the promise and opportunities the future poses.

Notes

1. Bush, George W. 'Oval Office Speech,' evening 11 September 2001, *September 11 news.com* at: http://www.september11news.com/PresidentBush.htm, accessed 23 October 2006.
2. Pew Research Center for the People and the Press, 'American Psyche Reeling from Terror Attacks,' released 19 September 2001. See: http://people-press.org/reports/display.php3?ReportID=3, accessed 23 October 2006.
3. Ibid.
4. Ibid.
5. Pew Research Center for the People and the Press, 'Terror Coverage Boosts News Media's Image but Military Censorship Backed,' released 28 November 2001. See: http://people-press.org/reports/display.php3?ReportID=143, accessed 23 October 2006.
6. Davis, Walter A. *Deracination: Historicity, Hiroshima, and the Tragic Imperative* (New York: SUNY Press, 2001), 141.
7. Ibid., 196.
8. Deleuze, Gilles and Félix Guattari. *A Thousand Plateaus: Capitalism and Schizophrenia*, trans. Brian Massumi (London: Athlone Press, 1988), 220.
9. Ibid., 508.
10. Ibid., 294.
11. Baudrillard, Jean. *The Spirit of Terrorism*, trans. Chris Turner (London: Verso, 2002), 31.
12. Ibid.
13. Indeed, postmodern artists consciously try to subvert individual and historical styles. For example, it is interesting to note that, after having started out in commercial art, Warhol acknowledged that his drawings during this time had a particular style to them which, in hindsight for him, was evidence of a certain 'feeling' carrying over into the picture (not to mention the fact that, as Warhol describes it, the people who commissioned the drawings were emotionally invested in the final products he produced for them). What this meant was the 'process of doing work in commercial art was machine-like, but the attitude had feeling to it.' Andy Warhol, cited in Goldsmith, Kenneth (ed.). *I'll Be Your Mirror: The Selected Andy Warhol Interviews* (New York: Carroll & Graf, 2004), 18. What Warhol wanted to do was abandon personal style

altogether and produce pictures that you neither had to understand nor feel. He succinctly stated: 'The reason I'm painting this way is that I want to be a machine, and I feel that whatever I do and do machine-like is what I want to do.' Warhol, Andy. 'Interview with Gene Swensen', in Harrison, Charles and Paul Wood (eds). *Art in Theory 1900–2000: An Anthology of Changing Ideas* (Oxford: Blackwell, 2003), 748. Being a 'machine' is not intended metaphorically, Warhol quite clearly sees himself *as* a machine: the camera connects to the eye, the assistant with the canvas, the silkscreen with paint, and so on. In this regard he seems to produce a legitimate connective synthesis picking up the pieces Rothko had left behind. See Jameson, Fredric. 'Postmodernism and Consumer Society,' in *The Continental Aesthetics Reader*, ed. Clive Cazeaux (London: Routledge, 2000), 283.
14. Jameson, 'Postmodernism and Consumer Society,' 293.
15. Ibid., 287.
16. Judd, Donald. 'Specific Objects,' in Harrison and Wood, *Art in Theory 1900–2000*, 825.
17. Foster, Hal. *The Return of the Real* (Cambridge, MA: MIT Press, 1996), 28.
18. Jameson, 'Postmodernism and Consumer Society,' 293.
19. Ibid., 286.
20. Marx writes in the *Manifesto*: 'When people speak of ideas that revolutionize society, they do but express the fact, that within the old society, the elements of a new one have been created, and that the dissolution of the old ideas keeps even pace with the dissolution of the old conditions of existence.' Marx, Karl. *Manifesto*, trans. Paul M. Sweeny (New York: Monthly Review Press, 1998), 37.
21. Ibid., 7.
22. Deleuze, Gilles and Félix Guattari. *Anti-Oedipus: Capitalism and Schizophrenia*, trans. R. Hurley, M. Seem, and H.R. Lane (Minneapolis, MN: University of Minnesota Press, 1986), 10.
23. Ibid.
24. Baudrillard, *The Spirit of Terrorism*, 48.
25. Deleuze and Guattari, *Anti-Oedipus*, 79.
26. Ibid., 78–9.
27. Freud, Sigmund. 'Beyond the Pleasure Principle,' in Peter Gray (ed.), *The Freud Reader* (London: Vintage, 1995), 595.
28. Ibid., 607.
29. Ibid., 612.
30. Peter Gray clearly points out that although some have provided an autobiographical interpretation of Freud's interest in developing a theory of death with his grief over the loss of his daughter Sophie, the manuscript of *Beyond the Pleasure Principle* was largely finished while Sophie was still alive and healthy. See Gray, *The Freud Reader*, 594 and 615.

31. Freud, 'Beyond the Pleasure Principle,' 618.
32. Freud, Sigmund. 'An Autobiographical Study,' in Gray, *The Freud Reader*, 36.
33. Ibid., 36. Davis points out there is a limit to how Freud perceives death as an instinct instead of 'work' and this accounts for Freud's claim that Thanatos has quiescence and not destruction as its goal. What Davis suggests is that Thanatos be liberated from instinct and understood as dynamic and active, as 'an energy seeking rituals not in order to bind and discharge the pressure that weighs on it but in order to celebrate itself and extend its scope.' According to Davis, Thanatos is driven by pleasure and a 'change of libidinal energy that has the annexing of Eros as its implied goal from the beginning.' See Davis, *Deracination*, 136. So far this is sounding very much like what Deleuze says but where he and Deleuze part ways is over the particularly human character Davis gives death work.
34. Žižek, Slavoj. *Organs without Bodies: Deleuze and Consequences* (London: Routledge, 2003), 102–5.
35. Pew Research Center for the People and the Press, 'Terror Coverage Boosts News Media's Image but Military Censorship Backed,' released 28 November 2001. See: http://people-press.org/reports/display.php3?ReportID=143, accessed on 23 October 2006.
36. Buchanan, Ian. *Deleuzism: A Metacommentary* (Durham, NC: Duke University Press, 2000), 4.
37. Ibid., 20.
38. Ibid.
39. Deleuze, Gilles. *Difference and Repetition*, trans. Paul Patton (New York: Columbia University Press, 1994), 19.
40. In *Anti-Oedipus* Deleuze and Guattari write: 'Freud never stopped trying to limit the discovery of a subjective or vital essence of desire as libido. But when the dualism passed into a death instinct against Eros, this was no longer a simple limitation, it was a liquidation of the libido.' They continue on, siding with Reich, explaining: 'Reich did not go wrong here, and was perhaps the only one to maintain that the product of analysis should be a free and joyous person, a carrier of the life flows, capable of carrying them all the way into the desert and decoding them . . .' See Deleuze and Guattari. *Anti-Oedipus*, 331.
41. Ibid., 332.
42. Deleuze and Guattari, *A Thousand Plateaus*, 296.
43. Deleuze, *Difference and Repetition*, 96.
44. Ibid.
45. Deleuze and Guattari, *Anti-Oedipus*, 9.
46. Ibid., 8.
47. Deleuze and Guattari, *A Thousand Plateaus*, 157.
48. Ibid., 158.

49. Deleuze and Guattari, *Anti-Oedipus*, 78.
50. Ibid., 76.
51. Ibid.
52. Deleuze and Guattari, *A Thousand Plateaus*, 54.
53. Pew Research Center for the People and the Press, 'American Psyche Reeling from Terror Attacks.'

CHAPTER 5

US Military Abuses at Abu Ghraib

On 28 April 2004 CBS *60 Minutes* aired a report on the brutalization of Iraqi detainees at the hands of US soldiers at Abu Ghraib prison; this was rapidly followed by an article on the same story that appeared in *The New Yorker* on 30 April 2004. These images flooded newsstands and media outlets worldwide, and the debate over moral culpability and immunity occupied talk-show radio hosts and news commentators alike. Needless to say, the then US Secretary of Defense, Donald Rumsfeld, responded to the media frenzy by quickly engaging a hermeneutic battle over the definition of 'torture' in an attempt to water down the legal ramifications of what had happened and save the face of his administration, demanding the actions be described as 'abuse' not 'torture.'[1] Our focus will be not so much on the problem of ideology – the hermeneutic hair splitting that went on over the definition of 'torture' – or even the subsequent legal arguments surrounding the moral responsibility of the military and/or the individuals involved; rather, carrying on from the previous discussion in chapter 4 concerning the media's role in producing an overabundance of memory, we will explore the effects of this situation, asking the question: how is collective memory put to work in the service of social subjection?

Using Foucault's notion of power as a form of disciplinary control in concert with Deleuze and Guattari's concept of desire as social, we will explore the sociality of memory in terms of a productive power. This means we will attend not so much to the problem of free will (the moral culpability of certain individuals) but we will start with the non-individual forces and affects operating in relation with other forces, such as collective memory, delving down deep to discover how these libidinal affects and energies are invested throughout the social field. It will be proposed that the potentially revolutionary social energies that the release of the Abu Ghraib images initiated were disciplined by another series of social forces: the collective memory of 9/11 still fresh in every American's mind and the deeper racist visual history that the Abu Ghraib images resonated with.

The report – *Taguba Report on the Treatment of Abu Ghraib Prisons in Iraq* – lists the following abuses during the period from October to December 2003:

> Punching, slapping, and kicking detainees; jumping on their naked feet; videotaping and photographing naked male and female detainees; forcibly arranging detainees in various sexually explicit positions for photographing; forcing detainees to remove their clothing and keeping them naked for several days at a time; forcing naked male detainees to wear women's underwear; forcing groups of male detainees to masturbate themselves while being photographed and videotaped; arranging naked male detainees in a pile and then jumping on them; positioning a naked detainee on a MRE Box, with a sandbag on his head, and attaching wires to his fingers, toes, and penis to simulate electric torture; writing 'I am a Rapest' on the leg of a detainee alleged to have forcibly raped a 15-year-old fellow detainee, and then photographing him naked; placing a dog chain or strap around a naked detainee's neck and having a female soldier pose for a picture; a male MP guard having sex with a female detainee; using military working dogs (without muzzles) to intimidate and frighten detainees, and in at least one case biting and severely injuring a detainee; taking photographs of dead Iraqi detainees.[2]

Evidence in support of the above findings included witness reports, photographs, and videotapes. Investigations revealed how the usual separation between the duties of military police and intelligence personnel had become blurred, concluding that violations against the prisoners was the result of an abuse of power.

When the images of Abu Ghraib entered mass media circulation they were theatricalized as they were ideologically inscribed by the following issues: who is morally culpable, this is not what the US represents, the debate over whether it was to be called 'torture' or 'abuse,' blaming the situation on a lack of military supervision, and so on. The images saturated the American landscape and the administration quickly admonished those responsible, all the while promulgating the virtues of the military, pointing out the actions of a few should be not be translated into an indictment of the military as a whole. The former situation fetishized the event, the latter attempted to confound ethical clarity, swiftly putting what the US administration promulgated as the incorrect interpretation of these events out to pasture. In a manner reminiscent of Rob Reiner's film *A Few Good Men* (1992) lawyers representing the court-martialed soldiers argued their clients were simply carrying out orders from their superiors.[3]

This argument purports that the mistreatment of the detainees was the result of power relations implicit within a dehumanizing chain of command. For instance, the will to extract intelligence information from some of the detainees by the CIA (Central Intelligence Authority) resulted in a vulgar loosening of moral guidelines that eventually perpetuated more and more violent behavior. Such an argument focuses on ideological tenets, that being the 'wrong' kind of ideology specific to military training, one that educated the individuals in question in uncivilized values.[4]

To focus purely on ideology though leaves the thorny question of spectatorial glee evidenced in the photographs unanswered. In this regard, others may prefer to insist that in the manner of William Golding's *Lord of the Flies* (1954), the images raised the problem of anonymity: when an individual identifies with the group they sacrifice individual responsibility and hence feel immune to any form of moral accountability whatsoever, though this too suggests the torture and accompanying documentation of this process was an instance of socialization gone wrong. As Žižek announces in his discussion against human rights: 'All big "public issues" are now translated into attitudes towards the regulation of "natural" or "personal" idiosyncrasies.'[5] Here public concern centers around social violence, but the activities of the pseudo-political realm shift the ground away from the struggle of politics proper onto the democratic process that argues over the meaning of torture, the responsibilities of the individual versus the institution, and the furious back-peddling of the US administration to save the face of virtue it propounded to the rest of the world, all of which, according to Žižek, serve social violence.

The images initially released by *60 Minutes* and *The New Yorker* documented the findings of torture and sexual humiliation listed in the *Taguba Report*. There was one of Private Lynndie England shown with a cigarette in mouth pointing to naked male Iraqi detainees as well as with what seems like her taking a nude detainee for a walk on a leash. One image depicted Sergeant Ivan Frederick atop a detainee. Some were of nude detainees struggling to form a human pyramid with US military posing behind them, smiling and giving a thumbs-up signal to the camera. Detainee Satar Jabar was documented with a black pointed hood and cloak standing on a box with his arms spread out and electrical wires attached to his body. There was the image of a male nude detainee tied up with women's underwear over his head, followed by another image of a detainee with a plastic hood over his head standing as another nude male inmate was forced to give him oral sex.

In her article, 'On the Torture of Others' published by the *New York Times Magazine*, Susan Sontag locates the revolutionary power of photographs in their ability to disseminate throughout the public arena in spite of ideological interests to censor such imagery and their circulation. She begins by making the point that photographs lay down the parameters for how conflict is judged and remembered and in this case the pictures not only reveal acts of torture, they portray a guilty America.[6] The power of this 'Western memory machine' comes from the content of these pictures for it is what they document that will define what we remember of the US invasion of Iraq. Indeed, she says it is because of the visual power of the photograph that the Bush administration desperately tried to curb the dissemination of the photographs. Going on to consider the content of the photographs as evidence of torture and not abuse, as Rumsfeld fumbled to redefine them, Sontag defiantly argues that we cannot separate the content of the pictures from the actual act of taking the pictures in the first instance and, more importantly, that the perpetrators chose to pose with their victims in the pictures. Noting similarities to the snapshots taken of the lynching of African Americans and of pornographic imagery she explains: 'What is illustrated by these photographs is as much the culture of shamelessness as the reigning admiration for unapologetic brutality.'[7] However, she concludes that even though the photos are disturbing in the extreme, like the countless other images documenting private erotic life spewing across the Internet they will continue to be taken and distributed regardless of how much the administration may try to censor their dissemination.

What Sontag does not address here is the way in which power is exercised as a mode of subjectification. To do this we need to first look to the mechanics of power Foucault describes in his study of 'docile bodies' in *Discipline and Punish*. This then prompts us to look at situational factors such as the dehumanizing architectural conditions of the seventh cellblock, where a majority of the abuses took place, and how these relations facilitated the mistreatment of detainees, and, more importantly in the context of our discussion here, the parameters of our problem widens to include the role of traumatic memory in the system of subjectification.[8] In *Discipline and Punish* Foucault proposes that what makes the Panopticon prison so effective in disciplining inmates is not just that it physically controls the behavior of inmates, as Jeremy Bentham was to put forward; what is important is that the prison environment also controls the psyche of the prisoner. Psychic control comes from being under the watchful eye of the prison guards from the central watchtower. Foucault's point is that although the guards may not actually be watching the prisoner in their cell around the clock, the prisoner himself is unable to ascertain when he is and isn't being watched. The body of the inmate is therefore disciplined by the threat of surveillance. Hence, the Panopticon environment can psychologically influence everyone from the inmate through to the prison guard. For example, the layout of the Abu Ghraib prison undermines effective supervision of the guards themselves and in this regard it is interesting to note that most of the torture at Abu Ghraib took place in the seventh block where there are 103 cells (each cell is six feet by ten feet) extending in single file down a long hallway. Hence, parts of the block remained invisible to supervision leading to an argument that suggests the guards need to be supervised just as much as the prisoners do. This line of argument forms a connection between the form of the prison and the coercive and punitive activities that took place in it.

Those who supervise, document, and initiate the torture of prisoners are in many ways what Foucault might call 'technicians of behavior,' in so far as their task is to 'produce bodies' that are 'both docile and capable' of providing intelligence information.[9] In other words, it is not so much that the military personnel at Abu Ghraib were not properly supervised – power understood as a system of control (such as when we ask what power is and where it comes from) – instead Foucault's analysis invites us to ask: how is power practised? Sontag touches upon a similar idea when she insists:

> The issue is not whether the torture was done by individuals (i.e., 'not by everybody') – but whether it was systematic. Authorized. Condoned. All acts are done by individuals. The issue is not whether a majority or a minority of Americans performs such acts but whether the nature of the policies prosecuted by this administration and the hierarchies deployed to carry them out makes such acts likely.[10]

However, contrary to Sontag, the idea Foucault advances is that power is not just ideological or coercive, nor is it simply the notion that power is located in the transcendent image of the state or the way state policy is administered. Foucault insists power is a system of subjectification that emerges out of social relations and that power can be revolutionary as much as it is coercive.

One very good example of imagery stirring revolutionary energies would be the graphic media coverage of the Vietnam War that not only swayed public opinion on the war but also fueled the antiwar movement. Actually Vietnam is an interesting point of comparison to the situation in Iraq: the Vietcong like the terrorist was hard to distinguish amid the local civilian population making it very difficult for American troops to clearly pinpoint the enemy. Further it was not just young men of military age that assisted the Vietcong; old men, women and even children were involved and it was this confusion of where the civilian ended and the enemy combatant began that led to a loosening of the Geneva Convention on the Laws of War (1949). As Belknap reports the Charlie Company was specifically indoctrinated in what came to be known as the 'Five S's': search, silence, safeguard, segregate, and speed.[11] The same Company under the direction of Lieutenant William Calley (known as 'Rusty') was later involved in the My Lai Massacre on 16 March 1968 for which Calley was accused of killing the majority of civilians.[12] The massacre was swiftly covered up by Congress, American President Nixon, and the military. Meanwhile, the press initially remained uninterested in the prosecution of Calley which also helped keep the issue under control.[13] Eventually, images of over 300 elderly, women, children, and babies who had been tortured, mutilated, and raped were released in America on 20 November 1969, leaving the nation choking back their tears, disgust, disbelief, and rage at the atrocities American forces had committed. In fact, the initial reaction of 43 percent of Minnesota residents to the massacre stories was that they were simply not credible.[14] As there is no image here it may be useful for the reader to hear the following description from Vernando Simpson, a soldier who partook in the massacre from the Second Platoon:

> I cut out their throats, cut off their hands, cut out their tongue [*sic*], their hair, scalped them. I did it. A lot of people were doing it, and I just followed. I lost all sense of direction.[15]

Once the graphic and brutal images of civilian slaughter persisted throughout the media and Americans started to absorb the story, pressure against the war began to mount. Furthermore, it wasn't just at the level of 'opinion' where the power of these images lay, it also disrupted the political sphere as public anger translated into concrete forms of resistance against the war (energizing the antiwar movement and prompting more draftees to publicly burn their draft notices): a revolutionary social force came into effect.

Following Foucault's conception of power we now engage a dialogical position that posits the social emerges out of a play of corporeal forces. Citing Foucault, Deleuze says:

> Violence acts on specific bodies, objects or beings whose form it destroys or changes, while force has no object other than that of other bodies, and no being other than that of relation: it is 'an action upon an action, on existing actions, or on those which may arise in the present or future'; it is 'a set of actions upon other actions.'[16]

For Foucault, social formations emerge through history and the open-ended concrete struggles that happen over the course of history. He claims a subject is constituted out of history and is subjected to all kinds of power relations that discipline and manage a body, teaching us that not only does the disciplinary system produce submissive individuals it also serves an epistemological function. It is a technique that concomitantly produces knowledge as it stabilizes the body. In turn, the authority of those who are supervising, judging, constraining, and coercing prisoners is obtained through the disciplinary mechanism itself. Hence, Sontag's argument that the Abu Ghraib images will define how the war in Iraq will be remembered may be highly questionable, because if Kendrick Oliver's analysis of the media coverage of the Vietnam War is any indication, the American public may find the ethical problems the events at Abu Ghraib raise just too difficult to address. The fact that the ethical context to which, for instance, the My Lai Massacre have been whitewashed by history is telling indeed. However, Oliver prefers to analyze the hazy place My Lai has in American memory in terms of an ideological battle, blaming the American military of institutionalizing some of the difficult lessons of Vietnam and for being a 'rather ambivalent guardian of the memory of the massacre itself, and of other American atrocities committed in Vietnam.'[17] The documentation of the abuses at Abu Ghraib can be seen as one way of knowing the 'enemy' and also as a way of deriving authority over the enemy, much like the photographs of medical experiments the Nazi's took during World War Two.

Sontag reports that many Americans began to feel that the continual coverage of the torture of Iraqi detainees at Abu Ghraib in the press seems to judge America in an unfavorable light, forgetting that 'they' (Osama bin Laden, Saddam Hussein, or whoever) attacked America first and doesn't America have the right to defend itself.[18] Indeed, the proliferation of these images did make America forget. However, it wasn't so much that America couldn't remember who 'started' the conflict; rather the images supplanted the sense of shame and insecurity of 9/11 (a majoritarian memory that had up until that point totally subjected the nation). To borrow from Deleuze's clarification of Foucault on this point, the power-relations of the events at

Abu Ghraib entail a 'pure disciplinary function,' whereby the power in question is 'simultaneously local, unstable and diffuse.'[19] Put differently, the traumas inflicted on the inmates 'do not emanate from a central point or unique locus of sovereignty, but at each moment move' from point to point in 'a field of forces, marking inflections.'[20] And that field of forces is historical. As such, Foucault advises a 'political anatomy must not be seen as a sudden discovery,' rather it is a 'multiplicity of often minor processes, of different origin and scattered location, which overlap, repeat, or imitate one another, support one another, distinguish themselves from one another according to their domain of application, converge and gradually produce the blueprint of a general method.'[21] Once again, Oliver raises an important point when he argues: 'If silence was impossible, then the next best thing would be acts of commemoration that case the massacre as aberrance.'[22] It is this kind of blinkered commemoration that constitutes an act of power in the Foucauldian sense: remembrance as a way of knowing the past and the present, and of forging a clear and unadulterated national identity.

Foucault attends to the process of historical narration and interpretation, arguing it is productive of identity. In his attention to context he avoids the model of historical authenticity, historicizing the discipline of 'history' itself. Accordingly, history is produced through knowledge that in turn is a discursive material practice of power relations. What history expresses are relations of power, for example the enlightenment emphasis on reason produced a set of disciplinary techniques that regulated the body and produced a passive subject. In other words, if we analyze the events of Abu Ghraib solely in terms of human rights and moral responsibility we remain blind to the *affective* dimension of forces in their sociohistorical relation. Inevitably, we forget that the documentation contains the possibility of supporting another historical narrative, one that doesn't repress the counternarrative of racist history. This history constitutes the active affects defining the power of historical forces to affect other forces. The key here is whether the organization of affects establishes a microfascism, for what makes fascism dangerous according to Deleuze and Guattari is its 'molecular or micropolitical power, for it is a mass movement: a cancerous body rather than a totalitarian organism.'[23]

Now the images of torture at Abu Ghraib are not viewed in isolation to the documentation of the Ku Klux Klan lynching African Americans and the videotaped beating of Rodney King by the Los Angeles Police, the carnage of Vietnamese civilians at My Lai, the 'dead valleys' as a result of American military activities in South Korea, or even the hooded head (draped with the American flag by US soldiers as they invaded Iraq) of the twenty-foot high Saddam Hussein statue as it was dethroned on 9 April 2003 (an image that resonated with another image taken at Abu Ghraib of a inmate with underwear over his head). On their own the images of Abu Ghraib are empty signifiers – an affective realm, filled with potential to produce meaning but ultimately signifying nothing specific. How they come to be invested with meaning and are organized influences how they circulate and are exchanged throughout the social field, or what Foucault otherwise calls the invention of a political anatomy. This position echoes the one put forward by Žižek who claims ' "society does not exist", its ultimate unity can be symbolized only in the guise of an empty signifier hegemonized by some particular content – the struggle for this content is the political struggle.'[24]

Žižek's point is that struggling over the content of the signifier is in itself political. The connection between the universal notion of the social and the particular content invested in the empty signifier is the effect of this struggle and for Žižek the concept of hegemony expresses the foundation of ideological control. A good example of this comes from the Pew Center for Research whose findings were: ideology and partisanship define individual media choices and attitudes toward news consumption. More specifically, the report noted in their 'nationwide poll of 3,000 adults, conducted April 19–May 12, 2004' that audiences for right-wing media sources, such as 'Rush Limbaugh's radio show and Bill O'Reilly's TV program remain overwhelmingly conservative and Republican,' meanwhile audiences for other more democratic 'news sources – notably NPR, the News Hour and magazines like the New Yorker, the Atlantic and Harper's – tilt liberal and Democratic.'[25] These statistics demonstrate that there exists a fragmented viewing demographic, one that is split along ideological lines, yet they also support another thesis: we view what will reinforce our own beliefs and in this way libidinal energies find investment in a fascistic desire: desire partakes in its own repression. Similarly, one thing is for certain and that is the media coverage of 9/11 created a global audience, one that overcame ideological partisanship. At this point we are now tempted to ask: if it is not ideology that produces the social field then what does?

When we shift our focus away from the free will of the individual we necessarily invoke a different conception of power. In the Spinozist sense this would be the difference between *pouvoir* (the power that belongs to an individual) and *puissance* (force). Deleuze and Guattari pick up on this distinction in their discussion of desire. They argue that desire is constituted via an exchange of libidinal intensities, energies, and affects, and the system that organizes these. They go on to characterize desire as self-sufficient, open, free flowing, and productive.[26] Affects and energies cannot be directly engaged because they do not move according to a fixed and determinate outcome. Libidinal energies and affects activate unforeseeable investments and these investments are entirely dependent upon the unpredictable activities of the libido that take place outside of an a priori structure. The productive dimension of the libidinal is the circulation and exchange of affects and energies. This is why Deleuze and Guattari prefer to think of power in terms of *puissance* instead of *pouvoir*. For with desire we are more open to being connected to the world in which we live and hence our power (which they understand is social) also increases. The idea is quite the opposite to that of liberal theory, which posits the freedom of the individual who makes choices on the basis of exercising their free will. Deleuzian *puissance* claims we don't actually choose a particular end result, rather our energies are capitalized upon in a way that does not fix the productive dimension of desire into a hegemonic structure, such as Freud does with the figure of Oedipus.[27]

Learning from Reich, who urges us to consider the character structure of social and individual bodies in conjunction with the social effects of mystical feeling, Deleuze and Guattari encourage us to look to the infrastructure of desire – social forces, energies, and affects that find investment in either a paranoiac or open subjectivity. Adding to Foucault and learning from Reich, Deleuze says the subject is the effect of particular investments of desire whereby they may actually desire the regulation Foucault speaks of.[28] Deleuze comments, 'force defines itself by its very power to affect other forces (to which it is related) and to be affected by other forces.'[29] For instance, the extraordinary character of 9/11 overrode ideological interest, and here it was because the social field watched and remained glued to their television screens (regardless of ideology) wherein the exceptional nature of the events of 9/11 emerged. That is, the power of photography to circulate publicly that Sontag outlines is the effect of a deeper investment of libidinal energies defining a given social field. In other words, whereas Foucault insisted power produces reality, for Deleuze and Guattari it is desire that organizes and produces reality (libidinal energies) and power is a dimension of that organization.

As Paul Patton comments, the political problem for Foucault is ultimately how resistance is possible, whereas for Deleuze and Guattari it is more a matter of explaining the complicity between desire and repression.[30] This is not to suggest that power and desire are not complementary; rather they are, as Patton outlines, a 'convergent phenomenon.'[31] In other words, it is a mistake to reduce the power of the photograph to an act of communication – whether that be a representation of real events, the dissemination of information, or a symbolic message – when in fact the very power we speak of is the effect of the social field investing its own time and energy in viewing such images. Without this investment of libidinal energies the images themselves would remain mute. For instance, in the Pew Research Center Report 'Iraq Prison Scandal Hits Home, But Most Reject Troop Pullout' the findings noted a shift in America's perception of the war in Iraq after the release of the Abu Ghraib images of torture.[32] It was reported that for the 'first time, a majority of Americans' (51 percent to be exact) said that the war on terror was not going well. Similarly, support for the decision to go to war began also to decline as did the approval rating of President Bush, which fell from 58 percent in January to 44 percent in May 2004.[33] Here we are noting a revolutionary power at work, one that threatens to destabilize the Bush Presidency. However, these findings are also a wonderful example of the way in which desire is complicit with its own repression. The Pew Center went on to report that on the whole the negative perception of the US mistreatment of Iraqi detainees and of the war *did not translate into public support* for the immediate withdrawal from Iraq.[34] What is even more interesting is that when four American contractors were murdered and their bodies defiled, Americans became the victims instead of the perpetrators of violence once more and public sentiment shifted accordingly toward a demand to withdraw from Iraq.

If public perception of the war in Iraq worsened as a result of the images taken at Abu Ghraib why wasn't this enough to prompt the demand for immediate withdrawal? Dare we surmise that the political struggle was not so much the specifically immoral content of the pictures themselves and those responsible, but the desiring-production of memory itself as a break was introduced into the intensive flow of traumatic memory post-9/11 and then captured. Put differently, the images of Abu Ghraib, while abhorrent and unacceptable to the majority of Americans, captured the work of 9/11 memories and their essentially regulatory function that produced a sense of powerlessness and the fearful American subject that was an effect of this. The affective enhancing of the energies of traumatic memory were recorded (the second synthesis of desire) when they were connected to the image of a robust America, repositioning Americans away from a weakened condition to that of fortitude.

The argument being made here is that the images of sexual humiliation and the physical coercion of Iraqis at the hands of US soldiers at Abu Ghraib produced a new memory of US might and power, one that invested the affects of fear and insecurity in the aftermath of the 9/11 terrorist attacks with a new image of strength.[35] In this sense, the cultural form traumatic memory takes is the effect of desire – the power to affect and be affected, changing from one affective condition to another – and this is why when images of US vulnerability reentered into circulation once more (the murder of US contractors) national support for the war quickly began to decline: invincibility was being recoded into a different configuration, one that emerged once again in connection with the flow of affective memory energies; however, this time it was images of US frailty and vulnerability that were exercised once more. In this context, the adverse impact the images of the contractors had on the public began to be translated into social and political outrage against the war: in 2006 Bush's Republican Party was dealt a heavy blow as the Democrats won an overwhelming majority in the Senate and the House.

The torture that took place at Abu Ghraib didn't simply represent an act of US domination in Iraq, it also energized a pre-existing authoritarian interplay between dominating and dominant social forces, exposing the violent social circulation and exchange of traumatic memory. Following Reich then and recalling our discussion from Chapter 1, the orgiastic glee evidenced in the documentary photographs of US military abuses of Iraqi detainees at Abu Ghraib prison produce and are produced by material psychic conditions; these in turn articulate the authoritarian nature of memory as part of the system of socialization. The images of Abu Ghraib relentlessly countered the images of 9/11 fresh in American minds, testifying to an infrastructure of desire operating at the pre-dialogical and prepersonal level of social memory. And nobody supports this idea better than the popular conservative American Radio Talk Show host, Rush Limbaugh. He exclaimed:

> There are probably some good people in the bad guys and some rotten apples in the good guys, and these people that did this so-called

> torture may in fact be the rotten apples of the good guy group. But it's like I said: it doesn't taint the whole military effort and it doesn't taint us, but the world is joining in now trying to taint us as a nation, as a people, and as a culture by virtue of these pictures on the basis that we have humiliated these people. What is hijacking our own airplanes and flying them into the World Trade Center and the Pentagon? How humiliating is it to blow up American civilians in a convoy and have their charred bodies dragged from the car and dragged through the streets? There seems to be no sensitivity, concern or outrage for any of this anywhere in the world. So pardon me if my patience is a little short.[36]

For Deleuze and Guattari desire is productive and inherently social; it is not an individual person or coherently defined group who desires power. Qualitatively different forces dynamically transform reality producing different investments of desire; these in turn define the possibilities for action and for being acted upon. Under these circumstances memorial culture doesn't just visually mediate between past trauma and the present, it records social energies – the collective memories of the Twin Towers falling, the bodies jumping to their deaths in clouds of smoke, the ash covering the streets of New York, and alarmed faces filled with horror and disbelief – then reconnects these to another configuration – US strength and dominance at Abu Ghraib.[37] As the media grabbed the news of torture at Abu Ghraib with ferocious frenzy, the story was put to work like a compulsive ritual: with 76 percent of Americans reporting they saw the images.[38] Now a political anatomy of desire emerges: Abu Ghraib may have weakened the public's perception of the US administration but it also empowered the social field, alleviating memories of national vulnerability as those of national prowess gained currency. In this way a mnemonic infrastructure of forces, energies, and affects came into play and the subjectivity that emerged was an indestructible national identity epitomized by the majority of Americans continuing to favor keeping troops in Iraq regardless of the decline in approval ratings for the war.

Given that the concept of memorial culture attends to the desiring-production at the heart of all social formations positing subjects are the effects of desiring-production, the power of collective memory lies in how memory is put to work by the social field. In the broadest sense of the term the reactive form of memorial culture can be likened to the infrastructure of desire that Deleuze speaks of, whereby it is not just the dead who hold a particular influence over the living, but the ritualistic emergence of the past as a desiring production working to subjugate revolutionary energies, creating new memories out of old ones in order to conquer uncomfortable memories. The photo may document reality, but as a cultural artifact once it enters a system of exchange it too has the power to produce reality. The kind of reality that emerges all depends on the kind of investment the social field gives the energies and affects traumatic memory produces. In this way, what we are faced with is another kind of realism, one that doesn't just represent the world but creates reality. This is where the importance of Deleuze and Guattari's concept of desire as social lies, for what is real is desiring-production: 'desire as in the irrational of every form of rationality, and not because it is a lack, a thirst, or an aspiration, but because it is the production of desire: desire that produces – real-desire, or the real in itself.'[39] What matters is not so much what a memory means, rather how the labor of memory is put to work: whether or not memorial culture is open to forging new connections with the past, so that the social field can be transformed from a reactionary and fascistic body into a more open and revolutionary one. Infusing Foucault's definition of power with Deleuze's concept of desire means we attend not so much to how free will was exercised by certain military individuals; rather we start with the nonindividual forces operating in relation to other forces delving down deep to discover the libidinal affects and energies at play throughout the social field.

In the previous chapter we saw how the postmodern aesthetic repeats the same images over and over again putting these to work in the service of a reterritorializing Memory machine, all the while comparing this to what the mass media does with circulating images of traumatic events. However, in all this we need to remember the viewer is not passive; as the Pew Center for Research statistics show, the public chooses to continue watching the material and thereby supports the continued coverage of such events. We concluded that in effect mass communications are very effective when it comes to commanding we do not forget. This chapter has continued this investigation of the power of memory to not forget, by focusing on when forgetting is put in the service of a paranoiac investment of desire. The events of 9/11 punctured America's sense of security, and the relentless media coverage of this loss and the public's involvement in this cultural venture reasserted deep-seated national feelings of powerlessness and victimization. Undoubtedly the images of 9/11 are not unconnected to those of Abu Ghraib, or even those of the My Lai massacre in Vietnam, or the lynching of African Americans carried out by the Ku Klux Klan. This chapter has not only tried to establish an aesthetic and historical connection between the documentation of these incidents but also proposed they all share a similar paranoiac investment of social desire. On that note, it is interesting that the American media and the US administration didn't even bother trying to get the public to forget what happened at Abu Ghraib. Instead, the volume on Abu Ghraib was amplified to the point where the incident was remembered with great ferocity throughout the social field. Therefore the argument is that this amplification of memory was in fact a way of countering the memory of 9/11 not on ideological grounds but as a way in which a battered nation saw a way out of the malaise. Public opinion in favor of the war declined but this did not translate into a will to withdraw from Iraq, simply because the images of Abu Ghraib swelled national confidence at a time when it was needed most.

Notes

1. The Abu Ghraib prison of the former Iraqi leader, Saddam Hussein, located twenty miles to the west of Baghdad, was converted by US armed forces into a military prison at the beginning of the Iraq War. It held everyday criminals along with others who were believed to be a security risk to coalition forces, including high-value leaders of the Iraqi insurgency.
2. *The 'Taguba Report' On Treatment of Abu Ghraib Prisoners in Iraq*, Article 15–6 Investigation of the 800th Military Police Brigade, Part One: Detainee Abuse Findings, 15. The report was compiled by Major General Antonio M. Taguba and completed in February 2004. See: http://news.findlaw.com/nytimes/docs/iraq/tagubarpt.html#ThR1.9, accessed 2 January 2007.
3. *A Few Good Men* is a court martial drama adapted for screen from the Broadway play by playwright Aaron Sorkin. It stars Tom Cruise, Jack Nicholson, Demi Moore, Kiefer Sutherland, and Kevin Bacon. In it Lt Daniel Kaffee, a military lawyer, represents Marines accused of murder. The defense argues that the Marines were simply obeying the orders of Colonel Nathan Jessup who had ordered a 'Code Red' to discipline PFC Santiago. Carrying out the orders of their superior the accused Marines murdered the soldier by accident.
4. The dominant analysis of Abu Ghraib is one that tends to focus on issues of moral culpability. If we look to the history of the law this is certainly the primary focus of most authors. For example, writing on the trial for murder of Lieutenant Calley in the context of the My Lai Massacre in Vietnam, Michal Belknap frames his discussion with the problem of

individual and group responsibility. He writes: 'Among those lessons are how and why good people do bad things, and who is responsible for crimes committed on the battlefield.' Belknap, Michal R. *The Vietnam War on Trial: The My Lai Massacre and the Court-Martial of Lieutenant Calley* (Lawrence, KS: University Press of Kansas, 2002), 2.

5. Žižek, Slavoj. 'Against Human Rights,' *New Left Review*, Vol. 34, July/August 2005, 117.
6. Sontag, Susan. 'Regarding the Torture of Others,' *New York Times Magazine*, 23 May 2004. See: http://www.nytimes.com/2004/05/23/magazine/23PRISONS.html?ex=1400644800&en=a2cb6ea6bd297c8f&ei=5007&partner=USERLAND, accessed 11 November 2006.
7. Ibid.
8. Foucault, Michel. *Discipline and Punish: The Birth of the Prison*, trans. Alan Sheridan (London: Penguin, 1977), 138.
9. Ibid., 294.
10. Sontag, 'Regarding the Torture of Others.'
11. Belknap, *The Vietnam War on Trial*, 47. Belknap also notes: 'Every soldier who fought in Vietnam heard stories about children who had supposedly supplied GIs with Coke containing ground glass or blown them up with hand grenades.' Ibid.
12. It is important to note that My Lai is a hamlet and the massacre in question took place in the village of Son My; however, as Kendrick Oliver points out, this is how American history represents the region. The area known by the Vietnamese as Xom Lang was in a hamlet called Tu Cung, not My Lai. It is slippages and displacements such as these that Oliver focuses his detailed and engaging study on. See Oliver, Kendrick. *The My Lai Massacre in American History and Memory* (Manchester: Manchester University Press, 2006).
13. Oliver explains that the 11th Brigade was allowed to investigate itself and as such the original military report of the incident was a small amount of accidental civilian casualties caused by 'long-range artillery bombardment and the crossfires of battle. Rumours and allegations of the deliberate massacre were dismissed as enemy propaganda.' Oliver, *The My Lai Massacre in American History and Memory*, 1–2. Belknap reports that 'The Nixon administration seemed interested mainly in minimizing the adverse impact of the story on support for its increasingly unpopular war in Vietnam, while Congress actually interfered with efforts to punish those responsible for the crimes committed at My Lai.' See Belknap, *The Vietnam War on Trial*, 118.
14. See Oliver, *The My Lai Massacre in American History and Memory*, 53.
15. Cited in Belknap, *The Vietnam War on Trial*, 65.
16. Deleuze, Gilles. *Foucault*, trans. Seán Hand (Minneapolis, MN: University of Minnesota Press, 1988), 70.
17. Oliver, *The My Lai Massacre in American History and Memory*, 251.

18. Sontag, 'Regarding the Torture of Others.'
19. Deleuze, *Foucault*, 72–3.
20. Ibid.
21. Foucault, *Discipline and Punish*, 138.
22. Oliver, *The My Lai Massacre in American History and Memory*, 251.
23. Deleuze, Gilles and Félix Guattari. *A Thousand Plateaus: Capitalism and Schizophrenia*, trans. Brian Massumi (London: Athlone Press, 1988), 215.
24. Žižek, Slavoj. *The Ticklish Subject: The Absent Centre of Political Ontology* (London and New York: Verso, 1999), 176.
25. Pew Research Center for the People and the Press, 'Online News Audience Larger, More Diverse: News Audiences Increasingly Politicized,' 8 June 2004, 4.
26. Lyotard makes a similar point with his concept of libidinal economy. He writes, the libidinal economy is 'not at all closed in the sense of a volume, it is infinite, and contrary to the representative cube, intensities run in it without meeting a terminus, without ever crashing into a wall of an absence, into a limit which would be the mark of a lack, there is nothing the libido lacks in reality, nor does it lack regions to invest . . .' See Lyotard, Jean-François. *Libidinal Economy*, trans. Iaian Hamilton Grant (Bloomington, IN: Indiana University Press, 1993), 4.
27. Similarly, Lyotard in his discussion of libidinal economy understands the economic dimension of libidinal activities as productive. As he puts it: 'The libido never fails to invest regions, and it doesn't invest under the rubric of lack and appropriation. It invests without condition. Condition is rule and knowledge'. Ibid. That is, free circulating energies are exploited and stabilized by structures that inevitably lead to the ossification of the sinuous libidinal band. Lyotard says: a 'force is amassed on these lines of contact which, thanks to its abundant investment, spread into new surfaces of so-called inscription.' Ibid., 21.
28. The shared philosophical project Deleuze and Guattari have with Foucault has been noted by many commentators of Deleuze, including Paul Patton who explains that just as 'Deleuze and Guattari develop a machinic theory of desire, so Foucault proposes an analysis of panoptic power as a machine for the production of homogenous effects of power.' See Patton, Paul. *Deleuze and the Political* (London: Routledge, 2000), 73.
29. Deleuze, *Foucault*, 71.
30. Patton, *Deleuze and the Political*, 74.
31. Ibid.
32. Pew Research for the People and the Press, 'Iraq Prison Scandal Hits Home, But Most Reject Troop Pullout,' released 12 May 2004. See: http://people-press.org/reports/display.php3?ReportID=213, accessed on 8 January 2007.

33. Ibid.
34. Ibid.
35. This is reminiscent of the visual souvenirs of lynchings carried out in the US during the late 1800s and early 1900s. But as Sontag points out there is a fundamental difference between the two. The photos of African American lynchings were intended as trophies, while the Abu Ghraib photos were intended for circulation, not to be saved in family albums. Sontag, 'Regarding the Torture of Others.'
36. Meyer, Dick. 'Rush: MPs Just "Blowing Off Steam",' *CBS News*, 4 May 2004. See http://www.cbsnews.com/stories/2004/05/06/opinion/meyer/main616021.shtml, accessed 8 January 2007. It is interesting to note that the Pew Research Center reported that believability for Rush Limbaugh was only 8 percent (on a scale of 1 to 4 with 1 being the highest rating) with 42 percent reporting at level 4 that they did not believe him. Yet, *The Rush Limbaugh Show* ranks as one of America's top talk radio host shows with over 13.5 million tuning in weekly. See Pew Research Center for People and the Press, 'TV News Viewership Declines,' 13 May 1996. See: http://people-press.org/reports/display. php3?PageID=444, accessed 8 January 2007 and 'The Top Talk Radio Audiences,' *TALKERS* Magazine, See: http://www.talkers.com/talkhosts.htm, accessed 7 January 2007.
37. Ian Buchanan expands upon this point in the context of militarism. He writes: 'Wars are spectacles in the traditional sense of being events staged to convey a specific message, but also in the more radical or postmodern sense that spectacle is the final form of war, the form war takes when it takes peace as its object.' See Buchanan, Ian. 'Treatise on Militarism,' in Buchanan, Ian and Adrian Parr. *Deleuze and the Contemporary World* (Edinburgh: Edinburgh University Press, 2006), 33.
38. Pew Research Center for the People and the Press. 'Iraq Prison Scandal Hits Home, But Most Reject Troop Pullout,' 12 May 2004. See: http://people-press.org/reports/display.php3?ReportID=213, accessed 8 January 2007.
39. Deleuze, Gilles and Félix Guattari. *Anti-Oedipus: Capitalism and Schizophrenia*, trans. R. Hurley, M. Seem, and H. R. Lane (Minneapolis, MN: University of Minnesota Press, 1977), 379.

CHAPTER 6

The Amish Shootings

> The Eternal Return as experience, and as the deterritorialized circuit of all the cycles of desire.[1]

If trauma is defined as an incommensurable experience or reality, then we can never ever really hope to use the logic of signification to interpret its meaning. How is it possible then to respond to traumatic memories if the fundamental presupposition of signification that semiotics, psychoanalysis, and structuralism all share in common no longer holds sway? Whereas in Chapter 4 our analysis of postmodern aesthetics and logic produced what Deleuze and Guattari might call an illegitimate disjunctive synthesis, in this chapter we will try to extract the sense of trauma by engaging the same synthesis in its legitimate form. The shootings of ten Amish schoolgirls and the community's response to this horrific event provides us with an important shift in focus away from either being an unrepresentable trauma figured as lack (void as content), or an uncompromising repetition of memory that refuses to forget a traumatic experience. The Amish response to the brutal killing of their children doesn't mask over the insurmountable difference trauma poses but, as will be argued, their response extracted the sense of trauma that emerges between appearances and copies, memory and history, all the while encouraging us to pose our question of traumatic memory in slightly different terms. That is, the question of what a traumatic event means or how it can be represented becomes redundant, because we no longer presuppose that a concrete experience or lived reality has to be represented in order to be real. The difficult question is now one of how the sense of trauma can be grasped in the absence of resemblance, imitation, or identification.

The Old Order Amish are a sectarian Anabaptist Christian community living in the US and Canada.[2] They lead a simple life defined by nonviolence, humbleness, and isolation. In an effort to not be 'tempted' by modern lifestyles they do not use electricity, heavy machinery, or drive automobiles. For instance, windmills power their water supply and their primary means of transportation is a horse and buggy, meanwhile all work is done with hand tools. Not wanting to participate in violent activities the Amish neither join the military, nor do they wear a mustache because of its association with the military.[3] Although they learn English in school, their community language is a version of German called Pennsylvania Dutch. They do not have churches, rather services are held in homes. There is an emphasis on modesty that translates into a self-effacing style of dress; the men wear broad brimmed black hats with black suits, and the women wear dresses that cover their arms and knees. As Amish scholar John. A. Hostetler succinctly puts it in the opening pages of his study on the Amish: 'Although the Amish have lived with industrialized America for centuries, they have moderated its influence on their personal lives, their families, their communities, and their values.'[4] The Amish way of life sets in play a series of paradoxes. As a community it is fiercely independent, yet it shuns the individualism defining the modern world. When compared to the rest of contemporary society it appears eccentric and unconventional, yet it firmly adheres to Amish law – *Ordnung* – where the community acts as both judge and jury for those who commit offenses. On the one hand the Amish welcome outsiders, yet as a community it is extremely insular, excommunicating and socially avoiding members who stray from its traditions and laws.[5] In the parameters of this book and more specifically this chapter we are unable to critically address the sociology of the Amish and some of the strict practices specific to their religious way of life; all we will be doing is examining how the Amish provide us with an interesting alternative when it comes to responding to trauma and the role of forgetting within the context of that response.

On Monday, 2 October 2006 Charles Carl Roberts IV, a thirty-two-year-old truck driver and father of three, took his children to school as usual then drove to the nearby West Nickel Mines Amish School in Lancaster County, Pennsylvania. In a suicide note left at his residence he expressed a continued anger at God for the death of his daughter, Elise, who had died twenty minutes after being prematurely born nine years earlier. In the note, he also admitted to assaulting family members twenty years ago, saying he had more recently experienced recurring feelings of pedophilia. In what seems like a planned attack (Roberts used several items for the shooting that appeared crossed-off on a list of supplies he had compiled) he entered the school with an automatic handgun and shotgun along with six hundred rounds of ammunition. He ordered the fifteen boys and three women (including the teacher) and infants to leave the school. Ten schoolgirls remained in the building. He then barricaded himself in the one room school building, nailing the doors shut, tying the girls up and binding their feet. He then made them face the blackboard, at which point he shot them close range – execution style – and then shot himself. Five girls died.

The sign outside the school – 'Visitors Brighten People's Days' – turned into a heartbreaking and cruel reminder of how the openness of the Amish was abused on that day. The desire of Roberts to molest children had twisted itself into the molestation of not just young girls but a community that is commonly defined by its nonviolence. Given the insularity of the Amish way of life, the shock of having someone enter their community, hijack their school unprovoked, traumatize their children and other adults in the school, then cold heartedly murder half of their schoolgirl population and seriously injure the others meant that day in October was a day like none other. It was a day when the men stopped work in the fields, the women left their home duties, and all rushed to the side of the families in their community who were suddenly and unexpectedly hit with grief. This was a day when the tourism objectifying the perceived eccentricity of Amish life exploded as the mass media noisily consumed their silence and sorrow across television screens, the Internet, and newspapers worldwide, attracting another kind of tourist culture: memorial culture.

Exactly one week after the shooting the surrounding community tolled its church bells at 10:45 a.m., the same time the school had been taken siege. Choosing to ignore the 'no parking' and 'no standing signs' at the site of the shootings, the surrounding community left flowers and messages along with a makeshift memorial that read 'Gods little Angels . . . In our hearts forever.' Spontaneous memorials are a common public response to death. Examples are numerous but some of the more well known ones would have to include the flowers, notes, and teddy bears flooding the gates of Buckingham Palace in London upon the sudden death of Princess Diana; likewise there was an influx of soft toys, letters, and drawings to the New York Fire Department in the aftermath of 9/11. How did the Amish respond to a similarly unexpected and violent act against some of the youngest members of their community?

Funerals for Naomi Rose Ebersole, seven years old, Anna Mae Stoltzfus, twelve years old, Marian Fisher, thirteen years old, and the two Miller sisters, Mary Liz, eight, and Lena, seven, occurred on family land. The girls were laid to rest in simple pine caskets and buried in hand-dug graves. The community rallied around in support, some raking the leaves in the front of the homes of the grieving families while others cooked meals. Within a week the schoolhouse was demolished and the debris taken to a nearby landfill. Grass and clover was planted at the site without plans for a commemorative structure to be placed there. Following in accordance with Amish tradition they did not commemorate the dead, the lives of the girls were not eulogized at their funeral, nor will their graves be visited in the future.[6] The Amish did not build anything, they did not leave memorabilia at the site, they did not publicly express their grief, in fact they did the very opposite of this. They were obviously deeply upset and yet they maintained their composure without traces of anger. All in all, there was a quiet feeling of strength the Amish expressed through their grief. Instead of building a permanent structure to memorialize the five dead girls the focus was on forgetting through forgiveness. Interestingly, the community made a concerted effort to reach out to the Roberts family, going so far as to mourn his death and establish a fund in the local bank for the family. The date 2 October 2006 was obviously an anomaly in the life of the Lancaster Amish community and they articulated this difference through their own communal specificity producing an individuating difference that was implicitly transformative.

Death was not embraced as a finite moment, it became a practical undertaking to participate in divine power and an exercise aimed at producing change for both their own community and the surrounding Lancaster County community. The Roberts family spokesman Dwight Lefever told CBS News correspondent Byron Pitts how an 'Amish neighbor came that very night, around 9 o'clock in the evening, and offered forgiveness to the family.'[7] The trauma experienced became another modality of being, being not as a finite individual but a being that transforms the moral view of the world into an ethical encounter. The Roberts family did not stand accused in the eyes of the Amish and in many senses nor did the murderer, because to the surprise of the general public the Amish grieved at Roberts' funeral. The ethical character of their response emerged as grief did not give way to invariable moral commands, whether that be in the form of 'never to forget' or a moral lesson on how we 'ought to' or 'should' represent trauma. Reality was not simply reordered by the events of that day; it was expanded. Construing death in this way means death is not monumentalized, for it is only when death is taken to be finite that it lends itself to a system of signification. Surpassing the dualistic structure that separates the victim from the victimizer, the past from the future, death from the present and forgetting from memory, the Amish response produced a different experience of trauma, one that brought into being what Deleuze might describe as the univocity of Being.

The ontological proposition Deleuze puts forward is that difference is the condition of Being. Setting out to clarify what constitutes the individuality of an existent, he begins by explaining the univocity of Being in contradistinction to the idea that Being is oppositional and limited. An example of this would be when we posit inside against outside or black against white (A does not equal B). Rather, for Deleuze, all Being is implicitly difference in and of itself regardless of whether it is of one genera or another. As he succinctly outlines: 'Univocal Being is at one and the same time nomadic distribution and crowned anarchy.'[8] Continuing on from here he clearly states that 'being cannot be supposed a common genus without destroying the reason for which it was supposed thus; that is, the possibility of *being* for specific differences.'[9] Univocal Being is therefore not a genus, it is an individuating difference and what is univocal is that this is the primary condition shared equally among all existents: becoming. This is why Deleuze insists: 'Univocity of being thus also signifies equality of being.'[10] In order to show this he uses the following distinctions originally put forward by Duns Scotus in *Opus Oxoniense*: *formal* and *modal*. When taken together, formal and modal distinctions demonstrate that univocal being is a condition of variation.

First, a formal distinction Deleuze says:

> . . . is a real distinction, since it is grounded in being or in the object; but it is not necessarily a numerical distinction because it is established between essences or senses, between 'formal reasons' which may allow the persistence of the unity of the subject to which they are attributed. In this manner, not only is the univocity of being (in relation to God and to creatures) extended in the univocity of its 'attributes', but, given his infinity, God can possess his formally distinct univocal attributes without losing anything of his unity.[11]

What this means is that we avoid the trap of presupposing that what we discriminate between is necessarily a fixed identity; furthermore, the essence at the heart of each distinction cannot be incorporated into one Being. This formal distinction allows us to distinguish between essences, all the while continuing to maintain that such differences persist in a univocal Being. On the other hand, a modal distinction is

> . . . established between being or the attributes on the one hand, and the intensive variations of which these are capable on the other. These variations, like degrees of whiteness, are individuating modalities of which the finite and the infinite constitute precisely singular intensities.[12]

Deleuze posits that although beings have attributes that vary in intensity, the variation in question here is not a distinction between fixed self-enclosed individuals. Yet the problem of the a priori nature of inherent variation persists. To solve this, Deleuze turns to Baruch Spinoza.

Spinoza's definition of the single substance of Being depends upon an ontological distinction formed between attributes and modes. The single substance of God or nature, for instance, has the attribute of infinity that is independent of the modes expressing the changes taking place in an attribute. However, the limitation of Spinoza is that identity is given primacy over and above difference and variation. He concludes *Difference and Repetition* noting that all Spinoza had to do was '*realise univocity in the form of repetition in the eternal return*.'[13] Deleuze understands the univocity of Being by the infinite differences of intensity a mode expresses. He goes on to amend Spinoza, proposing that what makes Being univocal is that attributes and modes persist together. Attributes are virtually undergoing variation and a Being expresses this as an actual intensity.

Using Nietzsche's concept of the eternal return, Deleuze extends the two distinctions laid out by Duns Scotus and also turns the univocity of Spinozism into an object of affirmation.[14] 'The form of repetition in the eternal return is the brutal form of the immediate, that of the universal and the singular reunited, which dethrones every general law, dissolves the mediations and annihilates the particulars subjected to the law.'[15] What keeps Nietzsche's wheel of the eternal return in motion is the creation of difference and the production of repetition through the affirmation of difference. The univocity of being here is said in the single sense of difference in and of itself, and the same sense that repetition returns. In this way, the eternal return doesn't just affirm univocal being it realizes it. Using the example of the throw of a dice, Deleuze explains that each throw is formally distinct and still ontologically unique. The outcomes of the throw of dice 'implicate, displace and recover their combinations in one another throughout the unique and open space of the univocal.'[16] The differences issued forth through the repetition of eternal return reject outright the dualisms of copy/original and model/reproduction that representation depends upon. Through the affirmation of chance and the invocation of the positive power of simulacrum, the representative grounding of difference in the identical or the subsuming of it into a model of the Same (or One), and the oppositional framework whereby difference is understood as the antithesis of the Same is rejected. Instead what Deleuze finds in Nietzsche is the possibility to articulate the positive power of simulacrum (as opposed to the Platonic dialectic formed between the Ideal forms and corrupt copies) whereby everything 'animal or being assumes the status of simulacrum.'[17] Simulacrum engages the difference at the heart of being while also summoning forth the repetition conditioning difference.

According to Deleuze and Guattari, simulation does not reference a moral order that uses the value of truth to judge one reality as 'more real' than an image. This raises the question of whether the self-referentiality of postmodern play and irony is necessarily negative (model versus copy), or doomed to being a self-canceling feat. With his concept of difference Deleuze would emphatically respond to such a question declaring: 'No, simulacra affirm difference and create the conditions of change!' In Deleuze's formulation, difference has classically been understood negatively. Put differently, to state that black is black because it is not white is to understand the difference between the two purely in terms of how one term negates the other. Implicit within this schema of recognition and identity formation is that difference is subsumed by the Same. Difference of this kind is anything but difference in and of itself simply because it lends support to an organic representational model, connecting 'individuation to the form of the I and the matter of the self.'[18] The whole point of Deleuze's study of difference and repetition, in his 1968 book bearing the same title, is to develop a concept of difference that is intensive.[19] This is a system of differences all communicating with one another, one in which 'different relates to different through difference itself.'[20] Imagine a repetition of differences that don't set out to produce a copy of a supposed original, differences that emerge through the process of repetition itself: an internal system of creation and variation. The limitations of Davis's critique of postmodern irony and his latent humanism previously discussed in Chapter 2 are now disclosed. Whereas for Deleuze the simulacrum is the difference that emerges through repetition, Davis denounces the simulacrum arguing it provides us with the perfect denial of reality by being endlessly 'autoreferential in ludic service to the spasms of non-meaning whereby it hollows out the subjects who embrace it.'[21]

At this juncture the fundamental question of how we can attend to trauma in a way that supports a schizoid sociality, instead of a fascist one, reappears. If memorial culture can be understood from the vantage point of desiring-production, isn't it possible to think of the representations of trauma that a culture produces as another way in which a collectivity is created? That is to say, a cultural activity that enunciates and expresses new modes of collectivization as part of the process of remembrance. Perhaps if we combine the material conditions of the concrete world with the utopianism offered by modernism, instead of thinking within the confines of subjective and objective experiences (an argument that uses the phenomenological presupposition of a bounded body as its point of departure and one that Davis advocates), we might be able to construct a critical and positive notion of representation. Deleuze's *Repetition and Difference* is a vital text in this context for it helps goad the negativity out of Adorno's dialectic without sacrificing the dialectic per se, as well as nudge the phenomenological premise Davis presupposes in another direction entirely. This allows us to construct a new concept of orgiastic representation, as Deleuze calls it, one that doesn't refuse outright the utopian dimension of representation.

To begin our discussion we need to first outline an important distinction between two kinds of representation, one that is organic and the other orgiastic, and as will later become apparent the idea of orgiastic representation also feeds another concept of Deleuze's, univocal Being, and the concept of becoming that he was to develop in collaboration with the psychoanalyst Guattari. These important concepts contribute to the formal theoretical structure defining the three syntheses of desiring-production (connective, disjunctive and conjunctive) that govern our overall analysis of schizoid and fascistic modes of memorial culture.

There is a common and ironical misconception that Deleuze 'represents' a philosophical position that is at odds with the theory of 'representation.'[22] This is not entirely correct. In *Difference and Repetition* he clearly forms a distinction between what he describes as *organic* representation and *orgiastic* representation. He states: 'When representation discovers the infinite within itself, it no longer appears as *organic* representation but as *orgiastic* representation: it discovers within itself the limits of the organised; the tumult, restlessness and passion underneath apparent calm. It rediscovers monstrosity.'[23] For Deleuze the problem of representation is not aesthetic, it is ontological. He concludes *Difference and Repetition* saying: 'Representation essentially implies an analogy of being.'[24] That said though, 'the only realised Ontology – in other words, the univocity of being – is representation.'[25]

While there is a lot of truth to Jameson and Davis's critique of simulation in the context of pop art and the endless repetition of the Twin Towers crashing to the ground displayed throughout the Western media, as was discussed in Chapter 4, this is largely a result of an illegitimate disjunctive synthesis at the level of organic representation and not simulation per se. The point here is, as Deleuze shows in collaboration with Guattari, that the repetition ad nauseam of trauma regardless of whether it is the result of media coverage or the style of postmodern play and appropriation does not turn orgiastic; it never really rubs shoulders with the monstrous dynamic that overrides imitation and identification. In large part this is because, as Jameson posits, it participates in the logic of postmodernism, understood as the logic of late capitalism. The Amish are a frugal people who do not participate in the logic of late capitalism. They are a self-governing group whose way of life is aimed at producing a spatial and psychological separation from the dominant model of multinational capitalism and the effects this has on culture. For instance, the strange Amish custom of using batteries to supply electricity but not public utility companies, as Amish scholar Donald B. Kraybill notes, 'eliminates access to mass media and helps to preserve traditional values.'[26] Their cultural practices are the result of a careful negotiation with mainstream popular culture. Visiting the website *Amish.net* it becomes readily apparent that the romanticized and idyllic vision many have of the Amish has given rise to a whole industry of Amish products – quilts, furniture, dolls, and other crafts. Yet, Amish society creates an interesting balance with popular culture so as to keep its way of life intact and how it does this is by putting the axiom of capital to work in the service of a different principle – not multinational capitalism but sociality. What this means is that the Amish system of social production is expanded by capital, in so far as an individual is not taken to be a means to another end (the generation of an abstract system of capital). Interestingly, the Amish use the nostalgia for a bygone era that is free of the logic of postmodernism, that Jameson speaks of, to their own advantage, carving out a radically different space and time to that on offer in the rest of the Western world. Amish difference, then, becomes the source of a creative discourse as economics is freed from the socially debilitating effects of late capitalism.

How the Amish respond to trauma is not answerable to the logic of postmodernism and it is for this reason that they provide us with an interesting case study in the context of memorial culture. They do not memorialize, commemorate, or eulogize the dead. Put differently, concrete experiences are used as an opportunity to activate an ethical encounter, one that both affects them as a community and in this instance, given that the perpetrator of the 6 October shootings was not Amish, the surrounding community as well. Yet, like their way of life, which has given rise to a prosperous tourism industry in areas where the Amish live, the difference characterizing how they respond to unprovoked murder was in another respect quickly appropriated by mainstream culture. Yet to the frustration of the media the Amish didn't play to the drama of the spectacle. In this way, the media tried to produce a fascistic investment for the libidinal charge trauma gives off, but the Amish in their choice of another more schizoid course opened the way for a becoming block.[27]

If we recall our earlier discussion of univocal being, Deleuze's task is to articulate a difference internal to Being itself, whereby difference is taken to mean the ontological condition of Being. As such the concept of becoming is an extension of this idea. Becoming is not the end result of a change, such as when we posit in the past we had X but this then evolved, or changed, into Y in the present. In *A Thousand Plateaus* Deleuze and Guattari outline their concept of becoming. They announce that a 'becoming is not a correspondence between relations. But neither is it a resemblance, an imitation, or, at the limit, an identification.'[28] Becoming is a dynamic movement of difference that can best be described as a non-goal-orientated movement and this is why Deleuze and Guattari explain becoming 'produces nothing other than itself.'[29] In light of our discussion of the Amish, the concept of becoming helps us out of a fundamental quandary to do with expressing the sense of trauma without resorting to a representational model that instigates an identity as the basis for that trauma, whether that be imitating or identifying with another's lived reality. This is because, the concept of becoming does not mean we start out with the events of 6 October 2006 and then move forward in time to the burial of the five Amish schoolgirls, all the while considering the differences between these two events, measuring how much or how little this changed both the Amish and Lancaster County communities. Nothing could be further from the concept of becoming advanced by Deleuze and Guattari than an analysis that takes perceived changes between the past and present as its primary point of departure. If we use the concept of becoming we do not start out with a finite state and trace how this changes into another finite state, moving from the everyday subject to that of the traumatized subject.

A change was not initiated by 6 October 2006, it was a return of difference that moved through the following social forces: Amish, Lancaster County, Roberts family, and popular culture. The different events making up that day along with subsequent days, not to forget the days prior to 6 October 2006, are all the effects of productions already evident in life. As these events and forces are produced in tandem with one another they undergo change. The becoming-ethical is what moves through all these states of affairs. The sense of trauma grasped in the response of the Amish community lies in its productive, not reproductive, character. Here trauma is conceived of as holding its own immanent, intensive advantages for the perpetuation of difference from within the duration of trauma. The ethical encounter is not at the expense of difference, or even despite difference, but is absolutely the result of a dynamic drive toward difference. The encounter is absolutely the product of this process of individuation occurring at the level of univocal Being.

Many members of the non-Amish community were quick to memorialize the deaths of five girls by identifying with the loss that the Amish were feeling. And while one cannot judge this display of public support and sympathy as 'wrong,' it needs to be noted that in their identification they produced a moralizing position that brought into play the age old dualism between good and evil. The spontaneous memorial clearly stated the girls were 'God's little angels.' Here the response was to fix the trauma into specific symbolic positions, and as such the trauma was Oedipalized (much like Rothko did when he made redemption the content of his pictures). Meanwhile, the Amish grieved at the murderer's funeral, moving beyond moral difference to create a monstrous coupling between victim and perpetrator. There is a different kind of self-referentiality at work in the Amish response, one that produces an involution as opposed to a repetition of the same. The involution is the effect of a block of becoming. That is, as Deleuze and Guattari might say, Amish remembrance was a symbiosis that brought 'into play beings of totally different scales and kingdoms, with no possible filiation.'[30] Trauma was clearly not turned into a source of social prohibition; symbolic positions gave way to affective connections. As Deleuze writes of Bacon:

> Life screams *at* death, but death is no longer this all-too-visible thing that makes us faint; it is this invisible force that life detects, flushes out, and makes visible through the scream. Death is judged from the point of view of life, and not the reverse, as we like to believe.[31]

The issue at stake is that trauma was not turned into an authoritarian situation, one that consumes an individual by reinstating their sense of separation from the world and others. The singularity of trauma was put to work to produce difference, a difference that opened itself up to individuation: the power of bodies to be affected by others and together they undergo change. In this regard, trauma was not Oedipalized in so far as the events of 6 October 2006 were not allocated an authoritarian position from which Amish identity could be signified.[32]

What is especially remarkable is not so much the private nature of the Amish response and their refusal to participate in the media's appetite to cover the incident every step of the way from the moment when Roberts left his house that morning right up to the raising of the schoolhouse; rather, the Amish didn't monumentalize what happened and this is largely because a legitimate disjunctive synthesis came into effect. To borrow from Deleuze and Guattari, they involved the community in their own incorporeal transformation by forming a block of forgiveness that 'runs its own line "between" the terms in play and beneath assignable relations.'[33] In this light privacy is taken to a different level entirely; it is not a case of extreme individualism subjugating the self in a self-encasing 'I' defined in contradistinction to the rest of the world. Amish privacy as it was practised after the shootings (we have to limit our discussion to this particular event) entailed a becoming-other that was implicitly social.

The Amish did not build a structure to remember the dead by, but what they did do was embrace the future and life as a way of remembering. Past, present, and future combine forces to imply a temporal difference conditioning Being. The object of affirmation was not the identity of trauma but the condition of difference that was practised as forgiveness, one that simultaneously produced an ethical encounter. What might appear to be an act of brutal erasure was more an anarchical gesture of incorporeal transformation. The response, along with the changes it effected, has its own duration in which all the incorporeal transformations constituting the sense of trauma unfold.

In *The Logic of Sense* Deleuze explains there are two planes of being; one consists of physical qualities and passions and how these coordinate one another – states of affairs; the other is an effect of the former and can be said to inhere in states of affairs – incorporeal entities.[34] Drawing inspiration from the Stoics, Deleuze clarifies that incorporeal entities are not 'physical qualities and properties, but rather logical or dialectical attributes' by which means they are events, the products of actions and passions that are verbs not adjectives or substantives.[35] Unlike states of affairs that are part of the present, incorporeals are infinitives that participate in the time of *aion* – nonchronological time – that belies the present. Hence, when we claim that the response to the Amish shootings stirred forth an incorporeal transformation, what we mean is that regardless of how grief, as a state of affairs, is actualized in the present, its sense can never be fully consumed (incorporeal dimension). What happens between states of affairs and the representation of these is the sense of trauma, the event of sense being the incorporeal effect Deleuze speaks of in *The Logic of Sense*.

The absolute and uncompromising forgiveness of the Amish becomes representative of a pure instant that moves beyond what the present state of affairs actualizes and turns into a block of becoming expressive of the dynamic movement of temporal difference – the sociality of an Amish way of life accumulated over time and the future-orientated position of unconditional forgiveness. Here, forgiveness is an incorporeal effect that is not entirely exhausted by its particular state of affairs. In this regard, the spontaneous memorials carried with them a little death sentence, telling us what to think in response to the shootings, designating an order-word to the incorporeal effect by closing that effect off to fresh connections in the future (which would allow a legitimate disjunctive synthesis to take place). Although spontaneous and provisional the memorialization of the area gave the life of trauma an order, and while some might like to retort that the piety of the Amish response could also be interpreted in this way, we cannot forget their silence amid the chaos of the media and the loud displays of grief by the surrounding community. The life of trauma 'does not speak; it listens and waits.'[36]

The Amish did not communicate their grief to the rest of the world with language and order-words, rather through incorporeal transformation. Grief can mobilize a statement such as 'We will not forget,' or the expression 'There is forgiveness.' It is the latter that expresses an incorporeal attribute of bodies that consists of both the victim and the perpetrator. The order-word 'designates this instantaneous relation between statements and the incorporeal transformations or noncorporeal attributes they express.'[37] As Deleuze and Guattari rightly say there are 'many passions in a passion, all manner of voices in a voice, murmurings, speaking in tongues,' and what the Amish response to the shooting of five of their children evokes is a case of what Manuel de Landa has described elsewhere in the context of his discussion of open-ended becoming as 'nonessentialist realism,' or what Deleuze might otherwise call an orgiastic representation and one that produces an inclusive and nonrestrictive use of memory (a legitimate disjunctive synthesis).[38]

Notes

1. Deleuze, Gilles and Félix Guattari. *A Thousand Plateaus: Capitalism and Schizophrenia*, trans. Robert Hurley, Mark Seem, and Helen R. Lane (Minneapolis, MN: University of Minnesota Press, 1983), 331.
2. The heritage of the Old Order Amish is traced back to the sixteenth-century Swiss Anabaptists. For more on the history of the Amish see Kraybill, Donald B. *The Riddle of Amish Culture* (Baltimore, MD: Johns Hopkins University Press, 2001), 3–6.
3. Amish men remain clean-shaven until they marry at which point they grow a beard in the absence of a mustache.
4. Hostetler, John A. *Amish Society*, 4th edn (Baltimore, MD: Johns Hopkins University Press, 1993), 3.
5. Ibid., 83–5.
6. The Amish do not have a memorial day and graves are often anonymous, reiterating the Amish belief and practice that each and every person is equal to the other in death as in life.
7. Pitts, Byron. 'Amish Forgive, Prey and Mourn,' *CBS News*, 4 October 2006. See: http://www.cbsnews.com/stories/2006/10/04/national/main 2059816.shtml, accessed 7 November 2006.
8. Deleuze, Gilles. *Difference and Repetition*, trans. Paul Patton (New York: Columbia University Press), 37.
9. Ibid., 38.
10. Ibid., 37.
11. Ibid., 39.
12. Ibid.
13. Ibid., 304.
14. Deleuze writes: 'it is not the Whole, the Same or the prior identity in general which returns. Nor is it the small or the large, either as parts of the whole or as elements of the same. Only the extreme forms return – those which, large or small, are deployed within the limit and extend to the limit of their power, transforming themselves and changing one into another. Only the extreme transforming themselves and changing one

into another. Only the extreme, the excessive, returns; that which passes into something else and becomes identical. That is why the eternal return is said only of the theatrical world of the metamorphoses and masks of the Will to power of the pure intensities of that Will which are like mobile individuating factors . . .' Ibid., 41.

15. Ibid., 7.
16. Ibid., 304.
17. Ibid., 67.
18. Ibid., 276.
19. A similar example would be the Seagram Building designed by architect Mies van der Rohe (in collaboration with architect Philip Johnson). Here we are presented with a thirty-eight storey building 157 meters high, a leading example of the International Style. Commenting on its dark bronze tinted windows Manfredo Tafuri likens the building to a 'Pop Art sculpture'; elucidating further, he says it 'obliges the American metropolis to look at itself reflected . . . in the neutral mirror that breaks the city web.' Cited in Jameson, Fredric. 'Architecture and the Critique of Ideology,' in *Architecture Theory Since 1968*, ed. K. Michael Hays (Cambridge, MA: MIT Press, 1998), 448. Taking a more phenomenological approach the architecture critic Kenneth Frampton explains that Mies's glass skyscraper stresses 'the tactility of material, as revealed under light . . . treating glass as though it were a kind of transparent stone.' See Frampton, Kenneth. *Studies in Tectonic Culture: The Poetics of Construction in Nineteenth and Twentieth-Century Architecture* (Cambridge, MA: MIT Press, 2001), 161.
20. Deleuze, *Difference and Repetition*, 277.
21. Davis, Walter. *Deracination: Historicity, Hiroshima and the Tragic Imperative* (New York: SUNY, 2001), 131.
22. Eugene Holland describes representation as repressive; Dorothea Olkowski frames her entire discussion of Deleuze quite literally as the 'ruin of representation.' See Holland, Eugene. *Deleuze and Guattari's Anti-Oedipus: Introduction to Schizoanalysis* (London: Routledge, 1999), 22; and Olkowski, Dorothea. *Gilles Deleuze and the Ruin of Representation* (Berkeley, CA: University of California Pres, 1999).
23. Deleuze, *Difference and Repetition*, 42.
24. Ibid., 303.
25. Ibid.
26. Kraybill, *The Riddle of Amish Culture*, 3.
27. The Amish response to their loss undermined what could be described as the phallocentric organization of capital. See Parr, Adrian. 'Assaulting the Phallocentric Organization of Capital,' *Women: A Cultural Review*, special edition on Guattari and Gender, Vol. 16, Winter 2005, 321–39.
28. Deleuze and Guattari, *A Thousand Plateaus*, 237.
29. Ibid., 238.

30. Ibid.
31. Deleuze, Gilles. *Francis Bacon: The Logic of Sensation*, trans. Daniel W. Smith (Minneapolis, MN: University of Minnesota Press, 2002), 52–3.
32. Arguing that the Amish identity was not signified against the trauma of the shootings is not to suggest that the community may not have used this as an example of why they remain separate to the modern world, nor is it to overlook the very non-Deleuzian emphasis that the Amish place on the world yet to come. There isn't the space here to critically evaluate the religious customs of the Amish and I don't pretend to be an Amish scholar. All we are trying to do here is consider and learn from a different way of responding to trauma, one that avoids turning traumatic memory into spectacle, reducing the lived reality of that day to a transcendent signifier. For anyone interested in researching the specificities of Amish life in more detail I would highly recommend Hostetler, *Amish Society*, and Kraybill, *The Riddle of Amish Culture*.
33. Deleuze and Guattari, *A Thousand Plateaus*, 239.
34. Deleuze, Gilles. *The Logic of Sense*, trans. Mark Lester with Charles Stivale (New York: Columbia University Press, 1990), 4–5.
35. Ibid.
36. Deleuze and Guattari, *A Thousand Plateaus*, 76.
37. Ibid., 81.
38. Ibid., 77; see De Landa, Manuel. 'Deleuze, Diagrams, and the Open-Ended Becoming,' in Grosz, Elizabeth (ed.). *Becomings: Explorations in Time, Memory, and Futures* (New York: Cornell University Press, 1999), 33.

CHAPTER 7

Ground Zero

> On October 3, 2006 the Gallup Poll found an increase in 'the view that terrorism or national security should be the top government priority.'[1]

The contemporary western urban environment is a transcultural locality, understood as a self-organizing entity producing and reproducing itself through the participation of sensorial and material movements. These include the smells and tastes of different localities, such as trees, gardens, parks, and eateries; the rhythms of wind flow, flashing street signs, the pulse of traffic, the circulation of people and goods, the throb of music vibrating throughout streets and buildings; the visual clamor of color, shape, texture, scale, lighting, shade, fashion, building density, branding, and the composition of all these elements; the soul of a neighborhood, whether that be the various places of religious worship, forms of sociality, traditions and rituals, or simply the overall tone of collective behavior; and finally modes of economic production and consumption, such as the types of commercial activity defining a particular landscape. At times these characteristics collide and in other instances they proliferate through or even participate with each other. There are differences in cultural specificity, social wealth, degrees of racial and ethnic segregation, as well as population density and quality (the local population of residents and the homeless or the semi-local population of visitors and commuters).

What has just been described is neither the model of a 'multicultural' urban environment, whereby each cultural space is independent of the other, nor is it a homogenous entity. Rather it is best characterized by the proliferation of various localities that are not places bound by fixed relations, in the territorial sense. The urban condition just described is one of praxis. In other words, the process of urban activity is what creates distinct urban realities. Hence, the vitality of the urban condition operates according to a principle of provisional stability. However, as this chapter will demonstrate, traumatic events can seriously destabilize the movement of urban life. Using Deleuze and Guattari's concepts of smooth and striated space this chapter will consider how traumatic memory can impact upon the vitality of the urban landscape by asking: what happens to the transcultural movement of an urban context once we begin to reduce that context to a problem of risk management?

One year after 9/11 US cities began conducting widespread emergency terrorism and bioterrorism response training; they also expanded surveillance systems and improved how information is shared. For example, Detroit, Austin, and Los Angeles identified potential terrorist targets throughout the city, while the Office of Emergency Management in Las Vegas instigated plans to simulate chemical attacks. Peter Beering, the coordinator of the Indianapolis Terrorism Preparedness, noted: 'We are dealing with an inherently elusive threat, and one where terrorists don't typically call and say, "We're going to attack you on Monday at 9 o'clock." '[2] Posed in this way though, the problem of threat detection seems a bit like asking, what does God look like? And the answer to this question is obviously arbitrary. Yet the demand to clearly detect and defuse security threats throughout the urban environment increasingly became the overriding principle in American urban design in the wake of 9/11. For example, after the New York Police Department (NYPD) released a report in May 2005 specifying security concerns for the Freedom Tower design that was to replace the old Twin Towers, architects Daniel Libeskind and David Childs quickly responded, presenting their new design on 29 June 2005 to the public. Primarily the findings of the NYPD concluded that the proposed Freedom Tower was vulnerable to attack for two reasons. First, it could easily be targeted from the air because of its height (1,776 feet). Second, it was a prime ground target since the proposed building design situated the Freedom Tower at the northwest corner of the World Trade Center Site, only twenty-five feet back from the very busy West Street. It was on this basis that New York Governor Pataki called for a complete redesign of the tower.

Unsurprisingly, the heavy-handed symbolism of the Freedom Tower persisted in the revised design: although the building height has been reduced to 1,368 feet the Metropolitan Television Alliance mast that stands atop the building brought the height back to 1,776 feet. For security reasons the new design for the base of the building was turned into nothing other than a bunker: a two-hundred-foot-high structure consisting of titanium and stainless steel. The symbolism is obvious: 1,776 harks back to the year of American Independence; the height of 1,368 feet is the same as the original tower that fell; and the mast, otherwise called the 'Beacon of Freedom', responds to the torch held by the Statue of Liberty on Liberty Island. At this point it may be worthwhile remembering one significant point: when the Twin Towers and Pentagon were attacked on 9/11 it was specifically American symbols that were assaulted. Specifically, these were American values, American military might, and western capitalism. With this in mind it seems a futile gesture for the designers to focus on repeating the selfsame symbolic vocabulary that came under attack in the first instance. On another note, the symbolic meaning tediously postulated throughout every nook and cranny of the World Trade Center site (WTC) design runs the risk of fortifying the site and the buildings on it against alternative civic activities spilling forth, as epitomized by Libeskind's intention to retain parts of the hole of ground zero as a place where people could descend into the depths of the past to remember and meditate. Here the memorial design – Reflecting Absence – of Michael Arad and Peter Walker made one very significant change to the master plan: raise the pit and bring the memorial site up to pedestrian level. In this way, Arad's proposal encourages civic activity not just in the area designated for the memorial but across the site as whole.

The symbolic charge of the ground zero master plan could be likened to what Deleuze and Guattari describe as a reterritorializing memory: the traumatic past will define and shape the area both in the present and for generations to come, collecting traumatic memories and treating these as colonial memories. Yet what about transitional spaces that create spaces filled with the potential for affective, not fixed symbolic value? These consist of spaces that tempt hesitation, delay, and rest, enticing spontaneous and provisional activities to appear, activities that continue unfolding and revitalizing the rest of the urban fabric. It is difficult to understand the extent to which design impacts upon the concrete life of the social without first recognizing that life is inherently unpredictable and any measure that sets out to manage its uncontrollable dimension is inevitably fascistic in spirit, in so far as these aspire to stabilize, order, and manage how life transmutes urban spaces. However, the insecurity that manifests itself throughout urban life doesn't need to be understood as simply negating social vitality, it can also be embraced as a source of sociality. Accordingly, the connection between traumatic memory and landscape design necessarily engages the following problem: how can a sense of security be engaged without eradicating the sparkle and dynamism of urban environments? Essentially, how we answer this question all depends on what we mean by 'security.'

During November 2002 American President Bush Junior announced: 'The continuing threat of terrorism, the threat of mass murder on our own soil, will be met with a unified, effective response.'[3] The response was the new 'Homeland Security Bill' signed by Bush on 25 November 2002. It inaugurated a new US cabinet-level department estimated to cost $40 billion. The department will house all the agencies and infrastructure believed to be responsible for keeping Americans safe: immigration, border control, intelligence analysis, and terrorism response. On another level though, the hackneyed term – 'Homeland Security' – actually produced very dramatic changes in urban design and the revisions to Libeskind's master plan for the WTC site that will be discussed further on in this chapter is just one example of this. But what does the term 'Homeland Security' mean? First, it presupposes that there exists a land that can commonly be called 'home'; and second, this so called 'land' – with its definitive territorial boundaries – needs to be secured. Put differently, the land commonly referred to as 'home' needs defending. But we forget that the physicality of 'land' has always been defended; in the past forts were built, moats were dug, and walls were constructed around entire cities. However, it was not only land and the territorial borders geographically demarcating it that Homeland Security attempted to 'secure', but key sights – symbolic and economic – that also increasingly came under the scrutiny of American security agencies after 9/11, not to forget the nonvisible dimension of biological terrorism that supposedly threatened to leak and contaminate entire populations. In this way, the traumatic memory of 9/11 became the point of view through which the urban condition was framed, judged, analyzed, and consequently designed. Put differently, and to borrow from Deleuze and Guattari, space became increasingly striated.

In Chapter 14 of *A Thousand Plateaus* Deleuze and Guattari describe the difference and connection between striated and smooth space. Turning to music, mathematics, and more loosely ancient Greek philosophy they propose striated space is inherently hierarchical, by which they mean we count such spaces in order to occupy them. This is not to suggest that striated space is inferior to smooth space; actually, in the context of design, some striation of space is necessary to allow for informed concrete design decisions to be made. For instance, the Lower Manhattan Development Corporation (LMDC) estimates that the working population of the WTC site prior to 9/11 was 50,000, with approximately 150,000 people such as commuters and visitors using the area on a daily basis.[4] The quantification and measurement producing such figures and statistics are an important part of any design and development process.

In contrast, Deleuze and Guattari insist smooth space is nonmetric in that it gestures to an incalculable mode of occupation. How we think about the implied smooth space of the WTC site would tend to address how space is used and what kinds of rhythms and flows produce different nodal points, not just over the site but throughout the city as a whole. What activities do a particular combination of buildings, open and covered areas, underground and overhead pathways encourage or discourage? The answer to these questions turns our attentions to urban intensities: the warmth and movement of the sun, shady spots for those hot summer New York days, wind levels, how traffic passes through the site, and so on. Does traffic decelerate or accelerate, stand still, sit, lie back, or walk briskly across the site? Does the movement take a diagonal direction or wander around the periphery? Do the building materials stimulate us to linger, look, and daydream, or do they shut down sensorial stimulation and fend us off?

Citing the French composer Pierre Boulez, Deleuze and Guattari clearly state that 'smooth space is occupied by intensities' and the examples they provide include: the sea, 'wind and noise, forces, and sonorous and tactile qualities, as in the desert, steppe or ice.'[5] For instance, how are 'horizontal melodic lines and vertical harmonic planes' produced in music? The simple answer is that these are striated because of the way in which sound is organized around order and succession: the octave. Smooth space, however, continually alternates in the fusion of harmony and melody, so that the form of the smooth is continually developing as rhythmic values are produced instead of a succession of fixed forms.[6] Borrowing from the ancient Greeks and their conception of open spaces as *nomos* – the antithesis of the *polis* (city) – Deleuze and Guattari suggest striated space has a *logos* that organizes, in other words they say it is a space that is 'canopied by the sky as measure and by the measurable visual qualities deriving from it.'[7] Meanwhile, the smooth space of the *nomos* is where 'one "distributes" oneself in an open space, according to frequencies and in the course of one's crossing.'[8] It is important to point out here that '*nomos*' is generally translated to mean 'law' and '*logos*' is taken to mean 'reason' or 'word.' However, in the context of Deleuze and Guattari's usage of these terms, *logos* refers to the Law of the Father or God, not *nomos*, which in the way they use it refers to nomadic law.

Not all smooth spaces are constructed the same way though. There are two types of smooth space. Although all smooth space is directional, meaning it is non-dimensional, smooth space can be either directed or non-directed. Ascertaining whether a smooth space is directed or not depends entirely on how it is produced. If, for instance, the 'nature of the journey itself' produces a change in direction, such as the 'nomads of the archipelagos,' then this is said to be a 'directed' smooth space.[9] If, on the other hand, smooth space is produced through the 'variability of the goal or point to be attained,' it is described as having been constructed out of a non-directed change in direction, as, for instance, the 'nomads of the desert who head towards local, temporary vegetation.'[10] Striated space, too, has its own differences that depend on how the modules of such spaces break and transform. If the modules are fixed and constant then we are left with straight striated space and this is certainly indicative of the NYPD security design criteria as well as the symbolism of the ground zero master plan design. For a curved striated space the modules change. Furthermore, if variation is regular it is a focalized *curved* striated space and if it is irregular it is a nonfocalized *curved* striated space.[11]

To help us understand the broader distinction between the smooth and striated, Deleuze and Guattari offer us a useful visual: the striated is like a line that exists between two points and the smooth is the inverse of this, it is the point between two lines. Interestingly, smooth space is considered to be haptic not optic, meaning it can be both an object of vision and a haptic space as well. Why haptic and not tactile? Once again they avoid engaging a dualistic understanding of the senses – optic versus aural – preferring to suggest instead that the eye can have a nonoptical function. But how exactly do smooth spaces appear out of striated ones? It almost seems as though smooth and striated spaces are at opposite ends of the spectrum and the only way they could possibly communicate with one another is through domination. This is not necessarily the case. Deleuze and Guattari remark that striated spaces do not just impose an order onto amorphous smooth space, because the relationship between the two is not juridical; that is, how the two interact cannot be understood negatively (regulated versus unregulated or law versus lack). Perhaps a better way to think about the smooth and the striated is in terms of a positive disjunction, whereby the hierarchical conceptual framework that presupposes a dominating or dominant reference point is kneaded and rubbed to the point where it becomes elastic.

For a brief moment, it seemed as if there was hope for *nomos* to distribute throughout the WTC site when the LMDC announced the cultural programming and building plans for the area, providing offers for space to the International Dance Center, International Freedom Center, the Signature Center, and the Drawing Center. Yet the striating forces implicit within the principle of 'security' saw that decision suspended. In June 2005 *The Daily News* reported that the Drawing Center, then housed in SoHo, had exhibited works critical of the war in Iraq. Spurred on by the outrage of some families who lost loved ones on 9/11, Governor Pataki threatened to withdraw the initial offer to house the Drawing Center on the WTC site if it could not guarantee not to exhibit works that may offend the sensibilities of New Yorkers and the families of the victims of 9/11. Here the operation of reterritorializing Memory begins to gather momentum, expanding as the memory of 9/11 was increasingly used to codify the site as a nationally sanctified area. It is this reterriorializing Memory that prompts such projects as the 'border watch operation' by the Minutemen. Led by Jim Gilchrist and Jerome Corsi the Minutemen use the site – which they refer to as 'sacred ground' – to stage their anti-illegal immigration demonstrations.[12] Voicing his opinion to the loud cheers of unionized construction workers and plumbers that 'September 11 was the result of not enforcing immigration laws, of not securing our borders,' Corsi uses memory to legitimate a connection between illegal immigration and the war on terror, all in an effort to control and reinforce the US–Mexico border.[13]

While many have argued that after 9/11 the wild and safe zones of the city, understood in terms of the territorial boundaries of place, have been made redundant as a result of the uncontrollable risks 9/11 unleashed, on the whole the principle of global markets and globalization has always operated in defiance of national borders.[14] What this latter point brings to the fore is that the global system of transnational cooperation feeds off preexisting security measures. In this way, we need to remember that surveillance was not introduced post 9/11, it was only exacerbated. Striated space, that is, was implicit within the smooth space of global capital. In fact, the 'post' of post 9/11 is only part of the problem as it conceptually frames the event in isolation to the events leading up to and preceding the attacks on the Twin Towers and the Pentagon. In this regard, we are automatically forced into a juridical theoretical framework when it comes to critically evaluating and analyzing design strategies in terms of 'security.' We need to remember here that border control did not begin after 9/11, it was simply tightened. Security measures, that is, were not implemented because of 9/11; instead, they were amplified. It is a fallacy and a sign of intellectual carelessness to argue that space has been striated post 9/11. The events of 9/11 legitimized the defensive interpretation of space in order to more effectively manage the smooth spaces that distribute and disrupt striated space.

Leaning upon the arguments advanced by Ulrich Beck and John Urry, urban theorist Jon Coaffee proposes that world risk society is negative and he defines this in the following manner: uninsurable risk, the threat of attack, and technological advances that have turned into the terrorist's toolkit.[15] Admittedly, Coaffee is detailing the spatial imprint of terrorism and the urban impact of the terrorist attacks of 9/11 in terms of infringements upon civil liberties due to counter terrorist measures in the city of London; yet in his discussion of conventional and nonconventional security measures he presupposes the problem of security to be the ground of urban design in a post-9/11 world. His analysis, in turn, marks the striation of urban design theory. To adopt a juridical framework is to use the selfsame logic that has seen the institutionalization of violence: Good versus Evil, safe and wild urban areas, freedom versus terrorism, and Liberalism versus Fundamentalism. At this point it may be helpful to give our memories a bit of a jog. The will-to-govern the autonomous and unpredictable character of life forces was *not* introduced post 9/11, it was simply aggravated. Border control did not begin after 9/11, it was merely tightened. All in all, the homogenizing force of striated space was already at work when 9/11 occurred; the traumatic memory of 9/11 simply became the excuse to increase and legitimize the interpretation and construction of space solely in terms of security.

Coaffee's position, while thorough in its analysis of policy and the urban ramifications of security measures implemented to counteract terrorist activities throughout the city, fails to elaborate on the possibility that in effect the problem of security is not the premise of design initiatives, it is the effect of how we think the terms and conditions of contemporary urban design. What this means is that, for instance, both Coaffee and the WTC design focus on criminal (aberrant) social activities and the curbing and controlling of these, more than generating new social activities and innovative ways of experiencing how we live our lives. For Coaffee it is a fait accompli that security management is placed in the foreground at the expense of unregulated sociality; all the while he advocates the importance of urban life. Considering social life from the vantage point of security management inevitably presupposes the delimitation of lived space. But what if the smooth space of accidental and irregular activities, for example, is not conceived of in absolute terms – as the polar opposite to the life of the city – and is rather embraced?

The principles used to both design for the security and symbolic weight of ground zero were simply punitive. That is, urban life was held accountable through the manner in which urban design took place. Structurally speaking there is not much difference between the aggression a group of bandits waged against the symbols of western democracy and the free market, and the aggression behind consciously building icons of Freedom and Capital in retaliation against these acts, not to mention the infantilizing memorial culture of patriotism such retaliation promotes: when taken together this is the work of reterritorializing Memory. The suffering of America imploded in a way that turned urban life into an object that is at once managed and then concomitantly used in the production of values and law. The aggression the American administration and the American Red States (those states whose residents primarily vote Republican) felt towards the 'axis of evil' and the so-called 'elusive threat' turned inwards and in the process many Americans were left asking 'Who are you – out there?' And 'Who are we – in here?' Posing the question in this way the social reinforces infantilizing paternalistic structures while rolling back social equality. No wonder President Bush Junior was surrounded by so many strong nanny-like figures such as Laura Bush, Condoleezza Rice, and Harriet Miers! But not to stray too far from the point at hand here, how can urban design help redirect memorial culture away from focusing on problems of identity, or Being, toward the more ethical problematic of 'how can we become other than the traumatic conditions thus far defining us?'

In her essay 'The End of Imagination' Arundhati Roy outlines to an architect friend that not all dreams are a matter of wealth and fame, that there are other dreams, namely, that is, to 'live while you are alive and die only when you're dead.'[16] To which her friend, with a taste of interrogation in her mouth, inquires what on earth she means by this. In response Roy writes the following on a paper napkin:

> To love. To be loved. To never forget your own insignificance. To never get used to the unspeakable violence and the vulgar disparity of life around you. To seek joy in the saddest places. To pursue beauty to its lair. To never simplify what is complicated or complicate what is

> simple. To respect strength, never power. Above all, to watch. To try and understand. To never look away. And never, never, to forget.[17]

Her friend remains 'somewhat unconvinced' by this. Roy goes on to say that she 'understood that it was nothing personal. Just a design thing.'[18] In effect what Roy is speaking of here is a difference in kind between *what* one dreams for and *how* one dreams. That is, for Roy's friend, the dream operates as the Ideal predicate of life. However, if one asks what is it that dreams *do*, as Roy's response invites us to consider, dreaming is broached as affection – the ability to be affected and affect the world around you. Roy suggests dreaming is something we *do* and therefore it is a pragmatic activity. In this way she qualitatively evaluates the praxis of dreaming in terms of love, modesty, empathy, strength, and joy. In other words, she invites us to understand dreaming productively. Or, as Jameson was to posit in the context of his discussion of utopia, the deeper truth of dreaming comes from 'what it reveals of the reality principle as such rather than in what it tells us about our wish fulfillments.'[19]

The issue of how collectivities dream and imagine life is particularly significant when thinking about memorial culture because in large part the capacity for collective remembrance feeds off a particular kind of imagination, one that is fixated on transcendent orders, or what Jameson describes as repressing fantasy mechanisms.[20] In *Difference and Repetition* Deleuze reworks the Kantian argument that the experience of space and time is the result of a coherent subject who synthesizes their sense impressions. Instigating a transcendent order, the world according to Kant is synthesized and organized from a fixed point that exists beyond the world: the Kantian subject. Calling into question the privileged transcendent position that the Kantian subject enjoys, Deleuze advocates that '[s]elves are larval subjects; the world of passive syntheses constitutes the system of the self, under conditions yet to be determined, but it is the system of a dissolved self.'[21] Essentially, 'larval subjects' are the outcome of syntheses and not the other way around. He further adds that the 'self does not undergo modifications, it is itself a modification.'[22] Subsequently, Deleuze directly challenges the notion of a Kantian subject by developing Kant's project into 'transcendental empiricism.' Combining empiricism (experience is the ground for knowledge) with transcendentalism, Deleuze insists experience is in a state of becoming. Experience, that is, has no origin or ground, as was the case with the Kantian subject whereby the faculties of the subject not only organize but also provide the conditions of possibility for experience. The philosophical preoccupation with 'being' is therefore radically challenged as Deleuze tosses out the transcendent ground of experience: the subject. For Deleuze, the utopian force of transcendental empiricism appears as affect, extending the limits of the faculties. Or, put differently and using Jameson's understanding of utopia: 'The attempt at a radically different system releases the imagination and the utopian fantasy in a radically different way from our own, one that includes different kinds of narrative possibilities.'[23] And to add to Jameson here, without these possibilities we are quite simply Oedipalized.

To briefly recap our discussion from Chapter 1, in *Anti-Oedipus* Deleuze, with Guattari, identifies the transcendence of the psychoanalytic subject as an Oedipalized subject. So what is the connection between the Oedipal fantasy and a transcendent subject? Primarily, for Deleuze and Guattari, the problem of transcendence in the context of psychoanalysis surfaces when the child's love for their parents is turned into a threat. The Oedipal law forbids the child's love for the parent and in so doing the child is brought into line – normative behavior – that is, unless they modify their desires the child is threatened with the possibility of loosing their parent's love. Hence, the Oedipal triangle of mommy, daddy, and me, namely the judicial role characteristic of the father who says 'no' and the imaginary space of the all-loving and all-giving mother, along with the child who forges and shapes their own identity in response to this originary lack by channeling their desires into a more acceptable avenue: the image of identity prescribed by the parents. Deleuze and Guattari point out that identity is the result of repressed desire. Put differently, in order for the child to feel accepted and consequently loved by its parents the unacceptable image of identity is sublimated in favor of a more suitable one.

However, what if desire was never really about just wanting the love of one's parents? What if desire was simply a matter of experimentation, one where the child plays with part objects without necessarily any object in particular being the primary point of reference (legitimate form of the connective synthesis)? These are the kinds of questions Deleuze and Guattari propose in *Anti-Oedipus* and later go on to develop further in *A Thousand Plateaus*. Further, how this scenario of the transcendent subject, as it appears in both Kant and psychoanalysis, plays out in the new world of heightened security designed to combat the constant threat of terrorism – constantly moving between orange and red – is that such security measures could be understood as a reterritorializing Memory, one that infantilizes the social body in much the same way as the omnipresent Oedipus complex infantilizes the subject. Just as the Kantian subject dominates the world with its own particular point of view using reason to synthesize the unreliable materiality of sense impressions, reterritorializing Memory dominates sociality (desiring production) with an image of acceptable and normative identity, closing off new narrative possibilities (to borrow from Jameson). This leaves us with the following question: how does urban design put transcendent subjectivity to work?

New security measures and the manifestation of these throughout the urban landscape are the effect of how we articulate and imagine contemporary urban life. This position presupposes there exists a higher authority (transcendent subject), one who knows what is best for you and by implication 'you' – the social body – 'lack' the necessary knowledge to ensure your own safety, in turn justifying the transcendent status of the all-knowing subject who will keep you safe. In other words, the transcendent subject infantilizes the social body by proclaiming the privileged status of being – as the only one who can and knows how to say 'no' to terrorism. Therein lies the potential violence of memorial culture: when trauma is put to work to produce a paternalistic framework for how life is expressed it strips the optimism out of the future and replaces it with dread. As Judith Butler points out, once the collective ethos has been deserted and is no longer collectively shared it turns violent. That being so, under such conditions the collective ethos can only become 'collective' once more by means of violence. Butler explains:

> In this sense, the collective ethos instrumentalizes violence to maintain the appearance of its collectivity. Moreover, this ethos becomes violence only once it has become an anachronism. What is strange historically – and temporally – about this form of ethical violence is that although the collective ethos has become anachronistic, it has not become past; it insists itself into the present as an anachronism. The ethos refuses to become past, and violence is the way in which it imposes itself upon the present. Indeed, it not only imposes itself upon the present, but also seeks to eclipse the present – and this is precisely one of its violent effects.[24]

To add to Butler, the focus on risk management and heightened security aspires to a largely utopian urban lifestyle. The violent effect of this aspiration resides in the failure to consider the necessary failure of any design that equates security with freedom; this refusal to confront the reality of unfreedom that such utopian design measures present is the very fantasy mechanism Jameson speaks of. Really the only way an urban design can authentically be utopian is if it doesn't feign to provide us with any guarantees but works to bring into focus the harsh reality that we can never be completely secure; moreover, why would we want to be!

According to Deleuze and Guattari freedom is an ontological condition tied to experimentation, joy, and unpredictability. In some forms of memorial culture this is not only discouraged, it is also seriously hindered by the transcendent subjectivity of trauma striating social space. The visual vocabulary used to account for 'Freedom' in the master plan for the WTC site in effect establishes a common ground where in fact no such ground can be presupposed. If the question of design is to really recognize and address the so-called 'elusive threat' it spawns then urban design and theory will be forced to face its own epistemological limit, all the while still offering the material conditions for economic productivity, social exchange, and cultural encounters: this is tantamount to massaging forth the smooth spaces that subsist within the imploded spaces of striation. To intensify smooth space within the forces of striation does not mean invoking the age-old dichotomy between urban and suburban, safe and wild, rich and poor, inside and outside, vertical and horizontal; rather it means turning the hierarchical organization of space inside out. They write:

> . . . smooth spaces arising from the city are not only those of world-wide organization, but also of a counterattack combining the smooth and the holey and turning back against the town: sprawling, temporary, shifting shantytowns of nomads and cave dwellers, scrap metal and fabric, patchwork, to which the striations of money, work, or housing are no longer even relevant.[25]

Clearly, smooth spaces invoke the forces of counteraction and counterattack. In the context of urban design this would mean designing in a manner that transforms how we experience, build and conceive the relation between traumatic memory and the spaces we inhabit, along with the diversity such spaces promote. As Roy acknowledges, primarily this has to do with how we imagine life and never forget our own insignificance, this being exactly the problem of design she speaks of. Meanwhile, Deleuze and Guattari insist the counterforce of smooth space inheres throughout striated space and life inevitably comes to a standstill the moment we try to standardize variation and summarize complexity with simplicity. But pinpointing the problem remains a reactive project if we don't also propose different ways of responding, or conceive of new directions that might provide the conditions for change. Creative practices can by no means solve the problem of 'terrorism' and 'security' as these materially manifest themselves in life, but in their experimental focus they are well placed when it comes to rendering striated space supple once more. Understanding the outside as terrifying and the source of contamination, against which the inside defensively freezes itself in an effort to contain and ward off encroachment, is the effect of reterritorializing Memory; accordingly the effect of this is the striation of urban space. What this chapter has proposed is that urban design start turning things inside out a little more, to distribute 'friendliness,' and imagine places filled with life in all its messiness, color, taste, smelliness, complexity, and restlessness.

Notes

1. Gallup Poll. 'Iraq Still Americans' Top Priority, but Terrorism Concerns Rise,' 3 October 2006. See: http://www.galluppoll.com/content/?ci=24835&pg=1, accessed 27 November 2006.
2. Siff, David. 'One Year Later: Security Tighter, Cities Stretched,' *CNN.com*, 12 September 2002. See: http://archives.cnn.com/2002/US/09/06/prepared.cities.overview/index.html, accessed 11 January 2007.
3. Siff, David and Patrick Cooper. 'Bush Signs Homeland Security Bill,' *CNN.com*, 26 November 2002. See: http://archives.cnn.com/2002/ALLPOLITICS/11/25/homeland.security/, accessed 11 January 2007.
4. Lower Manhattan Development Corporation. *Viewing Wall: Urban Scale*, 2002. See: http://www.renewnyc.com/PhotoArchive/viewingwall.asp, accessed 4 January 2007.
5. Deleuze, Gilles and Félix Guattari. *A Thousand Plateaus: Capitalism and Schizophrenia*, trans. Brian Massumi (London: Athlone, 1987), 479–80.
6. Ibid., 478.
7. Ibid., 479.
8. Ibid., 481.
9. Ibid., 478–9.
10. Ibid., 479.
11. Ibid., 477–8.
12. Winston, Ali. 'Ground Zero for Immigration,' *The Nation*, 18 August 2006. See: http://www.thenation.com/doc/20060828/winston, accessed 27 December 2006.
13. Ibid.
14. Beck, Ulrich. 'The Terrorist Threat: World Risk Society Revisited,' *Theory, Culture and Society*, Vol. 19, No. 4, 2002, 39–55; Urry, John.

'The Global Complexities of September 11th,' *Theory, Culture and Society*, vol. 19, no. 4, 2002, 57–69.

15. Coafee, Jon. *Terrorism, Risk and the City: The Making of the Contemporary Urban Landscape* (London: Ashgate, 2003).
16. Roy, Arundhati. *The Algebra of Infinite Justice*, with a foreword by John Berger (London: Flamingo, 2002), 15.
17. Ibid.
18. Ibid.
19. Jameson, Fredric. *The Seeds of Time* (New York: Columbia University Press, 1994), 75.
20. Ibid., 74.
21. Deleuze, Gilles. *Difference and Repetition*, trans. Paul Patton (New York: Columbia University Press, 1994), 78.
22. Ibid., 79.
23. Jameson, *The Seeds of Time*, 76.
24. Butler, Judith. *Giving an Account of Oneself* (New York: Fordham University Press, 2005), 4–5.
25. Deleuze and Guattari, *A Thousand Plateaus*, 481.

CHAPTER 8

Berlin and the Holocaust

There is an old Israeli joke of a Jewish mother who immigrated to Israel from Germany during the war. She is taking the bus through Jerusalem with her son Itzhak. She speaks animatedly to him in Yiddish and yet he keeps answering her in Hebrew. The mother insists he speak in Yiddish – 'No, no, no. Answer me in Yiddish mein sun.' Finally, an impatient Israeli leans over to her and exclaims: 'Lady, why on earth do you keep insisting that the boy speak Yiddish and not Hebrew?' To which the mother retorts with indignation and surprise: 'Why, I don't want him to forget he's a Jew of course!'

What this joke pokes fun at is the way the past is revered as a primary signifier of identity. This chapter intends to examine the problem of how memorialization might create a connection to the past without reinstating the Oedipal shadow of an original trauma, one that forces out an illegitimate conjunctive synthesis by compelling us to identify with one particular subjectivity. In order to argue this it will be proposed the past is not so much a tangible terrain, a demarcated and identifiable space, or a monumental time that acts as a warning or reminder both in the present and for future generations, but an admixture of times that affirm the present and future and in so doing encourage a more nomadic subjectivity that identifies with a variety of subjectivities.

When expressing grief over a violent event, a community often memorializes the area where the incident happened, paying tribute to the victims of violence. Certainly molding the landscape in order to respond to a shared loss is one way of reempowering a community. At what point though does this turn into a melancholic exercise in mourning? How might a violent event individuate a community instead of defining it both now and in the future? As the heirs of a traumatic history left behind by its Nazi forefathers, Germany is a good example of this situation. It would seem imprecise to claim that any sense of shame the current generation may feel is eclipsed by the atrocities their parents and grandparents committed in the lead-up to and during World War Two. Similarly, it would be a gross distortion to accuse young Germans of being guilty for the crimes of previous generations. However, since the latter part of the twentieth century the German landscape has been radically altered as the horrors of the concentration camps entered national consciousness and Germans tried to confront the difficult legacy their parents and grandparents dumped on them. One of the great challenges Germany has encountered since World War Two has been how to face the violence of the not so distant past in a nuanced and mature way, avoiding the segregative use of what Deleuze and Guattari call the conjunctive synthesis of desire – 'yes, I am one of you' – to produce what they describe as a 'hallucinating history, of reanimating the races in delirium' so as to cry out 'No, I am not of your kind, I am the outsider and the deterritorialized, "I am of a race inferior for all eternity" '.[1]

At the beginning of the twenty-first century holocaust memorials and other sites of remembrance for Nazi atrocities proliferate throughout Germany. In fact, one could say that the topography of the German landscape has been shaped by the following didactic indictment: 'You will not forget!' However, defining the land too rigidly along the lines of remembrance can close it off to other possibilities, especially if the unforgiving cry tensioning the terrain tenuously positions it between the urge to optimistically confront the future and an unforgiving glare back to the past. Berlin, for instance, was once the headquarters for the Third Reich and it was here where a largely assimilated Jewish population was almost completely eradicated. Walking the streets of Berlin today one cannot help but shudder at the thought of what took place during the late 1930s and early 1940s and in large part, as this chapter will later examine, this is because the topography specific to Berlin expresses the force of memory, a force that largely cannot be measured. Astonishingly, while the holocaust may have produced a series of fissures throughout Berlin life, this has produced an intensive topography, one that affirms new urban possibilities through which memory can express itself beyond the containment of a nostalgic turn to the past or even the incarceration of guilt, the specifics of which will become clearer once we explore Deleuze's concept of intensity.

There is no doubt that the holocaust is repeated throughout Germany in the form of exhibitions, museums, educational programs, the reconstruction of synagogues, the meager leftovers of Jewish culture, and extensive landscape memorialization. Geographer Kenneth Foote, for instance, understands landscape memorialization to be a platform whereupon the past is interpreted and given meaning. He examines how traditions are reinforced and even changed through what he describes as the sanctification of particular sites. Tragedy sites he writes are 'sanctified to highlight points of origin and great accomplishment and to celebrate the lives of heroes and the sacrifices ordinary people have made for city, state, [and] nation' producing a common history.[2] He develops an interesting categorical distinction between sanctification and rectification. Sanctification marks the 'traumas of nationhood' imparting an ethical or moral message that exceeds the loss of life. Although there are several reasons why a site comes to be sanctified the most important one he gives is whether or not the 'tragedy touches a single, relatively homogenous, self-identified community, one that comes to view the tragedy as a common, public loss.'[3] Here it would seem that the holocaust in the context of Berlin would be an appropriate example of what Foote terms sanctification. On the other hand, rectification, Foote explains, is when a site is cleared of blame and returned to use.[4] Having sought out sites where terrible accidents happened, he discovers he is unable to find empirical evidence that these events in fact took place.[5] This, too, would seem to be an appropriate assessment of Berlin since there are many parts of the city where Jewish life has disappeared to the point where even smells of Yiddish food and the sounds of Klezmer music have completely vanished. Nevertheless, the difficulty of this categorical distinction surfaces in the spatiotemporal conclusion Foote draws, for he says the reason why the rectified site is cleared of blame is because there exists one significant condition subtending it: innocence. The space itself remains pure regardless of time having supposedly contaminated it and yet the logic of this argument suggests that the event in question is merely a moment in time without simultaneity in the present or future. For a space to remain unblemished regardless of the movement of history not only presupposes an ideational space that recalls Plato's Ideal Forms, but by reducing the landscape to a historiographical distinction between the past, present, and future, Foote strips the intensive and affective dimension out of time. What this means is that when a site is considered free from blame it remains intact despite the force of time. Put differently, no longer considered as the cause of a given disaster the site doesn't become a lightning rod for communal healing. According to Foote's analysis, this situation absolves the innocent site from giving rise to questions concerning honor and guilt. So while the category of rectification denies the notion of an original trauma grounded in the landscape, through a displacement of the ground into a transcendent structure the ground returns as an Ideal space immune to history. This conclusion, however, produces some rather uncomfortable questions in the context of holocaust remembrance in Germany.

In this light, could the proliferation of holocaust memorials and museums dedicated to the memory of the Jews in Germany be a way of relieving future generations from the hushed tones of guilt, allowing it to live the landscape anew? This could certainly be the case if we examine the Monument Against Fascism (1986–93) by Jochen Gerz and Esther Shalev-Gerz. In 1983 the Gerz couple won the competition organized by the municipal council with their design for a twelve-meter high, galvanized steel square column weighing approximately seven tons covered in lead. Situated in Harburg, a working-class neighborhood of Hamburg, the column was to be lowered slowly over time until it completely disappeared, leaving behind a black square imprint in the ground. One part of the column was to remain exposed and today it is accessed through a window on a staircase. The idea behind the project was that the monument not simply be a fixed vertical structure defined against the ground plane (a common typology for monuments as noted in Chapter 3). Rather this would be a democratic event as the community could write on the lead surface of the column with a steel stylus spurred on by the following message presented on a plaque at the site:

> We invite the citizens of Harburg, and visitors to the town, to add their names here next to ours. In doing so we commit ourselves to remain vigilant. As more and more names cover this 12-metre tall lead column, it will gradually be lowered into the ground. One day it will have disappeared completely, and the site of the Harburg Monument against Fascism will be empty. In the end it is only we ourselves who can stand up against injustice.

Once full with messages the column was dropped into the ground until another clean writing area became available. It was lowered eight times in total, the final lowering occurring on 10 November 1993.

Interestingly, the result of the democratic dialogue was not just a series of messages against fascism. The stability of a steel form rearing up out of the landscape like an exclamation mark was destabilized by the social milieu filling its surface with an admixture of opinions: messages of peace, graffiti, and neo-Nazi notes and symbols. Why this skirts Foote's typology of landscape sanctification and rectification is that it shares a little of each, refusing to fully encompass one or the other. The Monument Against Fascism is so much more than just a moral message or the erasure of memory that leaves an uncontaminated area in its wake. Several different events define the stable structure with each act of communication taking place on the lead exterior, so that the intensity in question here appears between the stable structure and the metastable state of sociality. Here the event of social expression and the character of the memorial are simultaneously determined. In addition, the monument dictates the conditions of the social event as the act of sociality creates the final form of the monument – a blank square on the surface of the ground that penetrates the depths of the national landscape with all the ideological ambiguities of post-World War Two Germany. Although not in the context of Hamburg, this is an issue the heated exclamation of Herr Simmann (the Berlin building director appointed in 1992) reiterates: 'I'm sick and tired of all this Jewish history. We've got too much Jewish history in Berlin as it is. We don't need any more.'[6]

So, does the memorial typology developed by Foote become wobbly when thinking about the connection between Germany and holocaust remembrance? The moral lesson of sanctification is one of healing gained by putting the past to work as an original ground of national trauma. Although his case studies are American, when we transport his thesis into the context of German holocaust memorialization, Foote's typology and conclusions cripple us. We are unable to address the complicity between the sanctification of national land and the ideology of National Socialism where the past is used as a signifier of national unity. This issue is tackled head on by the Monument Against Fascism as it critically invokes monumental typology; using a vertical structure that engages the ground it subverts this typology by turning it into a self-referential gesture shifting from a positive (above ground) to a negative space (underground) concomitantly making that structure function differently. Further, the sanctification of the German landscape quite simply goes against the grain of responsibly confronting the full weight and shame many Germans felt their national history poses (that is, if we attend to the difficult arguments posed by the 1986 *Historikerstreit*). Yet, so too, does the idea of rectification. This is because the Nazis were intent on annihilating what they perceived to be sources of social and moral contamination (primarily the Jew). For Germany to rectify the landscape could also be perceived as cleaning up traces of the holocaust, a gesture that appeals to those selfsame principles of annihilation that led to the holocaust, another problem the Gerz's use of the vertical and horizontal plane employs. In effect, the Monument Against Fascism denationalizes the connection between memorialization and the landscape as it pries our eyes open to the topographical depths social ambiguity can take, regardless of how squeaky-clean the ground may seem. Although Foote points to unresolved meanings and the inability to come to terms with the more difficult and unheroic aspects of national history, arguing these are instances when memorialization sustains some memories at the expense of others, for him memorialization still removes the chaos out of trauma, making trauma serve a nationalistic and moral purpose, as well as regulating the function of memory in national consciousness.[7] Foote writes on the connection between remembrance and forgetting, noting it is just as important to look to what a society memorializes and the visual symbols and signs it uses to do this as it is to note what is left out of the picture. Yet he conceives the connection between landscape and memory as a problem of structure and what the site signifies, rather than function. The distinction between structure and function is one that Libeskind unabashedly confronted when he refused to follow the ninety-five-page-long competition brief to urbanize the former Sachsenhausen SS barracks on the outskirts of Berlin (1992).[8]

Choosing to completely ignore the program brief to develop housing, Libeskind's competition design – Mo~~u~~rning – demands the death camp not be hidden or severed from the 'site that formed its historical context and infrastructure' nor that the program for the site domesticate and trivialize its history.[9] His competition entry reserved an area alongside the concentration camp for cultural and economic production where retraining facilities for the unemployed and private sector could be established, along with a library and research facility, not to mention spaces for artists, musicians and, writers. Noting the monumental axis of the concentration camp administrative headquarters that lies at the apex of a triangular ground plan connecting the headquarters to the crematorium and the villa of the commandant, his design shifted this structure in order to generate a different relationship and orientation for the site. After flattening the buildings and exposing their foundations, he proposed the entire site be flooded so as to create a 'sunken archaeological zone.'[10] Then using the soil excavated to form the lake, his design created an 'ascending landform' adjacent to the lake, burying the 'remaining fragments of the past' so as to extend the 'circulation network from the water by tunneling through and out of the land to the context beyond.'[11] Furthermore, there was scope made for a rigorous replanting program that would create a wooded sanctuary and an area reserved for horticultural use.

In Mourning Libeskind uses the breaks and cracks of history as his point of departure refusing to create a domestic environment in the context of a concentration camp. He takes the totality of concentration camp topography and makes it function differently; shifting the emphasis away from structure and onto function he transfigures the triangular organization to produce a site of alterity. Employing a model of economic and cultural growth, the site articulates the simultaneity of present, past, and future in a way that exceeds historical visibility and interpretation as a succession of individuated moments in time. Libeskind argues for 'a history that should not be seen simply as an outline of a building' explaining that architecture 'should embody the invisible, the hopes and dreams in something we live in, we die in, and we remember.'[12] Returning to Foote once more we see a distinction emerging here; where Foote might see memorialization as the ground for what a community remembers and forgets, Libeskind's design for Sachsenhausen clearly takes memorialization as the result of this process of selection.

Ultimately, Foote asserts the primary significance of the ground for commemorative structures and in this way he substantiates a long-standing typology common to monument and memorial design. We now arrive at the first premise of an intensive topography: topographical coordinates are not determined by the ground plane; topographical coordinates are intensive. So, what might a memorial that denies the territorial focus on the ground look like? Architect Peter Eisenman notes that the 'ground has traditionally been a datum for architecture.' This is because architecture tends to be 'conceptualized through Cartesian coordinates, and the ground has been seen as an important reference for both upright man and architecture's object.'[13] The difficulty of reinforcing the ground in the context of memorial design is that it involves a patriarchal relationship to the landscape and by implication the past as well. When memorializing a site with the intention of honoring, mourning or simply reflecting on the past, how might the idea of a ground plane onto which a commemorative structure is placed be overcome? One possible solution is to refuse to work according to a top-down approach, to displace the emphasis given to space and the ground plane onto the event and other temporal relationships. In his Foreword to *A Landscape of Events*, by Virilio, architect Bernard Tschumi writes: 'For us, as architects, time is spatial because space is what we construct, and time is there to activate these spaces, occasionally to transform them by challenging the perception of their boundaries. Time is what allows us to measure space.'[14] Tschumi brings to our attention the manner in which architects tend to design first and foremost not in terms of events, rather they focus more on the spatial conditions of a design. What Tschumi finds especially exciting about the work of Virilio is his focus on the event-as-accident, simply because this encourages architects to begin thinking about 'designing conditions for events' instead of 'conditioning designs' whereby the event 'arises from the unlikely collision of generally uncoordinated vectors.'[15] Advocating an aesthetics of disappearance, Virilio conceives of accidents scenographically, explaining that this is 'a way of *showing what happens in what crops up out of the blue*,' the aim of which is to expose '*only what explodes and decomposes*.'[16]

In the context of his discussion of the anti-museum, Virilio proposes the exhibition consist of accidents and not objects. In the anti-museum visitors do not encounter objects on display but threshold situations that arise from experimenting and testing the limits of an object. Since time, not space, is the primary mode of perception for Virilio, Tschumi feels architects could benefit enormously from this shift in focus: away from being spatially situated in a place to being in the event of 'now.' Yet in describing an event as a happening or a state of affairs Virilio ultimately continues to think of a landscape constituted in terms of a series of lived presents. The moment he puts his concept of the event to work in the analysis of society and warfare he neglects what this state of affairs actualizes. The event for Virilio is the movement of forces in all their spontaneity and the world is a place in which events take place. Moreover, the landscape of events he conceives of is the virtual landscape of new telecommunication technologies; it is a vehicle for '*exposing what usually exposes us*.'[17] His image of the museum-goer testing and experimenting with an object so as to discover its limits presupposes a fixed object whereby events determine the object and this shares the premise of Foote's argument, that events shape the landscape.[18] For both Foote and Virilio what is specific about the landscape is the way in which it is characterized by an event that takes place *in* it. Neither takes the landscape as a transformative milieu. The upshot this conclusion has in the context of memorialization is that past traumas individuate the landscape. However, what if events unravel the identity of a site, giving rise to landscape-becomings instead? Rather than identifying a barren landscape, whereby the barrenness of the land is reduced to a description of a self-identical object – the land – we might try to think in terms of a barrening landscape, in so far as the present continuous verb 'barrening' explicates implicit forces of barrenness; when summoned these bring with them a whole new interplay of forces that in turn generate new and previously unforeseen milieus. It is not by turning barren that the continuity and essence of the landscape, previously defined as 'not barren,' is impacted upon. The landscape is just as much an event produced through a complex interpenetration of forces as is the process of barrening. Therefore the contention in this chapter is that both Virilio and Foote are not radical enough in their understanding of the event because in taking a top-down approach they not only forge a moralistic vision for the relationship between space and time but they also presume events organize a ready-made landscape. Here Deleuze's concept of the event, and more significantly his concept of intensities, is especially useful.

An event in the way Deleuze intends is the virtual dimension existent within a meeting of forces. An event does not change or happen to a fixed entity. When forces synthesize, events actualize, and although events may be realized in the present their time is not *of* the present. In brief, an event is an eternal truth. He writes events are 'ideational singularities which communicate in one and the same Event.'[19] It is in the 'unlimited Aion, the Infinitive in which they subsist and insist.'[20] Events attend to the immanent actualizations taking place through a given state of affairs. It is events that subsist throughout and produce the state of affairs in question. There is one particular characteristic of an event that can be said to take priority over others; however, it is imprecise to claim that the principle of succession in events is one of causal determinacy because an event does not have a dominant epicenter of power that causes one specific effect over and above other effects. The singularity of the event is one of affect – the imbrication of events and the forces constituting these – and zones of intensity – giving weight to the logic of succession that implies a theory of creative inheritance whereby difference in itself is affirmed. Zones of intensity, as will shortly be discussed in more detail, are ontologically distinct to their actualized states (qualitative, extensive, and extended magnitudes), yet they are still implicated in them. Carrying on from here Deleuze explains 'events bear exclusively upon problems and define their conditions,' which is not to be confused with claiming an event is problematical.[21] In this way, a landscape cannot represent the past because what makes the past 'past' is not that it precedes the present as an event in time; the past is a virtual realm consisting of the co-mingling of events, the entirety of which cannot be represented in present form. The present is a summary and contraction of an empirical moment in the present with a version of the virtual past. This virtual affirmation of the empty force of time as it exposes a landscape undergoing differentiation is what constitutes intensive topography.

In place of Virilio's landscape of events and the traumatic event that persists in the present as a shadowed ground that Foote purports, Deleuze prefers to think in terms of an ontology of the event, one that considers the virtual dimension of the event and its actualization. This was a project he began during the latter part of the 1950s with his study of the French philosopher Henri Bergson that he then took up and developed further in *Difference and Repetition*. In it Deleuze writes: 'The expression "difference of intensity" is a tautology.'[22] He goes on to explain that 'difference in itself is in fact intensity. This is because every intensity is differential, by itself a difference.'[23] Adding to this he points out everything that appears in the world is comprised of this differential. Taking this idea of 'intensity as difference' how does it help us consider the manner in which events correlate with a milieu of trauma? If memory can distribute, unstitch, and transform by its very movement – this being the deterritorializing capacity of memory – or inversely, memory reterritorializes once it is plugged into a filiative and linear system of relations, conjugating the open transversal process of deterritorialization through libidinal investment, then how does memory invoke either its deterritorializing or reterritorializing tendencies? We are unable to objectively calculate the difference between the two simply because they are not neatly opposed to one another. What we are speaking of here are tendencies that inform each other, or more broadly how a milieu is produced and the functions it carries out. For example, as already noted, the Monument Against Fascism produced an intensity in that it provided a context for an event to take place but the specificity of the event was what dictated the character of the memorial.

Ultimately, Deleuze's concepts of intensity and the event cancel out the standard topographical calculation that presupposes extensive qualities sufficiently define their intensive condition in the way that Foote purports, while also stripping the nostalgia out of Virilio's mourning for a pure landscape freed from the contaminating movement of real-time events. Classically, topography denotes a physical quality or extensive quantity. In the context of architectural practices topography entails a detailed physical description and calculation of a given site. It is commonly investigated as part of the research leading up to the design and building phases of architectural projects. Topography provides a grid of the physical contours of a site, following the peaks and abysses as they define the key features and patterns of a surface. The standard architectural use of topography is: either a building mimics the topographical form of its context, or it conquers it, or it independently floats above it. An example of the first would be the organic architecture of Frank Lloyd Wright's Fallingwater (1935) that neatly integrates with its waterfall context as the cantilevered layers of the house copy the pattern of the waterfall's rocky shelves. An example of the second is Le Corbusier's Ville Contemporaine (1922), an urban plan for Paris designed for three million inhabitants whose starting point was razing the city to ground zero and erecting in its place a rationalized collection of commercial buildings, streets, parks, housing, and transportation, the centerpiece being a collection of sixty-storey buildings where the wealthy would live and work. An example of the third would be Mies van der Rohe's modernist Farnsworth House (1951) situated in a rural setting alongside the Fox River. Elevated 5'3" above the ground the house does not interrupt its topographical context. Underscoring all these responses we have one fundamental dichotomy at work: natural versus artificial, whereby 'artificial' refers to man-made constructions (buildings, towns, cities, suburbs, parks). Here spatial organization, as Tschumi notes, is used to synthesize perception and in this manner it can be said to be extensive, leaving us with an objective view of a geographical area, producing a unified space that can be measured and whose qualities can be listed. Topography can be said to synthesize a *spatium* (the groundless space as pure intuition) when it inhibits the expression of pure percept and affect, rendering the landscape passive by imposing equality onto what is ultimately divisible. While we have difference – peaks and abysses – these are mapped across the terrain in a manner that assumes the differences in question are only differences by degree (proportion, location, and measurement). As Deleuze describes it we perceive space by passively synthesizing the *spatium*. What we therefore perceive is *extensio*, a homogenous and measurable space, not the *spatium*. In this regard, a topographical mapping in architecture not only produces a hierarchical spatial organization (what Deleuze and Guattari define as 'striated space' in *A Thousand Plateaus*) but also an a priori model that governs how a landscape is put to work.[24] The linear principle underpinning the organization of space produces a particular kind of perception of the landscape as an area to be conquered and, according to Deleuze and Guattari, one counts in order to occupy such space-times as opposed to occupying that space-time without counting.[25]

Attempting to combine the Deleuzian concept of 'intensity' with topography might at first glance seem like a gross distortion, given that 'intensity' in the way Deleuze intends it is anything but a form of extended magnitude. A Deleuzian intensity substitutes sensation for form. Rather than attending to the extensive it invites us to consider affective magnitudes. It is all a matter of how to allow an intensive trait to start working for itself, 'a hallucinatory perception, synesthesia, perverse mutation, or play of images' that together shake loose and challenge the 'hegemony of the signifier.'[26] Although intensities are virtual this is not the same as saying they are not real; for Deleuze we 'sense' intensities. That being so, intensities constitute states of affairs but they are not ontologically distinct from the actualities they generate. They are affective magnitudes in that they are entirely prepersonal. Intensities are not to be mistaken for a quality such as tall, soft, or dark in the sense that they are transtemporal: becoming-tall, becoming-soft, or becoming-dark. Memory is a field of intensity as is imagination. Separating himself from Bergson on this point, Deleuze notes that intensity is neither extensity nor quality, because even qualities subscribe to the law of representation. He announces Bergson may have 'wanted to free quality from the superficial movement which ties it to contrariety or contradiction,' explaining that this is why 'he opposed duration to becoming'; however, the problem is that Bergson achieves this opposition by 'attributing to quality a depth which is precisely that of intensive quantity.'[27] Deleuze outlines that intensity 'creates the extensities and the qualities in which it is explicated; these extensities and qualities are differenciated.'[28] What defines Deleuze's concept of intensity is therefore an internal difference, in so far as difference is neither a quality nor extensity simply because it *is* intensity. Unlike an extended magnitude, if we divide an intensity it changes in nature. The flow of the virtual being the differentiated and the actualization of this is what Deleuze describes as differenciation, bearing in mind what is differenciated is not a representation of the virtual realm, rather differenciation is implicitly creative in that it produces something new as it actualizes.[29] The intensity and its actualization are nonidentical. Put differently, if *extensio* is the critical condition of a metastable state – *spatium* – then *extensio* is best understood as the space we perceive. Hence, according to Deleuze, *extensio* is the spatial perception of a stable state. Yet, if intensities happen outside of the space we perceive, how is it possible to begin considering an intensive topography as an alternative process in the context of memorialization? Deleuze suggests that through the disjunctive use of our faculties of the understanding we are able to experience the groundless space of the *spatium*.

Why combine intensities with topography? Simply because the connection helps us grasp landscape not as given or neutral but as a becoming-milieu, an unpredictable depth constituted not just over time but *in* time, through the movement of differences in kind that present affects. In this regard, the milieu in question does not provide us with a preconceived form or meaning. In abbreviated form, that is: designing not with individually distinct elements or bringing each element into relationship with another, but using the principle of individuating connections whereby elements such as popular values and tastes, local identities, market forces, growth and settlement patterns, the physical features of a site, building orientation, ventilation flows, and so forth undergo change as they combine with one another. Here the unified perception of topographical identity is dismantled, setting the fully coherent plan or design that organizes the world out to pasture. The implication is that memorialization resists the moralizing top-down approach both Foote and Virilio fall prey to; that is, the memorial and events do not judge the landscape because these don't unify it. This is because the memorial no longer conquers the affects and intensities of a milieu or brings it under the control of a fully coherent territory. Intensive topographies are not a reactionary enterprise because topography no longer codifies the flows of intensity to create an image representative of a structure, subjugating its multiplicity. Intensive topographies can be likened to being more of a schizoid investment; they create deterritorializing lines of escape, decoding and producing nonfigurative directions that, in turn, create new paths and flows. This is the antithesis of a paranoiac desiring-investment that regulates as it codifies the landscape. An intensive topography is not considered the result of events shaping the land over time, or a landscape whose characteristics can be measured in relationship to how they have evolved over time; rather it is a topography that engages with the complexity of pure time and such an approach to topography looks to nonstructural functions in the way that Libeskind's Jewish Museum (1988–99) in Berlin does.

Invited to participate in a design competition for the new Jewish Museum in Berlin, Libeskind conceived the project as a lightning bolt cutting through the landscape. He began by looking up the

Gedenkbuch containing all the names of deported Berlin Jews. From here he compiled a list that he then used to archaeologically investigate the urban landscape of Berlin, discovering where each person lived, their occupation along with general details of their life. The addresses formed nodal points across the city, and when combined he was left with a series of fracturing landscapes that informed the design for the facades of the building. Extending this idea of archaeological history he improvised with the form of the Jewish star (a well known marker used by the Nazis to identify a Jew), repeating it so as to produce a differenciation with each repetition. It was these diagrams that then became the basis for the museum design. Cracking open the star three primary paths emerged, which when taken lead the visitor to the holocaust tower, the garden of exile, and along the path of continuity through the museum exhibition areas. The design emerges between two lines of thinking: organization and relationship. The original title for the design – 'Between the Lines' – reinforces this idea. Libeskind explains this is because the design involves 'a straight line, but broken into many fragments; the other is a tortuous line, but continuing indefinitely.'[30] He outlines three basic propositions used in the design process. First, in order to understand the history of Berlin the enormous intellectual, economic, and cultural contribution made by Berlin Jews needs to be addressed. Second, we need to physically and spiritually integrate the meaning of the holocaust into Berlin's consciousness and memory. Third, only by acknowledging and incorporating the void of Jewish life in Berlin can the city look to the future.[31] The result is not just a container housing inanimate objects in glass cases; rather it is an environment whereby the museum becomes a landscape of memorialization.

One enters the Jewish Museum through the old Baroque museum, moving underground then following the staircase up into the new wing. Here along the path of continuity one is presented with a combination of histories: the lives of both Berliner Jews and Berliner *goyim* (Yiddish for 'non-Jews'). Another path arrives at a dead end. This is a sterile, cold, concrete place. It is naturally lit by a few slits in the ceiling from where the sounds of outside life leak through. The void is not just empty, it emits a sense of disequilibrium and groundlessness in a way that defies phenomenological explication simply because the materials slowly fill the space with a sense of cold in color, texture, scale, light, and feeling. All the while heat darts rapidly throughout the body, solidifying throat muscles, tightening the stomach; accelerating the movement of blood at the back of the neck, in the armpits, and behind the knees. The blending of accelerated heating and the slow cooling follow different durations, both of which exceed the duration of the muted thud as the heavy entry door suddenly shuts, sealing the space off from the rest of the world. The void cracks open a variety of durations shaking one's sense of 'self,' in all its coherency. Exiting the room one enters another path that directs you outside into what seems like a park on the brink of collapse. Here, in the garden of exile, the unanchored milieu of the void reappears once more. The garden consists of a tilted ground plane from which projects forty-nine square concrete columns perpendicular to the tilted plate, each seven meters high. Forty-eight columns filled with soil from Berlin point to the inauguration of the State of Israel in 1948; one is filled with soil from Jerusalem.[32]

The whole point of Libeskind's use of the void is to suspend our ability to ground experience in habitual perception (unlike Rothko's use of the void as a point of identification). The void, for example, is not entirely dark although its emptiness produces a sense of darkness; the light emitted from above cools the space as it lingers against the concrete and yet panic produces bursts of heat. In this regard Libeskind notes:

> Light is the measure of everything. It is absolute, mathematical, physical, eternal. There is an absolute speed to it, you can't outrun it; that's what the theory of relativity is about. Stand here and remember what you can. What you remember is in light, the rest is in darkness, isn't it? The past fades to dark, and the future is unknown, just stars.[33]

As Deleuze might say a disjunctive synthesis takes place whereby our sensory experiences resist being assimilated by our categories of understanding and yet they still impinge upon each other in a way that pushes our faculties of understanding and our sense of self to the limit. Why phenomenology falls short here is because the disjunctive synthesis defies representation in a unified 'I' or 'self'; the perception in question is not that of lived experience but the manner in which we are exposed to a pre-individual experience beyond the consciousness of a human subject. A variety of affects and intensities permeate one another and none can be specifically located. There is a simultaneous interpenetration of different durations. Contrary to phenomenological interpretation which posits that the simultaneity in question is the result of individual events (each with their own succession) combining, a Deleuzian might say intensity is produced through the undecidable effect of intensity and affect, which exceeds existence in a fully coherent body or place. An undecidable milieu of problems is created, not simply a coherent solution. It is undecidable, in so far as it produces unanticipated futures that continue to blend with the present in all their virtuality, making the present a singularity. Hence, to state this is an undecidable effect is certainly not tantamount to saying the effect is indeterminate. In this way, Libeskind's use of the void is inextensive, making his design a novel rethinking of the significance of topography in the context of memorialization, consciously working against the organizational grain of extension and the frigid grid-like structure it lends support to. As Libeskind succinctly puts it: 'The tyranny of the grid! I fight against it all the time: buildings designed like checkerboards, with repetitive units that march along the same track. A marching grid is not what life is about.'[34] And yet curiously, the garden at the Jewish Museum uses a grid formation. The difference here is that Libeskind infuses a sense of the irrational into the grid the moment he shifts the base plate, causing a shift in the ground plane that in turn creates a sense of gravitational pull.

Just on the other side of town in the neighborhood of Friedrichstadt just south of the Brandenburg Gate and down the road from the German Parliament (*Reichstag*) is Eisenman's Memorial to the Murdered Jews of Europe (*Denkmal für die ermordeten Juden Europas*, 2003–2005).[35] It, too, has used the organization of the grid as a way of undermining the tyranny of a regulatory repetition of elements. This memorial derives from an intensive topography as Eisenman infuses life back into the lifeless order of the grid by introducing into *extensio* a sense of *spatium*. What this means is that the minimalist expressionism Eisenman uses, which Lin's Vietnam Veterans Memorial (1982) was a catalyst for, critically engages the memorial typology of a vertical structure set against the horizontal ground plane that together work to produce a homogenous entity. Like the Gerz monument, monument typology is used self-reflexively by Eisenman to release a feeling of groundlessness and vertigo. The limits of phenomenologically engaging with the 19,000-square-meter site, by relying too much on personal perception simply strips its intensive topography bare, for here there are a variety of intensities and affects commingling with one another. There is the stiff push from the weight of 2,711 falling columns, the pull of an undulating series of narrow paths and a ground plane that sinks below street level, the dizziness of shifting angles, the increasing pressure of moving amid a mass of slender concrete stelae as they thicken the landscape, the dilution of this heaviness on the outskirts of the piazza as the sun warms the site. The uniform grid pattern that the columns create slightly disperses along the fringes of the site producing varying degrees of enclosure and openness; at its edges sun and concrete combine inviting visitors to sunbake or pause to chat. Depending on how it is used the site eludes rigid definition; it has the solemnity of a memorial, the joy of a city park, and the flurry of a piazza. Children play hide and seek, others light Yahrzeit candles to honor the dead, and some use it as a meeting spot. The deeper in you go the quieter it becomes, the buoyancy of street sounds slow to a murmur as a gray narrow silence infuses the belly of the site. Through the language of abstraction, Eisenman drags the full weight of those anonymous bodies of history up from below the depths of the earth, enticing the visitor to take the place of those selfsame bodies by descending to where they were once buried. Those who criticize the project for reinforcing the stigma of the holocaust throughout the German landscape miss the point because in effect the holocaust-as-stigma is dislodged by Eisenman's intensive use of topography and, as Žižek might describe it, the reality we experience is never fully complete 'not because a large part of it eludes me, but because it contains a stain, a blind spot, which indicates my inclusion in it.'[36] The result is that Eisenman constructs an urban space that functions as a private and public space undermining their separation. His contribution to the intensive topography of Berlin is therefore a heterogeneous public sphere that works to open up subjectivity and the possibilities available for its social determination.

Ultimately the relationship between landscape and memory is fundamentally one of how the landscape is used; in this regard, the connection to the past as it transforms or creates blockages invites us to consider a more expanded definition of topography, to move beyond the verticals and horizontals and think about the thickening and thinning of diagonal movements, or the speed with which people move, and the blending of sense. Then there are other considerations that have to do with the way connections mutate and new directions come to the fore, like the trench consisting of the provisional memorial and exhibition titled 'Topography of Terror' – to which Eisenman's memorial is a peripheral element – taking visitors to the site of the former headquarters of the SS and Gestapo and the ruins of the National Socialist prison where torture took place. Here the directed lines of holocaust memory begin to disperse once other events are activated. The site meets with areas marking the rise and fall of the 96-mile-long Berlin Wall (1969–89) that left the city divided in two between East and West and where the longest stretch of the wall has been left intact. An alternative topography of terror is tapped into, one that emits the violence of the Cold War era as independent stalls crop up opposite the Eisenman memorial displaying images of spontaneous memorials that once defined the now imperceptible no-man's-land dividing East and West prior to German reunification in 1990.[37]

Here we return once again to Deleuze and Guattari's discussion of the Freudian death-instinct outlined earlier in Chapter 4. If Freud can be described as having once made the significant discovery of the Libido in terms of an 'abstract subjective essence of desire,' what exactly went wrong with his conception of desire? As Deleuze and Guattari point out, the moment Freud inserted this essence into a system of representation with his concept of the ego, desire was alienated from its productive potential. Furthermore, Freud set this alienation in concrete when he codified the essence of desire with the despotic signifier of Oedipus. Ultimately, Freud neutralized the life force by inverting life into death. So, perhaps then, if we read Adorno through the schizoanalysis of Deleuze and Guattari, what representation neutralizes is not so much the transcendent Truth of trauma, compromising the original force of systematically killing six million Jews, rather it is the opposite: organic representation inverts the affirmation of life turning it into the pure silence of the death-instinct, in other words a death principle that exists without model or experience. In this regard, the real crime of organic representation and the neutralization of trauma it produces comes from attempting to define the present and the past for future generations in terms of guilt, guilt being the territory upon which life in the future is preserved and out of which all life in some way represents the destructive force of an original wound. The anxious memorialization of the German landscape could be perceived in this way as it tries to relieve itself of the Oedipal force of original guilt by causing itself to grow in that very trauma.

We are left with the following questions: is the connection between the landscape and past events simply one where past ghosts endure within the present, defining the topography of the land according to the voids those selfsame ghosts left behind? Or does the act of memorial topography function as a mass grave into which the more unresolved aspects of past events are thrown? What this chapter has proposed is that the traumatic past should not be taken as the subject through which topography is surveyed, produced, or lived because traumatic memory can function as a topographical crack. In a nutshell, rather than define a landscape as tainted with guilt, Berliner life can be revitalized through the fault lines of Jewish life as Libeskind's Jewish Museum and Eisenman's Memorial to the Murdered Jews of Europe attest to. Topographically connecting the present to the past does not mean turning the landscape into a monument to the dead. It can be an optimistic move into the future that allows for the production of a future different to the past and, as Libeskind cautions, efforts to mark the landscape as a reminder 'should represent the future, not only the past; the beginning not only the end.'[38] Further, as Gerz's Monument Against Fascism demonstrates, a landscape can be conceived of as producing intensities as much as it is produced by them.

Landscape is never neutral, which is not tantamount to claiming it is ideological, this being the crux of Libeskind's competition entry for the development of the Sachsenhausen concentration camp. The connection between landscape and memory is implicitly ethical, in so far as it addresses the problem of what memory can do. More specifically though, there is the question of how landscape is not just scarred by an event, rather how it opens up to its own outside. In this way, landscape involves a becoming-other, an indeterminable experimentation with memory so that the designer doesn't use the land to interpret the past or turns it into a primary signifier of trauma. This constitutes what Deleuze and Guattari refer to as a legitimate conjunctive synthesis, one that is nomadic and polyvocal and is implicitly in opposition to the segregation fostered by its illegitimate counterpart.[39] Instead, with a look toward the future, the designer exposes the implicated durations of the land, affirming and celebrating the movement of the past in the present. This is not the same as demanding we celebrate the holocaust – an abhorrent claim – but we do need to put the past to work so as to optimistically embrace the future, to celebrate life over and above death. Here the quotation Deleuze and Guattari provide from Henry Miller's *Sexus* summarizes the problem with frankness: 'The phantasmal world is the world which has not been fully conquered over. It is the world of the past, never of the future. To move forward clinging to the past is like dragging a ball and chain . . . We are all guilty of crime, the great crime of not living life to the full.'[40]

Notes

1. See Deleuze, Gilles and Félix Guattari. *Anti-Oedipus: Capitalism and Schizophrenia*, trans. R. Hurley, M. Seem, and H. R. Lane (Minneapolis, MN: University of Minnesota Press, 1977), 105. With meticulous

commitment Germany has integrated the history of the holocaust by introducing it into the school curriculum, through the building of memorials and museums that document the mechanisms of Fascist Germany, and in the work of artists such as Anselm Kiefer, Hans Haacker, and Gerhard Richter (to name a few). We must not forget the efforts of intellectuals and in particular the heated 1986 *Historikerstreit* (Historians' Debate) between professional historians such as Jürgen Habermas, Ernst Nolte, and Eberhard Jäckel. These efforts all reveal the shared aspiration of a majority of Germans to fully take on the liability of their own history with maturity. Translations of the *Historikerstreit* arguments have been made by James Knowlton and Truett Cates, *Forever in the Shadow of Hitler? Original Documents of the Historikerstreit, the Controversy Concerning the Singularity of the Holocaust* (Atlantic Highlands, NJ: Humanities Press, 1993). See also *New German Critique 44: Special Issue of the Historikerstreit* (Spring/Summer 1988). James Young has provided a detailed study of the holocaust memorials shaping the German landscape. See Young, James E. *The Texture of Memory: Holocaust Memorials and Meaning* (New Haven, CT: Yale University Press, 1993).

2. Foote, Kenneth E. *Shadowed Ground: America's Landscapes of Violence and Tragedy* (Austin, TX: University of Texas Press, 2003), 293.
3. Ibid., 15.
4. In the context of Chicago, Foote explains that there is nothing 'marked at the site of a crash between a street car and a gasoline truck at 63rd and State Streets on 25 May 1950 that claimed 33 lives and injured many more; where two Illinois Central trains collided at the 27th Street station on 30 October 1972, killing 45 and injuring 322; at the Lake Street – Wabash Avenue curve of the Loop, where two elevated trains struck and derailed on 4 February 1977, killing 11 and injuring 200; or where a DC-10 crashed at O'Hare International Airport on 25 May 1979, claiming the lives of 258 passengers, 13 crew members, and 2 people on the ground.' Foote, *Shadowed Ground*, 309.
5. Ibid., 158.
6. Quoted in Libeskind, Daniel. *Breaking Ground: Adventures in Life and Architecture* (New York: Riverhead Books, 2004), 134.
7. For example, Foote notes that in America there are very few sites relating to the struggles of minority groups such as gays, women, Native and African Americans, or the violent clashes between the labor movement and the industrialists. For him, the absence of memorials dedicated to the fallen heroes of these groups is an issue of unresolved meaning in so far as it demonstrates how Americans have not really dealt with the violence of their own past. In the case of African American history, sites where lynchings and beatings took place remain unmarked because they 'carry such shameful connotations.' See Foote, *Shadowed Ground*, 322.

8. Although not originally designed to be a death camp, a gas chamber was constructed at *Konzentrationlager Sachsenhausen* (Sachsenhausen concentration camp) in 1943. Primarily Russian prisoners of war perished here as the Jews were moved east to Auschwitz for hard labor or to be systematically exterminated. Situated on the outskirts of Berlin, Sachsenhausen was unusual in that it was located on German soil. It was also a training ground for SS Guards prior to being posted in other concentration camps and a place where medical experiments and counterfeiting activities took place. In April 1945 the remaining inmates were ordered to evacuate the premises as the Allied forces neared. Those who collapsed were executed on the spot and, as the death march memorial reads, 6,000 prisoners perished. When the Soviet Red Army liberated the camp they promptly reconverted the site into a Soviet Special Camp housing former Nazi officials and political dissidents. It continued to be used in this capacity until the spring of 1950.
9. The 'u' in the title Mo~~u~~rning is literally crossed out to form a play on words between morning and mourning. Libeskind, Daniel. *The Space of Encounter* (New York: Universe, 2000), 90.
10. Ibid., 91.
11. Ibid.
12. Ibid., 90–1.
13. Eisenman, Peter. *Holocaust Memorial Berlin* (Baden: Lars Müller Publishers, 2005).
14. Tschumi, Bernard. 'Foreword,' in Virilio, Paul. *A Landscape of Events*, trans. Julie Rose (Cambridge, MA: MIT Press, 2000), viii.
15. Ibid., ix.
16. Virilio, *A Landscape of Events*, 59.
17. Ibid.
18. It should be noted that Virilio openly condemns the current situation where, as he says, events take place in real time resulting in a double event: one that happens in the here and now, the other in the transient encounter with the televisual. The reason for his criticism is that the televisual dimension of the event means that it doesn't actually take place. The result is that place is disconnected from time. The difficulty for Virilio arises out of the utopian implications this has for how human beings perceive the world around them, and in this regard his argument is implicitly phenomenological. Commenting on the speed of travel that contaminates how we perceive and measure geographical distances, Virilio lashes out against the priority given over to real-time experience. In rhetorical fashion he poses the problem in the following way: 'What will we look forward to when we no longer need to look forward in order to arrive?' See Virilio, *A Landscape of Events*, 65. The reason for concern comes from what Virilio calls *social quietism*, that is a sense of satisfaction that comes from no longer needing to move in order to engage in

social life. This is because we don't need to leave our homes anymore in order to come into contact with other people; a click of the mouse will suffice. He provides the following diagnosis: we end up turning into unproductive, immobile entities desiring absence at the expense of presence. Quoting the artist Paul Klee, he announces: 'To define the present in isolation is to kill it.' See Virilio, *A Landscape of Events*, 46. He laments the loss of the present and argues that the present and place are isolated from one another creating a world that is filled with physically inert and passive individuals. He likens the individual of real time to the exile, someone who is cut off from the sensory world around them. The forecast he leaves us with is obviously dire: sensory deprivation that comes from being in a 'place where nothing ever happens'! See Virilio, *A Landscape of Events*, 64. On the one hand he celebrates the spontaneity of events and yet he laments how 'phenomena that happen *here*, in common space, no longer happen *now*, in common time, but in an *other time* over which no one has any power, despite the tragic illusions of computer technology.' See Virilio, *A Landscape of Events*, 91.

19. Deleuze, Gilles. *The Logic of Sense*, trans. Mark Lester and Charles Stivale (New York: Columbia University Press, 1990), 53.
20. Ibid.
21. Ibid., 54.
22. Deleuze, Gilles. *Difference and Repetition*, trans. Paul Patton (New York: Columbia University Press, 1994), 222.
23. Ibid.
24. Deleuze, Gilles and Félix Guattari. *A Thousand Plateaus: Capitalism and Schizophrenia*, trans. Brian Massumi (London: Athlone Press, 1988), 474–500.
25. Here Deleuze and Guattari lean upon the composer Pierre Boulez to articulate this distinction. Ibid., 477.
26. Ibid., 15
27. Deleuze, *Difference and Repetition*, 239.
28. Ibid., 254.
29. See Parr, Adrian. 'Differentiation/Differenciation,' in *The Deleuze Dictionary*, ed. Adrian Parr (Edinburgh: Edinburgh University Press, 2005), 75–6.
30. Libeskind, *The Space of Encounter*, 23.
31. Ibid., 23.
32. The Kabbalistic significance of using the number forty-nine comes from multiplying the number seven by seven (seven being a holy number in Judaism).
33. Libeskind, *Breaking Ground*, 56.
34. Ibid., 124–5.
35. The original design for the memorial was the result of a collaboration between architect Peter Eisenman and the artist Richard Serra. Serra

withdrew from the project as the political process began and compromises were requested, feeling that these would undermine the project.

36. Žižek, Slavoj. *The Parallax View (Short Circuits)* (Cambridge, MA: MIT, 2006), 17.
37. A fascinating study on Berlin rebuilding programs as part of the process of German reunification from the perspective of film and one that includes an interview with the filmmaker Hubertus Siegert is Stern, Ralph. 'Berlin, Film and the Representation of Urban Reconstruction Since the Fall of the Wall,' in *Out of Ground Zero: Case Studies in Urban Reinvention*, ed. Joan Ockman (New York: Prestel, 2002), 117–31.
38. Libeskind, *The Space of Encounter*, 25.
39. Deleuze and Guattari, *Anti-Oedipus*, 110.
40. Ibid., 334.

CHAPTER 9

Trauma and Consumption

> THEY WAIT PATIENTLY, hands jammed in pockets, winter hats pulled low. They've been standing in the cold for nearly an hour, but they don't joke or shove or goof around the way people in lines usually do. They act as if they're in a church. Which, in a way, they are.
>
> They are waiting to see ground zero. They say they need to see it. And to accommodate the mourners, the well-wishers and the just plain curious from around the world, New York officials – after first discouraging visitors and then relenting and building a special viewing platform for them – have begun issuing free, timed tickets to the site of the World Trade Center bombings. (*Washington Post*)[1]

The journalist K. C. Summers comments that tickets to the ground zero viewing platform in New York City were available between 11 a.m. and 6 p.m. Although Summers turned up at 1 p.m. tickets for that day had run out and one was issued for 10 a.m. the next day. When arriving at the viewing platform it was noted that people should be prepared to be in line for at least 45 minutes. Similarly, and writing for the travel section of the *New York Times*, Joseph Siano reminds his readers that tickets for the viewing gallery were only valid for a half-hour time slot. He went on to warn readers to keep in mind that, since each time slot had 250 tickets, lines were long.[2] It is a hard pressed claim to assert that the labor of memory has an objective essence when we think about the reality of waiting in line for forty-five minutes and sometimes being told that the 250 tickets allocated for one day have now run out by lunch-time and yet people devotedly returned the following day to view the void 9/11 left behind. Under such circumstances the value of memory is obviously not objective but a subjective essence. What this chapter intends to do is trace what happens to the subjective essence of memory once the initial impact of trauma subsides, and the way in which this essence is then swiftly conjugated by the axiomatic of capital.

Before analyzing a capital-generating memory it is important we first look to the specific social conditions underpinning this situation. The Pew Center for Research has found that in the United States 73 percent of people in October 2005 followed the impact of Hurricane Katrina and Rita 'very closely' while in October 2001, 78 percent reported the same level of attentiveness for coverage of the terrorism attacks on the US. Are figures of this kind merely indicative of a media-driven culture or do they illustrate something else? For example, given the heavy impact government decisions for healthcare and education have on the quality of life of the average citizen in America it may be interesting to compare viewing attentiveness of disaster coverage with such issues, and to tighten the parameters of the manipulated variable here. One way to do this is to compare viewer attentiveness for non-catastrophic events to large-scale catastrophic events such as 9/11 and Hurricane Katrina. To begin, let us briefly look at the example of the Whitewater investigation that caused serious damage to the public's perception of the US President and First Lady, Bill and Hillary Clinton. Although criminally investigated the Clintons were not charged; however, charges were made against two of the principals of the Whitewater Development Agency. The CNN/USA Today/Gallup Poll reported that the American public had an 'overwhelmingly critical view of the pardons Bill Clinton gave just prior to leaving the presidency' with approximately 57 percent of those polled believing he had done something unethical and overall 75 percent of Americans gave a negative view of the pardons.[3] Strangely, this negative opinion of the President did not translate into public attention toward news coverage of the event. Further, the research findings state that only 11 percent in August 1995 and for January and March of 1996 followed the Whitewater investigation regardless of the political turmoil it caused.

The next question is how well American consumption of media disaster coverage fares in relation to popular entertainment. Quizzically, only 10 percent of Americans polled by the Pew Research Center reported high levels of attentiveness toward the real-life drama of television shows such as *Survivor* and *Big Brother* in July 2000. A decade earlier, only 10 percent said they closely followed the Academy Awards. So while significant political issues that would commonly be believed to be in the public's best interest to watch were not closely followed, nor were some of the most popular entertainment shows. Yet, using the category of 'high viewing attentiveness,' media coverage of traumatic events such as 9/11, the Challenger disaster, Hurricane

Katrina and the San Francisco earthquake all ranked in the top thirty percentile band among the American public.[4]

What do these statistics tell us? Overall, Americans seem more interested in following news coverage of trauma than they do important political events. This is further supported by the Pew report 'Young Americans and Women Less Informed: One in Four Americans Follow National News Closely' where it was noted that in the period 1989–95 the majority of Americans paid very little attention to news stories except, that is, those covering national calamities or the use of American military force. The report noted the following findings:

> Most attention went to stories of natural or man-made disasters and stories about wars and terrorism involving the United States or its citizens. Among the top 20 news stories in our data base, the Challenger disaster attracted the largest audience. Most of the other stories with huge audiences featured earthquakes, hurricanes, floods or American military actions. Exceptions are Rodney King and the story of baby Jessica who fell down a well in Texas in 1987.[5]

In general, cable and television news channels draw larger audiences than radio, newspapers, and the Internet. In the case of Hurricane Katrina, CNN actually improved its ratings with 31 percent of Americans reporting CNN to be their main source of international and domestic news. In fact, this figure was up 13 percent prior to Katrina.[6]

The above are all exemplary of the reification of trauma – market forces turning memory into an abstraction that culture then turns into a source of meaning. What the Pew Research Center figures highlight is that the public is not more interested in current events than popular culture, rather traumatic events seem to capture the public's attention more than any other news coverage. In this respect, it is no wonder that popular culture has jumped on the band-wagon: there is a lot of money to be made out of the social fascination with trauma. Put differently, the industry of memorial culture is semiological and traumatic memory provides new raw material for the market to expand.[7] In *A Thousand Plateaus*, Deleuze and Guattari describe the game of chess as semiological because it is an 'institutionalized, regulated, coded war, with a front, a rear, battles' all working to create binary relations between states.[8] In other words, memorial culture becomes semiological when traumatic memory is put to biunivocal use, or, put differently, when the differential and intensive power of memory is opposed and limited using the logic of organic representation (discussed in Chapter 6). What Deleuze and Guattari call 'biunivocal' are the relations that come to be as a result of a structural not strategic function. In the context of our discussion here this would be when the affects and energies of memory are coded and assigned an internal nature that governs how these are organized.

Tim Cole poignantly reminds us in his discussion of the industry that has popped up around the holocaust that we can't forget that the holocaust has also become big business. *Schindler's List*, for example, netted more than '$221 million at foreign box offices and [received] seven Academy Awards.'[9] Meanwhile, the Tourist Commission of Krakow now runs Schindler's List Tours featuring key sites from the movie and the old Jewish quarter, Kasimierz. Since the movie gentile-owned hotels named after key characters in the film such as Ariel and Alef have appeared. Similarly, and recalling our discussion of the Vietnam War in Chapters 3 and 5, Time-Life purchased the graphic photographs of the My Lai massacre taken by soldier Ronald Haeberle for $19,550 and once Haeberle had sold the rights to other countries (such as Germany, the UK, Sweden, Australia, and South Africa) the total figure came to a grand sum of $35,099.[10] Journalist Seymour Hersh later won a Pulitzer Prize for his coverage of the My Lai story.[11] Today, war tourism in Vietnam has become big business with hundreds taking tours through the Chu Chi tunnels (forty miles northwest of Ho Chi Minh City) of the Vietcong, or Ho Chi Minh's Military Museum and the War Remnants Museum, with some tours even visiting the rooftop of the Rex Hotel where former US officers and war correspondents used to pass the time. Meanwhile, with a budget of $15 million, the documentary style dramatization of Flight 93's crash into an empty field in Pennsylvania on 11 September 2001 premiered at a modest $11.6 million; by 29 July 2006 *United 93* had grossed $42,944,872 worldwide.[12] Following on from here, Hollywood Oscar-winning director, Oliver Stone directed the movie *World Trade Center* (2006) starring Oscar-winning actor, Nicholas Cage, with a generous budget of $65 million. With a tagline that reads 'The World Saw Evil That Day. Two Men Saw Something Else,' the film depicts Port Authority Officers trapped in the rubble of the WTC site on 9/11. Winning the 'best picture' and 'best director' awards at the Online Film Fans Awards, the box-office opening weekend figures for the United States were $18.7 million and in the United Kingdom £865,249; then coming in at number three on the movie charts in Australia it made AU$0.91million; within a few months the film grossed more than $141 million worldwide.[13]

In short, what these figures demonstrate is that there is an abstract subjective essence to remembrance and this essence (labor and production of remembrance) is reterritorialized in the private ownership of the entertainment industry, a situation that alienates the deterritorializing flows of libidinal mnemonic energies. As Deleuze and Guattari note: 'Production as the abstract subjective essence is discovered only in the forms of property that objectifies it all over again, that alienates it by reterritorializing it.'[14] There are countless examples of this phenomenon, whether we are talking about holocaust tourism or the appetite to view the events of 9/11 unfold and later the queues of people waiting to enter the ground zero viewing platform. The interesting issue is how the labor of memory is then separated from how memory is socially and culturally produced so that remembrance is then sold as a commodity. It is this process that turns memory into a subjective essence. Memory labor is coded as the property of entertainment industries or other forms of big business such as tourism. However, this is only because, as the above figures attest to, the social relations conditioning this process actively support it in the first instance. That is to say, the abstract subjective essence of memory is discovered through the very system of private ownership that alienates and objectifies traumatic memory by reterritorializing it as a determinate mode of capital-money production. Clearly, under such conditions the work of memory appears to be disposable as it is increasingly determined by conditions external to it (subordinated to the monolithic operation of capital) and yet those selfsame conditions are contingent upon the conjunction of social forces, relations, and affects. The first synthesis – the production of production, otherwise known as the connective synthesis – is where libidinal energy is turned into recording energy (Numen). When the Numen is transformed into consummation energy (Voluptus) we have the third conjunctive synthesis of consumption, one that also introduces us to the commodity character of cultural consumption and subject production.

If we recall our discussion in Chapter 2 that Adorno views mass culture as a sanitized aesthetic, his position is that the culture industry is monolithic and totalitarian. While this is largely an aesthetic criticism, it also invokes another more Deleuzian focus on what culture does. He clarifies that in the absence of aesthetic antagonism culture no longer produces conflict in the real world. He is clear to point out that the relationship between culture and conflict is paradoxical. That is, aesthetic truth depends upon the 'expression of the untruth of bourgeois society,' which is to say that art 'really only exists as long as it is impossible by virtue of the order which it transcends.'[15] For Adorno culture transcends this order dialectically, and here we get a brief taste of the Hegel in Adorno. The revolutionary force of culture makes its appearance as an extrinsic difference, a difference structured through contradiction and one that produces conflict. Adorno cautions us that the formal use of conflict by culture – whether that is its subject matter or even at the aesthetic level of color, line, and composition – is deceptive. All this ever does is present the possibility of conflict without disclosing the mechanism of cultural production that represses this very possibility. Satisfying the curiosity of the public, mass culture doesn't just serve the 'psychological economy of the subject,' it 'directly serves material interests as well.'[16]

In his discussion of musical fetishism in his essay 'On the Fetish Character' Adorno points to the limitations of a purely psychological interpretation that fails to recognize the commodity character of the music industry on the whole. He admits there are certain values and feelings that music unconsciously attracts in the consumer. However, these are secondary expressions of their commodity character. In order to actually hear the music there is a string of commodities we have to first purchase. This leads him to conclude, in a particularly Marxist fashion, that what is fetishized is not so much listening to the music itself but the amount of money that has been paid to attend the concert: 'He has literally "made" the success which he reifies and accepts as an objective criterion, without recognizing himself in it.'[17] For Deleuze, this situation turns into a territorial machine that curbs the independence of social economic reproduction wedding it to a social form of reproduction (human reproduction). The point of crossover for Adorno and Deleuze is that they both insist the integration of difference turns difference into an abstract quality, whereas for Adorno the problem is purely one of negativity – culture recodes difference as it homogenizes it. What makes this process totalitarian is that recoding negatively defines the organization of the social field. Meanwhile, for Deleuze there is a positive potential to this process. While the capitalist economy integrates difference (axiomatization) it produces cultural effects not just in the form of recoding (and like for Adorno, for Deleuze this is also negative) but also as decoding. It is the capacity for culture to decode the integrative process of the market where the rationalization and reification of culture is interrupted. What memorial culture shares in common with Adorno's negative dialectic is its capacity to also deterritorialize capital by making it 'pass over the plane of immanence as movement of the infinite' suppressing it as 'internal limit' by turning '*back against itself so as to summon forth a new earth, a new people.*'[18] Here the role of utopian memory thinking outlined in Chapter 2 is imperative when considering the productive power of desire, and to do this it is helpful to look to Marx for guidance.

Marx proves useful because he puts forward a slightly different understanding of the drives in his discussion of consumption and production. He explains that there are two ways in which consumption creates production: firstly, in the sense that 'a product becomes a real product only by being consumed'; secondly, in the sense that 'consumption creates the need for *new* production,' meaning that consumption presupposes production.[19] Clarifying this second point he notes that 'consumption *ideally posits* the object of production as an internal image, as a need, as drive and as purpose,' which is to say that we cannot have production without the drives; yet it is consumption that is responsible for the reproduction of those drives.[20] Whereas for Freud production is an imaginary order of the unconscious, for Marx it is the real that is produced. Advancing an alternative concept of desire Marx and Friedrich Engels argue consciousness is determined by life instead of saying life is determined by consciousness.[21] Meaning, the material conditions, and relations making up social modes of production are expressed ideologically.

Marx went on to replace the holy Oedipal trinity of mummy, daddy, and me that Freud advanced as the model of subject production with an economic trinity of social production – 'profit (profit of enterprise plus interest), land – ground-rent, labour – wages.'[22] That is, workers sell their labor while the capitalist buys their labor-power. Labor is best understood as the participation of human beings and nature, whereby the laborer appropriates the productive force of nature: 'acting on the external world and changing it, he at the same time changes his own nature.'[23] As capital increases so too does the working class and as wages are produced by the worker these products of labor become the worker's means of subsistence which can also be understood as feeding the capitalist machinery: subsistence produces the labor power that both reproduces the system of capital while also expanding that system. Expanding upon the thesis he advanced in the *Grundrisse* – consumption and production are implicated in one another – later in *Capital* Marx writes: 'Labour produces its own production conditions like capital, and capital produces labour in a wage-earning form as a means of realizing it as capital.'[24]

Obviously Marx was an uncompromising materialist in his analysis of capital formation and what he ultimately did was establish the productive aspect of desire while at the same time introduce desire into the system of capital.

Freud too hints at the economic production of desire but he never quite goes far enough. At one point he proposes that during childhood libidinal energy is tamed and socialized, and the primary motive of society in doing this is economic. He succinctly explains:

> The motive of human society is in the last resort an economic one; since it does not possess enough provisions to keep its members alive unless they work, it must restrict the number of its members and divert their energies from sexual activity to work.[25]

Clearly he believes the sexual drive is tamed through a process of signification and bodily inscription. That is, libido is given a reproductive meaning and a moral place within the social order. The barrier against the moral taboo of incest is

> . . . essentially a cultural demand made by society. Society must defend itself against the danger that the interests which it needs for the establishment of higher social units may be swallowed up by the family; and for this reason, in the case of every individual, but in particular of adolescent boys, it seeks by all possible means to loosen their connection with their family – a connection which, in their childhood, is the only important one.[26]

This introduces us to a dramatically different picture of consciousness, one that is closer to what Marx advances. For Marx claims consciousness is the product of social forces and these can be materially determined by the economic and technological circumstances of the times. It is this connection between Freud and Marx that Deleuze and Guattari examine closely in their first collaborative publication: *Anti-Oedipus: Capitalism and Schizophrenia.*

Although the reproduction process characterizing the family cannot be said to be directly economic, it is a process that involves noneconomic kinship features of alliance and filiation common to capital. Indeed, just as, Marx once noted, labor is enslaved through its external determination by capital, so too Freudian desire is subjugated within the form of the nuclear family by the abstract figure of Oedipus. In this way, the benefit of Deleuze and Guattari for our analysis comes from the way they advise that money is not just a matter of accumulation and exchange, as Marx was to posit, it is also how guilt is created. When Deleuze and Guattari fuse together the psychoanalytic observation of the family as a source of guilt with the Marxist analysis of the rise of the capitalist economy, they present a model not just where desire can rediscover its productive dimension once again (as outlined in Chapter 1) but a framework in which to understand the intimate connection between the family and capitalism. That is, the economy is not just driven by surplus and exchange-value it is also a system of debt; in this regard the role of the family in creating a deep-rooted sense of guilt and an eternal indebtedness is pivotal.

Furthermore, an Oedipal subjectivity results because the choices available for subject identification are restricted to either the father or the mother. This restrictive set of options produces a feeble and vulnerable subjectivity that needs to be revitalized by other social determinations. Rather than open subjectivity up to a multiplicity of social determinations – a primarily utopian exercise – new sources of identification also appear in isolated form – nationalism or memory extremism – and as such these simply fortify reproductive subjectivity. This segregation of reproduction from the sphere of production constitutes a particularly capitalist social formation. We now arrive at our third and final system of desire – the conjunctive synthesis.

The cultural condition of remembrance, mourning, and commemoration has shifted over time from the art of the symbolic elaboration or the narration of memory and history to capital production. Conceding that memorial culture has become a part of our staple diet the problem of how it manifests itself lies not so much in the genre of memorialization, rather in the way in which memory becomes a semi-autonomous force, one that reduces trauma to an object of reification – entertainment value – and as an avenue through which a capitalist axiomatic is propounded and reinforced. Remembering traumatic events has become another form of consumption, this being the third synthesis of the process of desire that Deleuze and Guattari speak of: the conjunctive synthesis.[27] What the conjunctive synthesis conjugates are series of decoded flows, this being a process that happens in and through the second synthesis that records energies. The conjunctive synthesis, or what they otherwise refer to as 'consumption,' produces intensities such as the 'intense feeling of transition, states of pure, naked intensity stripped of all shape and form.'[28] But where do these intensities come from? Simply put, they come from prior forces of repulsion and attraction along with the opposition between these. That is, desire consumes itself through supposed polar opposites such as self-enjoyment and suffering. In summary, it is this opposition that creates positive intensities that 'are never an expression of the final equilibrium of a system, but consist, rather, of an unlimited number of stationary, mestastable states through which a subject passes.'[29] What this means is that, unlike Marx was to posit, the economic base is not more important than the superstructure for our analysis of memorial culture; rather, both can be said to be effected because of contingent conjunctions of affect and desire.

Hence, to claim that the conditions defining memorial culture are economic is not to say that social interest in trauma is just an issue to do with money. Using the definition Deleuze gives of the economic in *Difference and Repetition* this would mean a 'theme or "problematic" always covered over by its cases of solution.'[30] Equally, the economic conditions of global capitalism constitute an economic social problem determining how a solution is found in very real social relations. This is why for Deleuze the social dialectic, which he understands as 'the totality of the problems posed to a given society, or the synthetic and problematizing field of that society,' is necessarily economic.[31] The particular kinds of investment trauma takes raises an interesting problem to do not just with what memory shares in common with desire but also social capital. This is why with Guattari he explains that 'the general theory of society is a generalized theory of flows; it is in terms of the latter that one must consider the relationship of social production to desiring-production, the variations of this relationship in each case, and the limits of this relationship in the capitalist system.'[32] Keeping in mind that the sociality of traumatic memory is never given but is the effect of processes of remembrance, the point is that remembrance is a differential field conditioning the social, and in this regard traumatic memory is the desiring production animating the affects, energies, and intensities that actualize how social capital is organized. The particular character social capital takes is not given because it is only ever an aggregate of effects of different traumatic memories that are in turn undergoing different processes of remembrance (albeit vaguely).

Memorial culture has come to the fore at a time when memory is increasingly being situated in connection to guilt by the market and culture. What ensues is that the market turns memory into capital – which helps account for our observation in Chapter 4 that it is not so much that the logic of postmodernism fosters amnesia as Jameson was to posit, rather it doesn't allow us to forget because there is money to be made off of the labor of memory and, more importantly, because the energies and affects of trauma are productive. Herein lies the isomorphic effect of traumatic memory when it is put to work in the service of capitalism. Deleuze and Guattari explain:

> To the extent that capitalism constitutes an axiomatic (production for the market), all States and all social formations tend to become *isomorphic* in their capacity as models of realization: there is but one centered world market, the capitalist one, in which even the so-called socialist countries participate. Worldwide organization thus ceases to pass 'between' heterogeneous formations since it assures the isomorphy of those formations. But it would be wrong to confuse isomorphy with homogeneity. For one thing, isomorphy allows, and even incites, a great heterogeneity among States (democratic, totalitarian, and, especially, 'socialist' States are not facades). For another thing, the international capitalist axiomatic effectively assures the isomorphy of the diverse formations only where the domestic market is developing and expanding, in other words, in 'the center.'[33]

With an illegitimate use of the conjunctive synthesis memorial culture turns abstraction (capital) into a point of social authority, restricting the lines of identification open for social organization, integrating the differential and potentially irruptive field of traumatic memory. For example, the isomorphy of Governor Pataki's warning outlined in Chapter 7 comes from capital organizing the different formations of traumatic memory so as to guarantee the integration of various memory configurations. However, it is at the level of the state (cultural policy, cultural institutions, the governor, demonstrations of relatives of 9/11 victims) whereby the flows and energies of traumatic memory that capital organizes are reemployed as a noncapitalist mode of production.

Pataki viewed the ground zero site as 'sacred ground,' likening it to the 'beaches of Normandy or Pearl Harbor, and we will not tolerate anything on that site that denigrates America, denigrates New York or freedom, or denigrates the sacrifice or courage that the heroes showed on Sept. 11.'[34] Ominously, he went on to point out that he would use his power as New York Governor to block the tenancy of any cultural institution that did not toe the line with politically themed artwork that took the memory of the site as its critical point of departure. The governor's ultimatum was a direct response to demonstrations protesting against the inclusion of the Drawing Center at the ground zero site that included approximately 200 relatives of 9/11 victims. Deleuze and Guattari are instructive in helping us understand the segregative form of this kind of memorial culture in their comments on literature:

> Here again, oedipalization is one of the most important factors in the reduction of literature (in this case memory) to an object of consumption conforming to the established order, and incapable of causing anyone harm. It is not a question here of the personal oedipalization of the author and his readers, but of the *Oedipal form* to which one attempts to enslave the work itself, to make of it this minor expressive activity that secretes ideology according to the dominant codes.[35]

In other words, it is through the production of traumatic memory consumption where subjectivity appears. And as our above example of protests against the inclusion of the Drawing Center at the ground zero site attests to, it is not just consumption at the level of money-capital but also at the level of social-capital; furthermore, in the context of memorial culture the process of consumption also includes memory-capital.

The nationalistic sentiment behind the rallying call to eliminate any cultural institution that is deemed unpatriotic in its focus is a segregative and illegitimate use of the conjunctive synthesis. It is one that projects the force of memory onto a paternalistic memory, not vice versa as a psychoanalytic interpretation might posit. In other words, it is Oedipus that relies upon such nationalistic fervor. The revolutionary energies of a deterritorializing memory appear too frightening and it seems better to 'fall back under the law of the signifier, marked by castration, triangulated in Oedipus,' the effect of which is that the crowd displaces the 'limit, they make it pass into the interior of the social formation, between the social production and reproduction that they invest, and the familial reproduction that they fall back on, to which they apply all the investments.'[36] Under such circumstances a fully paranoid and fascistic subjectivity is constructed, one that is dominated by the segregative form of a reterritorializing memory. According to Deleuze and Guattari this constitutes an illegitimate conjunctive synthesis because it is isolationist. In other words, there is a biunivocal use of memory that produces segregation (one that is nationalistic and racist), the result of which is the integration of difference and the construction of a fixed subject. However, we need also to remember that although the deterritorialized and decoded flows of traumatic memory are conjugated, this does not happen without those selfsame flows 'forging farther ahead; without their escaping both the axiomatic that conjugates them and the models that reterritorialize them . . .' so that a revolutionary remembrance of struggle can reappear once more.[37]

Notes

1. Summers, K. C. 'Ground Zero 101,' *Washington Post*, Sunday, 3 March 2002, E02.
2. Siano, Joseph. 'Travel Advisory; Tickets (Free) Required for Ground Zero,' *New York Times*, 20 January 2002. See: http://query.nytimes.com/gst/fullpage.html?sec=travel&res=9F03E1D91338F933A15752C0A9649C8B63, accessed 18 October 2006.
3. Gallup Poll, 'Americans Overwhelmingly Criticize Pardons, But Few Think Clinton "Did Something Illegal," ' 14 March 2001. See: http://www.galluppoll.com/content/?ci=1906&pg=1, accessed 27 November 2006.
4. Pew Research Center for the People and Press, 'Public Attentiveness to News Stories: 1986–2006.' See: http://people-press.org/nii/, accessed 27 November 2006.
5. Pew Research Center for the People and Press, 'Younger Americans and Women Less Informed: One In Four Americans Follow National News Closely: Times Mirror News Interest Index: 1989–1995,' released 28 December 1995. See: http://people-press.org/reports/display.php3?ReportID=134, accessed 27 November 2006.
6. Pew Research Center for the People and Press, 'Main Source of Disaster News,' 8 September 2005. See: http://72.14.203.104/u/peoplepress?q=cache:5mglLc3U5IoJ:people-press.org/reports/pdf/255.pdf+hurricane+katrina&hl=en&gl=us&ct=clnk&cd=8&ie=UTF-8, accessed 27 November 2006.
7. Since the latter part of the twentieth-century a powerful culture industry devoted to the remembrance of traumatic events has cropped up. So what might the material conditions of this phenomenon be? During the latter part of the twentieth century the last remnants of welfare capitalism began to crumble; now in the early part of the twenty-first century it has all but disappeared (that is if we take the Scandinavian countries and a few other pockets of Europe as an exception). After the political leadership of US President Ronald Reagan and Prime Minister Margaret Thatcher in the United Kingdom, later followed by the fall of the Berlin Wall in 1989, the US Presidencies of both Bush senior and junior, and media magnate Silvio Berlusconi in Italy (just to name a few), western sociopolitical realities have increasingly unified around the axiomatic of global capitalism.
8. Deleuze, Gilles and Félix Guattari. *A Thousand Plateaus: Capitalism and Schizophrenia*, trans. Brian Massumi (London: Athlone Press, 1988), 353.
9. Cole, Tim. *Selling the Holocaust: From Auschwitz to Schindler* (New York: Routledge, 1999), 1.
10. Belknap, Michael R. *The Vietnam War on Trial: The My Lai Massacre and the Court-Martial of Lieutenant Calley* (Lawrence, KS: University Press of Kansas, 2002), 120.

11. Ibid., 119.
12. Germain, David. 'R.V passes United 93 to win box office,' *Reuters Associated Press*, 30 April 2006. See: http://www.ktvb.com/shared content/features/entertainment/broadwire/050106ccjccwEntRV.8bac50c9.html, accessed 25 June 2007. One viewer noted: 'Never has a movie stunned me as much as "United 93." I was literally shaking during the final minutes of the film. Even though I knew the outcome I tried to fight it. I kept yelling under my voice "come on guys, PUSH PUSH . . ., KEEP FIGHTING." But unfortunately none of us can escape the eventual tragedy. I didn't leave the auditorium until the final credits ended. When I walked out of the theater, I felt like I felt on that dreadful day of September 11th, 2001 . . . Numb.' IMDb User Comments for United 93, p. 1. See: http://www.imdb.com/title/tt0475276/usercomments, accessed 28 July 2006. With a production budget of $15 million worldwide by 29 July 2006 *United 93* had grossed $42,944,872. Directed by Paul Greengrass *United 93* presents the story of the passengers who seized control of the plane away from its Muslim hijackers. United 93 at: http://www.boxofficemojo.com/movies/?id=united93.htm, accessed 29 July 2006.
13. Allocine Newsletter. http://www.allocine.co.uk/film/boxoffice_gen_cfilm=61772.html; Infilm Australia. http://www.infilm.com.au/boxoffice.htm, accessed 28 November 2006.
14. Deleuze, Gilles and Félix Guattari. *Anti-Oedipus: Capitalism and Schizophrenia*, trans. R. Hurley, M. Seem, and H. R. Lane (Minneapolis, MN: University of Minnesota Press, 1977), 259.
15. Adorno, Theodor. W. *The Culture Industry: Selected Essays on Mass Culture* (London: Routledge, 1991), 77.
16. Ibid., 83.
17. Ibid., 38.
18. Deleuze, Gilles and Félix Guattari. *What is Philosophy?*, trans. Graham Burchell and Hugh Tomlinson (London: Verso, 1994), 99.
19. Marx, Karl. *Grundrisse*, trans. Martin Nicolaus (London: Penguin, 1973), 91.
20. Ibid., 92.
21. Marx, Karl and Friedrich Engels. *The German Ideology: Including Thesis on Feuerbach* (New York: Prometheus Books, 1998).
22. Marx, Karl. *Capital*, ed. David McLellan (Oxford: Oxford University Press, 1999), 465.
23. Ibid., 115.
24. Ibid., 394.
25. Freud, Sigmund. 'The Sexual Life of Human Beings,' *Introductory Lectures on Psychoanalysis*, trans. James Strachey (London: Penguin, 1991), 353–4.
26. Freud, Sigmund. 'Three Essays on the Theory of Sexuality,' *The Freud Reader*, ed. Peter Gray (London: Vintage, 1995), 290.

27. I would like to firmly point out that the connection drawn between memory, desire, and capital here is not meant to be in sympathy with Norman G. Finkelstein's claim that the holocaust is used ideologically in a self-serving rational manner by Jews to 'deligitimize all criticism of Jews' and that 'criticism could only spring from pathological hatred.' See Finkelstein, Norman G. *The Holocaust Industry* (New York: Verso, 2003), 37.
28. Deleuze and Guattari, *Anti-Oedipus*, 18.
29. Ibid., 19.
30. Deleuze, Gilles. *Difference and Repetition*, trans. Paul Patton (New York: Columbia University Press, 1994), 186.
31. Ibid., 186.
32. Deleuze and Guattari, *Anti-Oedipus*, 262.
33. Deleuze and Guattari, *A Thousand Plateaus*, 436.
34. Healy, Patrick D. 'Pataki Warns Cultural Groups for Museum at Ground Zero,' *New York Times*, 25 June 2005. See: http://www.nytimes.com/2005/06/25/nyregion/25rebuild.html?ex=1277352000&en=feecbc648d8a45af&ei=5090&partner=rssuserland&emc=rss, accessed 14 December 2006.
35. Deleuze and Guattari, *Anti-Oedipus*, 133.
36. Ibid., 135.
37. Deleuze and Guattari, *A Thousand Plateaus*, 472.

Conclusion

> For Christianity the fact of suffering in life means primarily that life is not just, that it is even essentially unjust, that it pays for an essential injustice by suffering, it is blameworthy because it suffers . . . Saved by that suffering which a little while ago accused it: it must suffer since it is blameworthy. (Deleuze)[1]

During the Jewish period of mourning over the destruction of the first and second temples – *Tishah B'av* – it is written in the *Siddur* that Plato accompanied King Nebuchadnezzar when he destroyed the First Temple. Once the building was in ruins Plato encounters the wailing prophet Jeremiah near the Temple Mount. Aghast that such a preeminent and wise sage should be weeping over a pile of ruins, Plato asks him why on earth he is crying, explaining to him that it is pointless to cry over the past. He goes on to ask Jeremiah what good his tears can possibly do now that the building is just a pile of sticks and stones. Jeremiah answers by exclaiming Plato couldn't possibly understand because this was where he acquired his wisdom. According to Jewish tradition, Jeremiah demonstrates the key attributes of anyone worthy of being a prophet and the lesson drawn from the story is that Jeremiah is neither wallowing in self-pity, nor is he consumed by feelings of injustice or even personal suffering. This is because, as Rav Simcha Zissel of Kelm clarifies, Jeremiah is not mourning over the past but out of hope for the future. Every tear shed contributes to the reconstruction of the next Temple.[2] Put differently, for Jeremiah the past is a source of inspiration, not a burden. For this reason Jeremiah exclaims Plato cannot possibly understand why he cries, for his tears are future oriented; they inaugurate an act of social remembrance aspiring to put the present to work for a future yet to come. During *Tishah B'av* the social lesson is not to suffer over the past; instead emphasis is given to the active power of mourning to foster courage, hope, and a sense of joy in the future: remembrance as struggle. In this regard, memory is used by the social field in a distinctively non-Oedipal way so that the past is not a blueprint for the future.[3]

Activating memory in order to seek out, as Deleuze and Guattari describe it, a 'different solidity, other bases and other blocs,' is possible only in so far as memorial culture lets loose a pre-individual memory, a utopian mnemonic practice that is both productive and passive.[4] Under such circumstances how collective memory is put to work throughout culture neither supposes a universal memory, nor a past with a determinate identity. Such a mode of social remembrance inaugurates a new way of remembering as a mode of willing, not just producing new memories or taking memory to be the result of something that once happened. In this respect, in the course of remembering the social field is prompted to connect what previously seemed to be disparate events, giving rise to a memorial cultural activity that aspires to explore the material of the past with the understanding that collective remembrance is productive and real as compared to being expressive and symbolic.

In so far as desire is social and collective memory presupposes a social situation, the phenomenon of memorial culture is a configuration and investment of desire. To say memorial culture is a mode of desiring production is to also claim that it can turn either schizoid or fascistic, and like Jeremiah's tears it has everything to do with the effects of collective remembrance. Does memorial culture foster a fascistic or schizoid investment of memory? To answer this it is important to note the reterritorializing movement driving the fascistic investment and the deterritorializing movement underpinning the schizoid investment of memory. For if reterritorializing Memory posits a movement of signification as Deleuze and Guattari describe it in *A Thousand Plateaus*, we look to the contents of the past in order to discover what the past means. In effect, as collective memory finds fascistic investment in modes of cultural production it mutates into a reterritorializing relation because culture attempts to resolve the contradiction between present and past realities by forming a fixed relation between these. What this means is that collective memory is used to reinforce the past as different to the present and in so doing past, present and future are codified according to their difference from one another (purely negative difference), or the distinction between the past and present is confounded (difference is erased). Both reinforce a homogenous and determinate representation of the past (what Deleuze would call an organic representation).

In many respects the idea of a schizoid investment of memory expands upon and critiques the Freudian concept of *Nachträglichkeit*. In brief, *Nachträglichkeit* posits that subjectivity is historical and is constructed through the reconstruction of traumatic events.[5] According to Freud, the velocity of memory can be likened to a complex drive that takes place in history. Becoming a fully socialized subject happens once unruly and socially unacceptable desires are brought under control through a system of signification. In this regard, Freud inaugurates an important shift away from the concept of a fully constituted subject who brings their desires into the world, onto a divided subject (unconscious and conscious) established as the effect of psychic energy. In response, Deleuze writes that with 'regard to memory, it is not similitude in the reminiscence but, on the contrary, the dissimilar in the pure form of time which constitutes the immemorial of a transcendent memory' and it is this pure form of time that is most instructive when attempting to think a distinction between traumatic memory and the remembrance of trauma.[6] Hence, when he and Guattari insist in *What is Philosophy?* that art is a monument, they are not suggesting that the monumentality of art lies in its size and weight, rather it is the independence of art to stand its own ground by conserving, not commemorating, the being of sensation. Hence, the 'artist's greatest difficulty is to make it *stand up on its own*.'[7]

Memorialization is distinct from the traumatic event that gave rise to it, the designer who created it, and the collective that sponsored and supported its coming into existence. Memorialization is an enduring activity of public remembrance that is conserved and activated throughout cultural activities, but the actual force of trauma is distinct from the very materiality of memorial culture. In this respect, we can claim that traumatic memory is singular, it is unspecified, and yet it appears (monstrously) as an orgiastic representation unleashing the revolutionary force of trauma in all its dappled tones, stammering rhythms, fractured reflections, and strangling silences.[8] This is what Deleuze and Guattari mean when they insist:

> A monument does not commemorate or celebrate something that happened but confides in the ear of the future the persistent sensations that embody the event: the constantly renewed suffering of men and women, their re-created protestations, their constantly resumed struggle. Will this all be in vain because suffering is eternal and revolutions do not survive their victory? But the success of a revolution resides only in itself, precisely in the vibrations, clinches, and openings it gave to men and women at the moment of its making and that

> composes in itself a monument that is always in the process of becoming, like those tumuli to which each new traveler adds a stone.[9]

For instance, in the thousands of taped oral holocaust testimonies around the world there are innumerable accounts of holocaust survivors who years after their terrible experiences in the concentration camps are overcome by inexplicable, yet overwhelming physical sensations that impinge upon, albeit sometimes only briefly, their ability to function in the world. Some of these sensations take shape as a feeling of suffocation and others as anxiety.

Let us take the example of an otherwise happy survivor living in Melbourne, Australia with her husband and children who gets on a bus to go to the supermarket only to be suddenly overcome with a sense of uncontrollable choking. She quickly gets off the bus at which point her breath returns to normal. Thinking about what might have triggered this attack, she recalls having similar feelings fifty years ago when she was taken in a cattle car transport from Hungary to a work camp. It may have been a particular smell combined with the tactile sensation of confinement in connection with an overcrowded bus and the heat of sweaty bodies that intensified the corporeal movement of memory. We are now left asking: is the a priori activity of memory a unified ground from the past that reproduces itself in the present for this survivor? Can the struggle between the interior life of traumatic memory and the forces of remembrance in the present possibly be articulated by culture?

To posit a determinate memory that returns to the present in the same way undermines the creative connection happening between different bodies and temporalities and this movement is entirely without priority. Indeed, at this juncture a distinction between what Deleuze and Guattari describe as a reterritorializing Memory in *A Thousand Plateaus* and another more messy, pre-individual, decodifying memory connection needs to be made. This is why art after the holocaust can no longer truthfully express interior life because that interior life is the deterritorializing force of trauma. Now a tension emerges with Deleuze and Guattari's understanding of memory as reterritorializing and what could otherwise be described as 'singular memory.'[10]

Singular memory is not *given*, meaning it does not denote a finite moment in time; it is an involution that necessarily implies deterritorializing movements that are not subject to the individual will of a 'self.' As such, singular memory is pre-individual as opposed to being an experience constituting the 'self' or located within the *cogito*; it is a modality of individuating differences prior to any given individual difference. As a differentiating force singular memory undergoes change *in* time but does not evolve *over* time. Singular memory is not a distinct or fixed entity or time, it is the deterritorializing dimension of history and of reterritorializing Memory; both are disjunctive and secondary in respect to singular memory. Deleuze and Guattari propose there is 'no history but of the majority, or of minorities as defined in relation to the majority.'[11] They add that although minorities such as women, children, or blacks may have memories these are collected by a 'virile majoritarian.' In this regard, reterritorializing Memory is the colonizing memory of childhood memories, rather than the blocks of becoming memory. When singular memory comes into play it effects a different memory but one that retains traces of the whole of memory. Such memory could be best likened to a deterritorializing movement, one that shares a great deal in common with Deleuze and Guattari's first synthesis of desire: the connective synthesis. For example, to return to our example of a holocaust survivor's memory, it is neither the environment of the bus that completely causes the physical sensations of choking, nor even the individual herself who suddenly remembers the past; that is, memory is already in movement with its own temporality and these movements simply intensify within a specific social situation. 'Social' here means the affective and intensive energies of bodies that constitute a mode of desiring production.

Singular memory is unilateral such that the holocaust survivor's memory on the bus distinguishes itself from a specific space (the cattle car transports) and time (the holocaust); however, it brings with it that which it distinguishes itself from. For this reason, in relation to memory, trauma may best be understood as a particular arrangement of differences and degrees of intensity that generates its own temporality, and it is the singular movement of memory that creates the conditions for this auto-temporality. This is why the logic of a reterritorializing Memory fails to adequately account for the singular, affective, and intensive potential of traumatic memory. The singularity of memory is 'singular' to the process of remembrance and the field in which this process takes place. By distinguishing the memory from remembrance we can argue that the singularity of memory (much like Deleuzian intensity) may not actually be delimited within a given remembrance. However, it is still that which produces it, in so far as this comes to be because of the specificity memory poses. It is the intensive difference amid memories that fade away once a remembrance comes to be that constitutes singular memory.

In so far as the concept of singular memory is a pre-individual memory, it draws on Deleuze's discussion of Nietzsche and expressivism – the idea that life consists of pre-individual singularities. In the spirit of Deleuze's use of Nietzsche, singular memory does not relate to a unified ground or experience of the subject. As such, to speak of reterritorializing Memory is not to assert that memory is exercised by a subject with either misplaced or authoritarian intentions, it is an activity resulting from a combination of illegitimate syntheses: connective, disjunctive, and conjunctive. These syntheses of desire seize upon the energies, or force, of singular memory (herein lies the significance of the Freudian notion of libido), organizing it into distinct periods, causes, identities, and hierarchical temporal relations. The activity of a reterritorializing Memory forces a dualistic separation between the past and present, a split that is no different to the separation of being from becoming. Accordingly, the whole notion of 'historical trauma' that Freud posits with his concept of *Nachträglichkeit* is an effect of this split. The past, however, cannot be located in a fixed and determinate point or ground, one that takes form in the present as a unified temporal entity. Singular memory thus conceived is neither the original memory out of which the present is merely a faint copy, nor are the qualities of singular memory determined by a prior cause. Singular memory is a differentiating force; it is an operative function that combines an aggregate of differences. Trauma is one possible aggregate. As univocal memory, trauma elides the negative position commonly ascribed to it. In this light, trauma no longer poses an irresolvable negation of Being or of life and it can be said to persist over time. However, this is not to suggest trauma persists in the same way over time. The differentiating power of singular memory is one of internal difference, and if we were to follow Deleuze's Nietzsche, it could be said to be ultimately creative.[12] That is, the activity of singular memory is untimely, not historical; it is positive, not negative, positive in so far as it is not different to the present and future – it is a mode of both – and it is also the condition necessary for future difference.

This situation introduces the issue of how forces are repeated and which ones are selected (this is an activity that takes place at the level of desiring production). It is here where Deleuze's use of Nietzsche's concept of force is most instructive:

> In Nietzsche the essential relation of one force to another is never conceived of as a negative element in the essence. In its relation with the other the force which makes itself obeyed does not deny the other or

> that which it is not, it affirms its own difference and enjoys this difference. The negative is not present in the essence as that from which force draws its activity: on the contrary it is a result of activity, of the existence of an active force and the affirmation of its difference.[13]

The point is that remembering a traumatic event doesn't entail mimicking or describing that event as truthfully as possible, rather it entails a mode of composition and endurance that actualizes the overwhelming force of trauma in all its difference. This is largely a problem of how to extract the singularity of memory out of a mix of memories so as to tap into the expressed form of trauma, whereby its force endures in us only because we have willed it to. Memorial culture stutters with a schizoid investment of memory, presenting memories the social field affects in the selection and connection of different memory singularities. A fascistic investment occurs when the social field resists the endurance of traumatic memory, finding investment for this wound in an authoritarian image of the sublime or through repressive modes of remembrance, what Deleuze and Guattari might otherwise call a paranoid investment of desire.

For memorial culture to move beyond a fascistic investment of trauma, a utopian trajectory of memorialization needs to be put into practice. It has been argued, with the help of Deleuze's concept of orgiastic representation and Jameson's discussion of utopian failure, that the inability of memory to fully represent utopia is implicitly a utopian gesture of sorts. Within the utopian dimension of memory lies the impulse to imagine a better future. In the context of memorial culture this entails engaging memory in a way that eludes trauma fetishism so that singular memory can retain a critical edge, activating both the past and future from the standpoint of the present. In this light an affirmative memorial culture would be one where the work of singular memory would mean '*discovering, inventing, new possibilities of life*.'[14] By the same token, it is simply as Deleuze says of Nietzsche, that life 'struggles with *another kind* of life.'[15] Accordingly, in view of the weeping prophet Jeremiah, the struggle of remembrance is one that constructs a revolutionary connection to the future. His tears are a sign of how collective trauma endures throughout the social only in so far as we will it to, which is to say his are the tears of a witness and they are the effect of a fundamental choice not to remain a mere bystander. Interestingly, the witness inaugurates the sociality of memory as they choose to allow trauma to passively endure inside of them; the passive endurance of traumatic memory is what eventually compels them to act. Hence, the struggle of remembrance lies in discovering a way to conserve the force of trauma as it endures in the witness without preserving it in a transcendent or repressive structure. This is the struggle that defines the ethical significance of memorial culture for the human condition; ultimately we cannot afford to be shy or hesitant when trauma appears for it inheres in all of us. Essentially, we are faced with a choice of whether or not traumatic memory compels us to act, meaning that we record this memory not to counter injustice but because we choose not to suffer in the face of it.

Notes

1. Deleuze, Gilles. *Nietzsche and Philosophy*, trans. Hugh Tomlinson (New York: Columbia University Press, 1986), 15.
2. Feuer, Rabbi Avrohom Chaim and Rabbi Avie Gold (trans.). *The Complete Tishah B'av Service* (Brooklyn, NY: ArtScroll Mesorah, 1991), xii–xiii.
3. Judaism does not advocate a transcendent realm whereby the world is merely a poor copy; rather life is filled with practical principles and as such the materiality of life needs to be embraced. This can be achieved by focusing on how the concrete world can be put to work to enrich individuals and the community (including the environment) as a whole. This is largely a principle of sustainability; it aspires to benefit life both in the present and for the future.
4. Deleuze, Gilles and Félix Guattari. *What Is Philosophy?*, trans. Graham Burchell and Hugh Tomlinson (London and New York: Verso, 1994), 165.
5. Hal Foster used this idea in *Return of the Real* to revitalize the critical force of postmodernism. See Foster, Hal. *The Return of the Real* (Cambridge, MA: MIT Press, 1996).
6. Deleuze, Gilles. *Difference and Repetition*, trans. Paul Patton (New York: Columbia University Press, 1994), 144.
7. Deleuze and Guattari, *What is Philosophy?*, 164.
8. At the risk of sounding jargonistic this would mean that the schizoid investment of memory works to deterritorialize the fixed relation between the past and present, as well as the determinate representation of the past, both of which characterize a fascistic investment of memory and its reterritorializing movement.
9. Deleuze and Guattari, *What is Philosophy?*, 177.
10. I would like to extend my special thanks to Ian Buchanan here for suggesting I use the term 'singular memory' as opposed to what I was originally calling 'pure memory.'
11. Deleuze, Gilles and Félix Guattari. *A Thousand Plateaus: Capitalism and Schizophrenia*, trans. Brian Massumi (London: Athlone Press, 1988), 292.

12. For Nietzsche this is the crux of his concept of Will to Power. Similarly for Bergson it is the key to understanding his concept of *élan vital*.
13. Deleuze, *Nietzsche and Philosophy*, 8–9.
14. Ibid., 101.
15. Ibid., 8.

Bibliography

Adorno, Theodor W. *Can One Live after Auschwitz?*, ed. Rolf Tiedemann (Stanford, CA: Stanford University Press, 2003).

——. *The Culture Industry: Selected Essays on Mass Culture* (London: Routledge, 1991).

——. *Negative Dialectics*, trans. E. B. Ashton (London: Routledge, 1973).

Adorno, Theodor W. and Max Horkheimer. *Dialectic of Enlightenment: Philosophical Fragments*, trans. Edmund Jephcott (Stanford, CA: Stanford University Press, 2002).

Agamben, Giorgio. *State of Exception*, trans. Kevin Attell (Chicago: Chicago University Press, 2005).

——. *Homo Sacer: Sovereign Power and Bare Life*, trans. Daniel Heller-Roazen (Stanford, CA: Stanford University Press, 1998).

Alexander, Jeffrey C., Ron Eyerman, Bernhard Giesen, Neil J. Smelser, and Piotr Sztompka (eds). *Cultural Trauma and Collective Identity* (Berkeley, CA: University of California Press, 2004).

Allocine Newsletter. http://www.allocine.co.uk/film/boxoffice_gen_cfilm=61772.html. Accessed 28 November 2006.

Appy, Christian. *Working Class War: American Combat Soldiers and Vietnam* (Chapel Hill, NC: University of North Carolina Press, 1993).

Arendt, Hannah. *On Violence* (San Diego, CA: Harcourt, Brace & Co., 1970).

Bal, Mieke, Jonathon Crewe and Leo Spitzer (eds). *Acts of Memory: Cultural Recall in the Present* (Hanover, NH and London: University Press of New England, 1999).

Baudrillard, Jean. *The Spirit of Terrorism*, trans. Chris Turner (London: Verso, 2002).

Beck, Ulrich. 'The Terrorist Threat: World Risk Society Revisited,' *Theory, Culture and Society*, Vol. 19, No. 4, 2002, 39–55.

Belknap, Michal R. *The Vietnam War on Trial: The My Lai Massacre and the Court-Martial of Lieutenant Calley* (Lawrence, KS: University Press of Kansas, 2002).

Bilton, Michael and Kevin Sim. *Four Hours in My Lai* (New York: Penguin, 1992).

Blair, Tony. 'Transcript of Tony Blair Speech,' *CBS News Online*, 7 July 2005. http://www.cbc.ca/news/background/london_bombing/blair_speech.html. Accessed 10 October 2005.

Bogue, Ronald. *Deleuze's Wake: Tributes and Tributaries* (Albany, NY: State University of New York Press, 2004).

Bonnefoi, Christian. 'Louis Kahn and Minimalism,' *Oppositions 24*, Spring 1981, 2–25.

Buchanan, Ian. *Deleuzism: A Metacommentary* (Durham, NC: Duke University Press, 2000).

——. 'Metacommentary on Utopia, or Jameson's dialectic of hope,' *Utopian Studies*, Vol. 9, No. 2, 1998, 18–30.

Buchanan, Ian and Adrian Parr. *Deleuze and the Contemporary World* (Edinburgh: Edinburgh University Press, 2006).

Bush, George W. 'Oval Office Speech: September 11, 2001,' *September 11 news.com*. http://www.september11news.com/PresidentBush.htm. Accessed 23 October 2006.

Butler, Judith. *Giving an Account of Oneself* (New York: Fordham University Press, 2005).

Caruth, Cathy. *Unclaimed Experience: Trauma, Narrative and History* (Baltimore, MD: Johns Hopkins University Press, 1996).

—— (ed.). *Trauma: Explorations in Memory* (Baltimore, MD: Johns Hopkins University Press, 1995).

Cazeaux, Clive (ed.). *The Continental Aesthetics Reader* (London: Routledge, 2000).

Coafee, Jon. *Terrorism, Risk and the City: The Making of the Contemporary Urban Landscape* (London: Ashgate, 2003).

Cole, Tim. *Selling the Holocaust: From Auschwitz to Schindler* (New York: Routledge, 1999).

Cooper, David. *Existentialism: A Reconstruction* (Oxford: Blackwell, 1999).

Davis, Walter. *Deracination: Historicity, Hiroshima and the Tragic Imperative* (New York: SUNY Press, 2001).

Deleuze, Gilles. *Desert Islands and Other Texts: 1953–1974* (New York: Semiotext[e], 2004).

——. *Francis Bacon: The Logic of Sensation*, trans. Daniel W. Smith (Minneapolis, MN: University of Minnesota Press, 2003).

——. *Negotiations: 1972–1900*, trans. Martin Joughin (New York: Columbia University Press, 1995).

——. *Difference and Repetition*, trans. Paul Patton (New York: Columbia University Press, 1994).

——. *The Fold: Leibniz and the Baroque*, trans. Tom Conley (Minneapolis, MN: University of Minnesota Press, 1993).

——. *Expressionism in Philosophy: Spinoza*, trans. Martin Joughin (New York: Zone Books, 1992).

——. *Bergsonism*, trans. Hugh Tomlinson and Barbara Habberjam (New York: Zone Books, 1991).

——. *The Logic of Sensation*, trans. Mark Lester with Charles Stivale (New York: Columbia University Press, 1990).

Deleuze, Gilles. *Cinema 2: The Time Image*, trans. Hugh Tomlinson and Robert Galeta (Minneapolis, MN: University of Minnesota Press, 1989)

——. *Foucault*, trans. Seán Hand (Minneapolis, MN: University of Minnesota Press, 1988a).

——. *Spinoza: A Practical Philosophy*, trans. Robert Hurley (San Francisco: City Light Books, 1988b).

——. *Nietzsche and Philosophy*, trans. Hugh Tomlinson (New York: Columbia University Press, 1986),

——. *Kant's Critical Philosophy: The Doctrine of the Faculties*, trans. Hugh Tomlinson and Barbara Habberjam (Minneapolis, MN: University of Minnesota Press, 1984).

Deleuze, Gilles and Félix Guattari, *What is Philosophy?*, trans. Graham Burchell and Hugh Tomlinson (London and New York: Verso, 1994).

——. *A Thousand Plateaus: Capitalism and Schizophrenia*, trans. Brian Massumi (London: Athlone Press, 1988).

——. *Kafka: Toward a Minor Literature*, trans. Dana Polan (Minneapolis, MN: University of Minnesota Press, 1986).

——. *Anti-Oedipus: Capitalism and Schizophrenia*, trans. R. Hurley, M. Seem, and H. R. Lane (Minneapolis, MN: University of Minnesota Press, 1977).

Felman, Shoshana. *The Juridical Unconscious: Trials and Traumas in the Twentieth Century* (Cambridge, MA: Harvard University Press, 2002).

Feuer, Rabbi Avrohom Chaim and Rabbi Avie Gold (trans.). *The Complete Tishah B'av Service* (Brooklyn, NY: ArtScroll Mesorah, 1991).

Finkelstein, Norman G. *The Holocaust Industry: Reflections on the Exploitation of Jewish Suffering* (New York: Verso, 2003).

Foote, Kenneth E. *Shadowed Ground: America's Landscapes of Violence and Tragedy* (Austin, TX: University of Texas Press, 2003).

Foster, Hal. *The Return of the Real* (Cambridge, MA: MIT Press, 1996).

Foucault, Michel. *Discipline and Punish: The Birth of the Prison*, trans. Alan Sheridan (London: Penguin Books, 1991).

——. *The Archaeology of Knowledge and the Discourse on Language*, trans. Alan Sheridan (New York: Pantheon Books, 1972).

Frampton, Kenneth. *Studies in Tectonic Culture: The Poetics of Construction in Nineteenth and Twentieth-Century Architecture* (Cambridge, MA: MIT Press, 2001).

Freud, Sigmund. *Introductory Lectures on Psychoanalysis*, trans. James Strachey (London: Penguin, 1991).

——. *The Standard Edition of the Complete Psychological Works of Sigmund Freud*, Vol. XI, trans. James Strachey (London: Vintage, 2001).

Gallup, Jane. *Feminism and Psychoanalysis: The Daughter's Seduction* (London: Macmillan, 1982).

Gallup Poll, 'Americans Overwhelmingly Criticize Pardons, But Few Think Clinton "Did Something Illegal,"' 14 March 2001. http://www.galluppoll.com/content/?ci=1906&pg=1. Accessed 27 November 2006.

Germain, David. 'R.V. passes United 93 to win box office,' *Reuters Associated Press*, 30 April 2006. http://www.ktvb.com/sharedcontent/features/entertainment/broadwire/050106ccjccwEntRV.8bac50c9.html. Accessed on 25 July 2007.

Goldsmith, Kenneth (ed.). *I'll be Your Mirror: The Selected Andy Warhol Interviews* (New York: Carroll & Graf, 2004).

Gray, Peter (ed.). *The Freud Reader* (London: Vintage, 1995).

Grosz. Elizabeth (ed.). *Becomings: Explorations in Time, Memory, and Futures* (New York: Cornell University Press, 1999).

——. *Volatile Bodies: Toward a Corporeal Feminism* (Sydney: Allen & Unwin, 1994).

Harrison, Charles and Paul Wood (eds). *Art in Theory 1900–2000: An Anthology of Changing Ideas* (Oxford: Blackwell, 2003).

Hays, Michael K. *Architecture Theory Since 1968* (Cambridge, MA: MIT Press, 1998).

Healy, Patrick D. 'Pataki Warns Cultural Groups for Museum at Ground Zero,' *New York Times*, 25 June 2005. http://www.nytimes.com/2005/06/25/nyregion/25rebuild.html?ex=1277352000&en=feecbc648d8a45af&ei=5090&partner=rssuserland&emc=rss. Accessed 14 December 2006.

Hersh, Seymour. *My Lai 4: Report on the Massacre and Its Aftermath* (New York: Random House, 1970).

Holland, Eugene. *Deleuze and Guattari's Anti-Oedipus: Introduction to Schizoanalysis* (London: Routledge, 1999).

Horkheimer, Max and Theodor W. Adorno. *Dialectic of Enlightenment*, trans. Edmund Jephcott (Stanford, CA: Stanford University Press, 2002).

Hostetler, John A. *Amish Society*, 4th edn (Baltimore, MD: Johns Hopkins University Press, 1993).

Huyssen, Andreas. *Twilight Memories: Marking Time in a Culture of Amnesia* (New York: Routledge, 1995).

Infilm Australia. http://www.infilm.com.au/boxoffice.htm. Accessed 28 November 2006.

Irigaray, Luce. *Speculum of the Other Woman*, trans. Gillian Gill (Ithaca, NY: Cornell University Press, 1985a).

——. *The Sex Which Is Not One*, trans. Catherine Porter with Carolyn Burke (Ithaca, NY: Cornell University Press, 1985b).

Jameson, Fredric. *Archaeologies of the Future: The Desire Called Utopia and Other Science Fictions* (London: Verso, 2005).

——. *The Seeds of Time* (New York: Columbia University Press, 1994).

——. *Postmodernism: Or, the Cultural Logic of Late Capitalism* (Durham, NC: Duke University Press, 1991).

Jameson, Fredric. *The Political Unconscious: Narrative as a Socially Symbolic Act* (Ithaca, NY: Cornell University Press, 1981).
——. *Fables of Aggression: Wyndham Lewis, the Modernist as Fascist* (Berkeley, CA: University of California Press, 1979).
——. *Marxism and Form: Twentieth-Century Dialectical Theories of Literature* (Princeton, NJ: Princeton University Press, 1971).
Knowlton, James and Truett Cates. *Forever in the Shadow of Hitler? Original Documents of the Historikerstreit, the Controversy Concerning the Singularity of the Holocaust* (Atlantic Highlands, NJ: Humanities Press, 1993).
Kraybill, Donald B. *The Riddle of Amish Culture* (Baltimore, MD: Johns Hopkins University Press, 2001).
Kwon, Heonik. *After the Massacre: Commemoration and Consolidation in Ha My and My Lai* (Berkeley, CA: University of California Press, 2006).
LaCapra, Dominick. *History and Memory After Auschwitz* (Ithaca, NY: Cornell University Press, 1998).
Lang, Berel. *Writing and the Holocaust* (New York: Holmes & Meier, 1988).
Libeskind, Daniel. *Breaking Ground: Adventures in Life and Architecture* (New York: Riverhead Books, 2004).
——. 'Memory Foundations,' *Studio Daniel Liebskind*, 2002. http://www.lowermanhattan.info/rebuild/new_design_plans/selected_libeskind/default.asp. Accessed 18 September 2006.
——. *The Space of Encounter* (New York: Universe, 2000).
Lin, Maya. *Boundaries* (New York: Simon & Schuster, 2000).
Lobell, Mimi. 'Kahn, Penn and the Philadelphia School,' *Oppositions 4*, October 1974.
Lower Manhattan Development Corporation. 'Viewing Wall: Urban Scale, 2002,' *LMDC*. http://www.renewnyc.com/PhotoArchive/viewingwall.asp. Accessed November 2006.
Lukacs, John. *Historical Consciousness: The Remembered Past* (New Brunswick, NJ: Transaction Publishers, 2004).
Lyotard, Jean-François. *Libidinal Economy*, trans. Iaian Hamilton Grant (Bloomington, IN: Indiana University Press, 1993).
MacDonald, Paul (ed.). *The Existentialist Reader* (Edinburgh: Edinburgh University Press, 2000).
Marx, Karl. *Capital*, ed. David McLellan (Oxford: Oxford University Press, 1999).
——. *Manifesto*, trans. Paul M. Sweeny (New York: Monthly Review Press, 1998).
——. *Grundrisse*, trans. Martin Nicolaus (London: Penguin, 1973).
Marx, Karl and Fredrich Engels. *The German Ideology: Including Thesis on Feuerbach* (New York: Prometheus Books, 1998).
Meyer, Dick. 'Rush: MPs Just "Blowing Off Steam,"' *CBS News*, 4 May 2004. http://www.cbsnews.com/stories/2004/05/06/opinion/meyer/main616021.shtml. Accessed 8 January 2007.

Michaud, Eric. *The Cult of Art in Nazi Germany*, trans. Janet Lloyd (Stanford, CA: Stanford University Press, 2004).
Mintz, Alan. *Popular Culture and the Shaping of Holocaust Memory in America* (Seattle, WA: University of Washington Press, 2001).
Mock, Freeda Lee (dir.). *Maya Lin: A Strong Clear Vision* (New York: American Film Foundation, 1994).
More, Thomas. *Utopia* (Cambridge: Cambridge University Press, 1975).
Nacos, Brigitte. 'Terrorism, the Mass Media, and the Events of 9/11,' *Phi Kappa Phi Forum*, Spring 2002, 13–19.
Nietzsche, Friedrich. *The Will to Power*, trans. Walter Kaufman and R. J. Hollingdale (New York: Vintage, 1968).
Norberg-Schulz, Christian. 'Kahn, Heidegger, and the Language of Architecture,' *Oppositions*, Vol. 18, Fall 1979, 29–47.
Ockman, Joan (ed.). *Out of Ground Zero: Case Studies in Urban Reinvention* (Munich: Prestel, 2002).
Ockman, Joan and Edward Eigen (eds). *Architecture Culture 1943–1968* (New York: Columbia Books of Architecture/Rizzoli, 1993).
Oliver, Kendrick. *The My Lai Massacre in American History and Memory* (Manchester: Manchester University Press, 2006).
Olkowski, Dorothea. *Gilles Deleuze and the Ruin of Representation* (Berkeley, CA: University of California Press, 1999).
Palmer, Laura. *Shrapnel in the Heart: Letters and Remembrance from the Vietnam Veterans Memorial* (New York: Random House, 1987).
Parr, Adrian (ed.). *The Deleuze Dictionary* (Edinburgh: Edinburgh University Press, 2005a).
——. 'Assaulting the Phallocentric Organization of Capital,' *Women: A Cultural Review*, special edition on Guattari and Gender, Vol. 16, Winter 2005b, 321–39.
——. *Exploring the Work of Leonardo da Vinci within the Context of Contemporary Philosophical Thought and Art* (New York: Edwin Mellen Press, 2003).
Pataki, Governor. 'Design Plan for Freedom Tower: Introduction,' *Lower Manhattan Development Corporation: Remember, Rebuild, Renew*, 30 June 2005. http://www.renewnyc.com/plan_des_dev/wtc_site/new_design_plans/Freedom_Tower/freedom_tower_intro.asp. Accessed 10 May 2006.
Patton, Paul. *Deleuze and the Political* (London: Routledge, 2000).
Pew Research Center for the People and the Press. 'Main Source of Disaster News,' 8 September 2005. http://72.14.203.104/u/peoplepress?q=cache:5mglLc3U5IoJ:people-press.org/reports/pdf/255.pdf+hurricane+katrina&hl=en&gl=us&ct=clnk&cd=8&ie=UTF-8. Accessed 27 November 2006.
——. 'Iraq Prison Scandal Hits Home, But Most Reject Troop Pullout,' 12 May 2004. http://people-press.org/reports/display.php3?ReportID=213. Accessed 8 January 2007.

Pew Research Center for the People and the Press. 'News Audiences Increasingly Politicized: Online News Audience Larger, More Diverse,' 8 June 2004. http://people-press.org/reports/display.php3?PageID=833. Accessed 27 November 2006.

——. 'American Psyche Reeling from Terror Attacks,' 19 September 2001. http://people-press.org/reports/display.php3?ReportID=3. Accessed 23 October 2006.

——. 'Terror Coverage Boosts News Media's Image but Military Censorship Backed,' 28 November 2001. http://people-press.org/reports/display.php3?ReportID=143. Accessed 23 October 2006.

——. 'TV News Viewership Declines,' 13 May 1996. http://people-press.org/reports/display.php3?PageID=444. Accessed 8 January 2007.

——. 'Younger Americans and Women Less Informed: One In Four Americans Follow National News Closely: Times Mirror News Interest Index: 1989–1995,' 28 December 1995. http://people-press.org/reports/display.php3?ReportID=134. Accessed 27 November 2006.

——. 'Public Attentiveness to News Stories: 1986–2006.' http://people-press.org/nii/. Accessed 27 November 2006.

Pitts, Byron. 'Amish Forgive, Prey and Mourn,' *CBS News*, 4 October 2006. http://www.cbsnews.com/stories/2006/10/04/national/main2059816.shtml. Accessed 7 November 2006.

Plato. *Republic*, trans. Desmond Lee (London: Penguin Books, 1987).

Rawls, Walton (ed.). *Offerings at the Wall: Artifacts from the Vietnam Veterans Memorial Collection* (Atlanta, GA: Turner Publishing, 1995).

Reich, Wilhelm. *The Mass Psychology of Fascism* (New York: Farrar, Strauss & Giroux, 1970).

Richter, Jean Paul. *The Notebooks of Leonardo Da Vinci: Volume 2* (New York: Dover Publication, 1970).

Rothko, Mark. *Writings on Art* (New Haven, CT: Yale University Press, 2005).

Roy, Arundhati. *The Algebra of Infinite Justice*, foreword John Berger (London: Flamingo, 2002).

Scarry, Elaine. *The Body in Pain: The Making and Unmaking of the World* (Oxford: Oxford University Press, 1985).

Schiff, Hilda. *Holocaust Poetry* (New York: St. Martins Press, 1995).

Siano, Joseph. 'Travel Advisory; Tickets (Free) Required for Ground Zero,' *The New York Times*, 20 January 2002, http://query.nytimes.com/gst/fullpage.html?sec=travel&res=9F03E1D91338F933A15752C0A9649C8B63. Accessed 18 October 2006.

Siff, David. 'One Year Later: Security Tighter, Cities Stretched,' *CNN.com*, 12 September 2002. http://archives.cnn.com/2002/US/09/06/prepared.cities.overview/index.html. Accessed 18 October 2006.

Siff, David and Patrick Cooper. 'Bush Signs Homeland Security Bill,' *CNN.com*, 26 November 2002. http://archives.cnn.com/2002/ALLPOLITICS/11/25/homeland.security/. Accessed 18 October 2006.

Sontag, Susan. 'Regarding the Torture of Others,' *New York Times Magazine*, 23 May 2004. http://www.nytimes.com/2004/05/23/magazine/23PRISONS.html?ex=1400644800&en=a2cb6ea6bd297c8f&ei=5007&partner=USERLAND. Accessed 11 November 2006.

Summers, K. C. 'Ground Zero 101,' *Washington Post*, Sunday, 3 March 2002, E02.

Taguba, Maj.-Gen. Antonio M. *The 'Taguba Report' On Treatment of Abu Ghraib Prisoners in Iraq*, February 2004. http://news.findlaw.com/nytimes/docs/iraq/tagubarpt.html#ThR1.9. Accessed 2 January 2007.

TALKERS Report. 'The Top Talk Radio Audiences,' *TALKERS Magazine*, 28 October 2005. http://www.talkers.com/talkhosts.htm. Accessed 7 January 2007.

Tate Gallery Catalogue, *Mark Rothko 1903–1970* (London: Tate Gallery, 1987).

Thiis-Evensen, Thomas. *Archetypes in Architecture* (Oslo: Norwegian University Press, 1987).

Till, Karen E. *The New Berlin: Memory, Politics, Place* (Minneapolis, MN: University of Minnesota Press, 2005).

Urry, John. 'The Global Complexities of September 11th,' *Theory, Culture and Society*, Vol. 19, No. 4, 2002, 57–69.

Virilio, Paul. *A Landscape of Events*, trans. Julie Rose (Cambridge, MA: MIT Press, 2000).

Young, James E. *At Memory's Edge: After-images of the Holocaust in Contemporary Art and Architecture* (New Haven, CT: Yale University Press, 2000).

——. *The Texture of Memory: Holocaust Memorials and Meaning* (New Haven, CT: Yale University Press, 1993).

Young, Marilyn. *The Vietnam Wars, 1945–1990* (New York: Harper, 1991).

Žižek, Slavoj. *The Parallax View* (Cambridge, MA: MIT Press, 2006).

——. 'Against Human Rights,' *New Left Review*, Vol. 34, July/August 2005, 115–31.

——. *The Ticklish Subject: The Absent Centre of Political Ontology* (London and New York: Verso, 1999).

Index

EU Authorised Representative:
Easy Access System Europe Mustamäe tee 50, 10621 Tallinn, Estonia
gpsr.requests@easproject.com

Printed and bound by CPI Group (UK) Ltd, Croydon, CR0 4YY
14/09/2026
02216780-0001